D1601159

Ending Mass Incarceration

Ending Mass Incarceration

Why it Persists and How to Achieve Meaningful Reform

Katherine Beckett

OXFORD
UNIVERSITY PRESS

Oxford University Press is a department of the University of Oxford. It furthers
the University's objective of excellence in research, scholarship, and education
by publishing worldwide. Oxford is a registered trade mark of Oxford University
Press in the UK and certain other countries.

Published in the United States of America by Oxford University Press
198 Madison Avenue, New York, NY 10016, United States of America.

CIP data is on file at the Library of Congress
ISBN 978-0-19-753657-5

DOI: 10.1093/oso/9780197536575.001.0001

1 3 5 7 9 8 6 4 2

Printed by Sheridan Books, Inc., United States of America

For Jesse and AnnaRose, and the future you enable me to believe is possible

Contents

Acknowledgments

This book covers topics I began working on over a decade ago. I have accumulated many debts along the way. To the men and women at the Washington State Reformatory: you teach, by example, the value and meaning of redemption, and I am deeply grateful for the opportunity to know and work alongside you. To those of you who shared your personal stories: thank you. Your generosity, perseverance, and courage are deeply appreciated. Special thanks to Nick Hacheney, Devon Adams, Eugene Youngblood, and Vincent Sherill for connecting me to the Concerned Lifers Organization and the Black Prisoners' Caucus at WSR and for welcoming me in those spaces. To the people, both inside and out, who run University Beyond Bars (UBB), much appreciation for creating the opportunity to teach and learn alongside such fantastic scholars, and for putting up with our collective overcrowding of the UBB office. Thanks also to Steve Herbert, whose work in and on prisons paved the way, whose questions, suggestions, and observations are invariably helpful, and whose ongoing support is deeply appreciated. The ideas and companionship of Megan Francis made many of my visits to prison all the richer.

Some of the research discussed in this book was made possible by Lisa Daugaard's unending propensity to make trouble and her commitment to always be working toward a solution; thank you for inviting me on this journey and for sharing your brilliance along the way. Thanks also to Martina Kartman for enabling me to immerse myself in the world of restorative justice, for embodying the work, and for connecting me to so many others whose work and lives are inspirational to me. I am indebted to Heather Evans for saying yes, over and over again despite all the lost sleep, and for being such a wonderful collaborator, and to Joel for putting up with all of this. Exchanges with many other colleagues, including Monica Bell, Forrest Stuart, and Bruce Western, are always generative; I am especially grateful for Bruce's comprehensive feedback and suggestions regarding an earlier version of this book. Craig Haney's work and example have also been an important source of inspiration. Thanks also to Michele Storms and Jaime Hawk for creating an opportunity to shine a light on the problem of long and life sentences in Washington State. Chelsea Moore's unwavering belief that we can make a difference is an inspiration.

I have learned much about the challenge and promise of developing alternative ways of responding to substance use disorders and behavioral health issues from everyone at LEAD, Co-LEAD, and JustCARE, especially Jesse Benet and Tara Moss. I have also had the good fortune to work with a number of outstanding (present and former) graduate students, including Lindsey Beach, Marco Brydolf-Horwitz, Emily Knaphus-Soran, and Anna Reosti, who have allowed me to draw on our coauthored work here. I also appreciate the contributions of other current graduate students, especially Devin Collins, Allison Goldberg, and Aliyah Turner, whose work on alternative ways of responding to unsheltered homelessness and behavioral health has been so illuminating. I am thankful for the example of my colleagues in the departments of Law, Societies and Justice and Sociology, especially Angelina Godoy, who conduct research that addresses pressing human rights concerns and gives voice to those who are affected by them. And I am grateful for the support of Michael Tonry, Meredith Keefer, and others at Oxford University Press.

Last but by no means least, I am thankful for the generous support of the Miyamoto family, which has made much of this work possible, and for my colleagues at the University of Washington who value hands-on, publicly engaged, and problem-solving scholarship. Some of the research presented here was funded by the National Science Foundation's Law and Social Sciences program (#1456180), the Public Defender Association, The Ford Foundation, the University of Washington West Coast Poverty Center, the ACLU of Washington, and Laurie Black and Stafford Mays, whose generosity is deeply appreciated.

1

Introduction

As I write these words at the close of 2020, over 10 million people living in the United States have been sickened with COVID-19. Nearly half a million have died as a result, and many of those who were hospitalized are now contending with long-term health challenges and massive medical debt.[1] Video-recorded evidence of police killings and near-killings of Black men, including, most recently, George Floyd, Jacob Blake, and Daniel Prude, continue to emerge at a regular and heartbreaking pace. Democracy and the right to vote are under assault.[2] Millions of people are unemployed.[3] Evictions are on the rise and are expected to become even more common.[4] Recently, the western United States was ablaze: millions of residents were smothered under toxic air for months, and tens of thousands were evacuated.[5]

The events of 2020 have made it abundantly clear that public safety is inextricably bound up with health and welfare. Yet this capacious understanding of public safety is at odds with popular usage of the term. For decades, conservative political actors have argued that there is just one significant threat to public safety—interpersonal violence—and that the restoration of tough criminal penalties was the (only) appropriate response to this problem. This emphasis intensified in the 1960s and 1970s, as conservatives argued that government responsibility for public safety required nothing more than a muscular state response to so-called street crime. As many observers have pointed out, these calls for "law and order" treated protest against racial inequality as a form of violence and were part of an effort to discredit the civil and welfare rights movements,[6] just as President Donald Trump's donning of the law-and-order mantle in the summer of 2020 was a clear rejoinder to the Black Lives Matter movement.

Calls for "law and order" were also a component of a larger struggle over the proper role of government in economic affairs. Throughout this period, conservatives argued that it is *not* the government's responsibility to provide for the public welfare. Some even made the argument that welfare *causes* crime. It is no coincidence that in 1964, the same year that President Lyndon B. Johnson signed the Civil Rights Act and in the context of the War on Poverty, Republican presidential candidate Barry Goldwater relied heavily on the rhetoric of "law and order." Those who mobilized this rhetoric not only emphasized the threat of "street crime" and conflated protest with violence; they also emphasized government's role in maintaining a "free" economy and invoked racist images of "welfare queens" to delegitimize the movement to expand welfare rights.[7]

This political strategy has, for decades, been a useful way of tapping into the racial biases and stereotypes that are inextricably bound up with attitudes about crime, punishment, and poverty in the United States.[8] In fact, racially charged rhetoric about crime and punishment and welfare[9] was key to this effort to woo socially conservative White voters to the GOP. This use of such "subliminal" racial appeals and coded racial rhetoric remains a powerful means of tapping into racial resentments for electoral benefit, particularly among those in the electorate who were prioritized in the wake of partisan realignment.[10] This strategy continues to be central to Republican Party op- erations. For example, despite broad popular support for Deferred Action for Childhood Arrivals and opposition to construction of a border wall, GOP candidates relied heavily on racially charged immigration-related rhetoric in the run-up to the 2018 midterm elections in an attempt to secure the votes of electorally crucial and socially conservative White voters.[11] Similarly, on the eve of the 2020 presidential election, the Trump campaign issued numerous calls for "law and order" in an attempt to capitalize on racial tensions and in a desperate bid to shift attention from his disastrous handling of the pandemic and its economic and social consequences.[12]

Unfortunately, this impoverished understanding of public safety has gained a strong toehold in our increasingly fragile and fractured democracy, to the point that justice is often presumed to be synonymous with tough punish- ment. Over the years, and particularly in the 1990s, many liberal lawmakers also came to support this tough crime talk and policy. The results of this po- litical convergence are well known, and include the widespread adoption of policies that created the largest prison population the world has ever known. Spending on courts and corrections increased notably and the number of people under the supervision of the criminal legal system increased more than fivefold while the safety net became more porous.[13] The United States has been the world's leading jailer for many years now; it is also characterized by extraordinarily high levels of poverty and inequality compared to other wealthy nations.[14]

The increased reach of the U.S. criminal legal system has been so profound, and so consequential, that researchers now treat penal institutions as a key mechanism by which social inequality is reproduced over time.[15] But the problem is not only a matter of scale. At its core, mass incarceration reflects the tenuousness of our commitment to racial equity, to human rights, and to social justice. It is also testament to our reluctance to recognize the innumerable ways that violence has shaped our country, our people, and our way of doing "justice." It is in this context that calls to reimagine public safety from Black Lives Matter activists have resounded across the country.

Redefining Public Safety

The narrow understanding of public safety just described artificially separates public welfare, public health, and public safety. It also rests on the erroneous assumption that interpersonal violence is the preeminent threat to safety—and the only kind of threat to which governments are compelled to respond. Assault, robbery, and other violent crimes do undermine public health and well-being, and the risk of these types of violence remains unacceptably high in disadvantaged urban neighborhoods, despite recent drops in national crime rates. Sadly, current policies do little to reduce these kinds of harms. Moreover, other equally serious threats to safety, health, and well-being are also pervasive, especially in marginalized communities. These include past and present discrimination, high levels of poverty and extreme poverty, pervasive housing instability and homelessness, limited access to healthcare, police harassment and violence, unsafe water and air, mass incarceration, global pandemics, the climate crisis, and, for noncitizens, the risk of family separation and deportation.

Recognition of the varied nature of these threats to our well-being necessitates a broader understanding of the meaning of public safety. To feel—and be—safe, people need not only to be protected from interpersonal violence and other crimes but also to know that they will not be killed by the police and that the government is doing what it can to address the threat of climate change. They must have access to housing and healthcare and be free from harassment and discrimination. This more capacious understanding of public safety recognizes that investments in public health, healthcare, education, child care, substance abuse treatment, green energy and technology, and housing are simultaneously investments in public welfare, public health, and public safety.

From this broader perspective, poverty is itself a form of violence: it entails various forms of psychological and physical deprivation that impair health and well-being. It also fuels interpersonal violence because families living in poverty contend with a variety of structural and contextual challenges that are consistently associated with higher levels of crime and violence.[16] Given this association of poverty with interpersonal violence, it is unsurprising that investments in social and child welfare not only improve people's quality of life but also reduce crime and violence.[17]

In short, a thin conception of public safety that focuses only on freedom from "street crime" obscures the fact that many people—and especially people of color, people living in poverty, undocumented immigrants, and disabled people—contend with numerous and often overlapping threats to personal safety. It also ignores evidence that some of these other threats to well-being and safety fuel interpersonal violence and, relatedly, that investments in public welfare and public health reduce crime and violence. By contrast, a thick conception of public safety recognizes the wide array of social conditions that undermine safety and well-being, and prioritizes the health and well-being of all members of the public, including the incarcerated.

Despite the increasingly visible and obvious array of threats to public health and safety that were on full display throughout the pandemic, the idea that harsh criminal penalties represent a meaningful way of addressing and ensuring public safety has become common sense for many Americans. In addition to erroneously assuming that crime is the only significant threat to our safety, this approach rests on the misleading premise that the tough policies that fueled mass incarceration effectively reduce crime. This is inaccurate. In fact, harsh penalties do not deter crime and violence more effectively than less severe sanctions. Long and life sentences are an inefficient, inhumane, and ineffective way of reducing crime, and many societies with less draconian criminal penalties enjoy comparatively low rates of crime.[18] As is discussed throughout this book, it is simply untrue that tough anticrime policies keep us safe. In fact, it has become abundantly clear that mass incarceration itself constitutes a threat to public safety and health.

Mass Incarceration as a Threat to Public Health and Safety

Critics on both the left and the right use the term "mass incarceration" to call attention to the unprecedented scale of the U.S. criminal legal system and racial inequities in it—and the havoc they wreak.[19] The U.S. incarceration rate began an unprecedented ascent in the 1970s. This trend continued through 2007, when nearly one in one hundred adults lived behind bars, 5 million others were on probation or parole, roughly 10 million spent time in jail, and nearly one in three—between 70 and 100 million people—were living with a criminal record.[20] Immigrant detention has also increased dramatically: on an average day in 2020, nearly fifty thousand immigrants were detained in the United States, up from a few thousand in 1980.[21] The scale of confinement sharply differentiates the United States from comparable democratic countries, where incarceration rates range from 38 per 100,000 residents in Japan to 188 per 100,000 in New Zealand. By contrast, the U.S. incarceration rate remains remarkably high, at 644 per 100,000 residents in 2020.[22] The United States is the world's leading jailer, and has been for some time now.[23]

In 2001 the legal scholar David Garland coined the term "mass imprisonment" to call attention to the "unprecedented expansion of prison populations" in the United States and to racial inequities in it, including the "systematic imprisonment of whole groups of the population."[24] Since that time, the use of the similar term "mass incarceration," which also includes the jail population, has exploded. Much of the literature that explores mass incarceration's causes and consequences pays particular attention to the tail-end of the criminal legal process—namely, incarceration—and to the policy developments that have fueled the use of prison and jail. This extensive body of research shows that mass incarceration has had far-reaching effects that work to enhance—and mask—racial and economic inequalities.[25] For the formerly incarcerated, these effects include reduced earnings and employment, increased housing instability and indebtedness, and impaired physical health and mental well-being.[26] Criminal legal system involvement undermines the life chances not only of those who experience incarceration but their families and loved ones as well.[27] Given pronounced racial and ethnic disparities in criminal legal system involvement, families and communities of color have been especially hard hit.[28] One recent study, for example, found that nearly half of all Black women have a family member in prison.[29]

As Garland notes, studies that focus on the causes and consequences of mass incarceration are distinct from efforts to "trace all of the forms in which state power is exercised through the criminal justice apparatus."[30] Studies aimed at this broader objective often use the terms "carceral state" or "mass criminalization" to call attention to the expanding role of police and criminal legal institutions—broadly defined—in communities of color and in the lives of people contending with poverty. This broader conception of the problem is bolstered by the fact that while roughly 2 million U.S. residents live behind bars, more than 4 million are on probation or parole, and tens of millions who have completed their criminal sentence remain saddled with debilitating criminal records and oppressive legal debt.[31] It has become abundantly clear that aggressive policing and non-confinement-based forms of criminal legal supervision—including, increasingly, electronic home monitoring—also cause significant harm by imposing a vast array of burdensome rules and restrictions, enhancing debt, and generally failing to assist people as they seek to stabilize their lives.[32]

Yet even a focus on all forms of criminal legal supervision captures just the tip of the criminal justice iceberg: contact with the criminal legal system often has destabilizing and debilitating effects even if people are never convicted or sentenced to jail or prison.[33] For example, sociologist Devah Pager's seminal work reveals that low-level felony convictions (even absent evidence of incarceration or criminal legal supervision) reduce job applicants' prospects. The effect of the "mark of a criminal record" interacts with and is compounded by racial discrimination to enhance inequality over time.[34] Similarly, other sociological studies indicate that people who are stopped, frisked, arrested, fined, and surveilled are harmed by their contact with police and the criminal legal system even if they are neither convicted nor confined. For example, aggressive policing adversely affects the health and well-being of targeted individuals and communities.[35] In fact, living in neighborhoods where the police rely heavily on "stop and frisk" and similar techniques amplifies psychological distress and undermines the well-being of male residents, including those who are not stopped by the police.[36] Arrest and the involvement with the lower court system that it often triggers can be enormously time-consuming and create a variety of burdens, including reporting and program requirements, fines, and more. Even where misdemeanor courts depend on high dismissal rates to manage large caseloads, and where conviction is relatively uncommon, arrest and court involvement can be quite exacting.[37]

Criminal legal system contact and surveillance have adverse effects on people's lives not only because they lead to punishment, but also because they impact residents' everyday lives, including the routes they travel, the institutions they can access (or must avoid), the balance of power in their personal relationships, their financial resources, and more, in consistently unhelpful ways.[38] The presence of the police in hospital emergency rooms, for example, induces some people who have had contact with the criminal legal system to leave the hospital without receiving treatment, a pattern that likely reproduces health inequalities over time.[39] Similarly, people who have had any form of contact with the criminal legal system are significantly less likely to interact with organizations that engage in formal record-keeping (such as medical, financial, labor market, and educational institutions) than people who have not. Insofar as access to these institutions is an important means by which people improve their quality of life and achieve upward mobility, this "system avoidance" may be an important mechanism by which the criminal legal system reproduces social inequality over time.[40]

The dramatic uptick in the assessment of legal financial obligations further illustrates how contact with the criminal legal system can adversely affect people and exacerbate inequality even when conviction and incarceration do not occur. The imposition of fees, fines, and other legal obligations has increased notably as courts and other criminal legal institutions struggle to fund their expanded operations. This trend, combined with the increase in the number of people who are convicted, means that millions of (overwhelmingly poor) people now carry legal debt.[41] In fact, many people who have never been convicted also carry the burden of legal debt. For example, a recent study in Alabama found that fines imposed on people who were arrested but not convicted of a misdemeanor offense or traffic violation outstrip those imposed on people convicted of a felony offense.[42] Similarly, parents are charged for the cost of their children's detention in at least nineteen states and in numerous counties.[43]

In short, while confinement in jail or prison is especially harmful, some of the negative effects of the criminal legal system do not depend on incarceration or even conviction. At the same time, the increased reach of the criminal legal system means that a variety of control-oriented institutions, including court supervision programs, probation, and parole, play a significant and often harmful role in the everyday lives of people who are poor. For these reasons, some scholars and advocates use the term "carceral state" to highlight the expanded power and reach of criminal legal institutions. The term "mass criminalization" similarly underscores the fact that "aggressive policing and incarceration are our default tools for dealing with a wide array of social problems that can and should be solved by other means," as advocate and writer Deborah Small notes.[44] Although it is clear that criminal legal institutions can and do create significant harm even in the absence of incarceration, I use the more familiar term "mass incarceration" throughout this book to refer to the broad expansion of the state social control apparatus and the myriad ways in which it penetrates and shapes the lives of far too many people in the contemporary United States.

If mass incarceration made us safer, weighing the harm it causes against its public safety benefits would be a tricky business. But mass incarceration does not make us safer. Although the policies and practices that have fueled the expansion of the criminal legal system are routinely justified as crime-fighting measures, mass incarceration is a short-sighted, ineffective, costly, and inhumane approach to public safety. Many countries with far lower incarceration rates experience far less crime and have enjoyed declines in crime rates similar to those that have taken place in the United States.[45] U.S. states that decreased their imprisonment rates the most in recent years have enjoyed the largest drops in crime rates.[46] Research further shows that short sentences deter as much as long ones, and that the vast majority of people age out of crime. In fact, incarceration is often criminogenic, actually *causing* crime.[47] For these and other reasons, the National Research Council recently concluded that "statutes mandating lengthy prison sentences cannot be justified on the basis of their effectiveness in preventing crime."[48]

Mass Incarceration and Criminal Justice Reform in Twenty-First-Century America

While mass incarceration persists and carceral state power remains robust, notable shifts have occurred in the criminal legal landscape. Twenty or thirty years ago, criticizing harsh sentencing policies would have been political suicide for elected officials; today many politicians express concern about the expansion of prison and jail populations.[49] Perhaps most surprising, after years of advocating "tough" approaches to crime and drugs, some conservatives have come to believe that prisons and jails have grown too large. In fact, political scientists David Dagan and Steven Telles attribute the recent increase in state-level reform measures to the mobilization of conservative critics of mass incarceration who "tied what had been a handful of scattered state-level reforms into a broader narrative that cast decarceration as a matter of conservative principle, then marshaled their political networks to spread the message, and plotted strategic initiatives at the state and federal levels to bring around potential allies."[50] For Dagan and Telles, the significance of these developments lies not only in the novelty of conservatives' revised position and their ability to capitalize on the "Nixon goes to China" dynamic, but also in the role that conservatives play in presenting evidence of mass incarceration's costs to other conservatives, thereby spreading the new gospel. Indeed, Dagan and Telles suggest that this process was so effective that criminal justice reform has become the new "conservative orthodoxy."[51] While the election of Trump to the presidency in 2016 cast doubt on this thesis, it is clear that the politics surrounding the issue have shifted, and not only among conservatives. In 2020, many Democratic presidential candidates, including Joe Biden, fought to position themselves as more progressive on criminal justice issues than their competitors and to distance themselves from their prior statements and actions on related issues.

A notable shift in media discourse has also occurred. In the 1980s and 1990s, news stories about crime and punishment were ubiquitous and often framed crime as a consequence of the failure of the criminal legal system to punish adequately. These stories often suggested criminals escaped punishment because of legal technicalities, liberal judges, and permissive laws.[52] This framing of the crime problem clearly implied that the best way to reduce crime is to impose more certain and severe penalties. Omnipresent, racially coded, and fear-inducing stories about crime, as well as the repeated claim that crime and violence were on the rise as a result of judicial "permissiveness" and that remorseless teenage "superpredators" were ubiquitous, amplified anxiety and ushered in an era in which Americans were increasingly "governed through crime."[53]

Fast-forward a few decades and news media discussions of crime and punishment reveal a different sensibility. One meta-analysis of recent studies of discourse about punishment, for example, states, "Readers and viewers of mainstream media are learning about nationwide efforts to reduce prison populations, about substandard prison conditions, and about the negative consequences of 'zero tolerance' school disciplinary policies, among other things."[54] Contemporary newspaper stories about criminal reform often highlight the fiscal costs associated with mass incarceration.[55] In this context, and in the wake of substantial crime drops and reduced political attention to crime-related problems, public support for punitive policies has fallen noticeably.[56]

At the policy level, too, changes are apparent. At least forty-eight states and the District of Columbia have enacted some type of criminal legal reform aimed at reducing incarceration. In fact, research shows that decarcerative reforms intended to reduce prison sentences have outnumbered incarcerative measures by a substantial margin in recent years.[57] Drug policy reform has been especially popular, and nearly all states have adopted significant drug law reforms in recent years. In 2004 and again in 2009, for example, New York State revised its notorious Rockefeller drug laws.[58] Michigan abolished its automatic "life without parole" sentence for those convicted of selling 650 or more grams of a controlled substance, and Texas expanded diversion options for drug possessors.[59] In the context of the opioid crisis, many states have reduced penalties for drug possession; drug courts have continued to expand; and media accounts increasingly humanize those struggling with addiction and emphasize the possibility of recovery.[60] By the end of 2020, eleven states and the District of Columbia had legalized recreational marijuana use for adults.

There is, then, considerable evidence that the criminal legal zeitgeist is in flux, that the need for change is widely appreciated, and that significant reform is underway. And at first glance, it appears that these reforms have made a dent in mass incarceration. Confinement rates have fallen modestly but steadily since their peak in 2007. Although still remarkably high by international standards, by 2018, the U.S. incarceration rate had fallen by more than 15 percent to reach its lowest level in twenty years.[61] The number of people under any form of correctional supervision also fell to levels not seen since 1992.[62]

Upon closer inspection, however, it becomes clear that matters are more complicated than this narrative of incremental progress implies. Reliance on incarceration rates alone as a measure of reform efficacy ignores the fact that crime rates have been plummeting for decades. We would expect incarceration rates to fall in the context of dramatically falling crime rates, even if the intensity of the criminal legal system response to crime remained constant. However, comparatively small declines in incarceration rates may mask *increases* in the intensity of the criminal legal system's response to law violations when crime is dropping. More sophisticated measures of the criminal legal response to law violations therefore take crime rates into account when assessing the strength of the penal system over time.[63]

Toward this end, Figure 1.1 compares the cumulative change in crime and incarceration rates since 2000 with two alternative measures of penal intensity

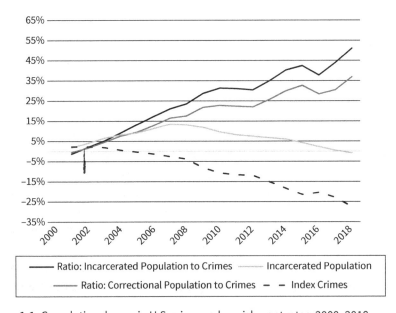

Figure 1.1 Cumulative change in U.S. crime and punishment rates, 2000–2018.

Sources: Author's analysis of Bureau of Justice Statistics National Prisoner Statistics program data accessed through BJS's Corrections Statistical Analysis Tool, Bureau of Justice Statistics, *Correctional Populations in the United States*, Table 1, and FBI Uniform Crime Reports.

Note: Crimes include the eight Part I "index" crimes that are most likely to trigger a prison sentence.

that include information about crime trends. The first measure compares the number of incarcerated people to the number of felony crimes known to the police. The second compares the number of people under any form of correctional supervision (including prison, jail, probation, or parole) to the number of felony crimes known to the police. If penal intensity were holding steady, we would expect that these ratios would remain constant. If the criminal legal response to crime was becoming less intense, as the narrative of incremental progress implies, these ratios would be falling. But as Figure 1.1 makes evident, the strength of the penal response to crime continued to increase even as incarceration rates fell.

In short, if we focus on the incarceration rate alone, we see a modest decline, which creates the impression that recently enacted reforms have "worked" and that the system of mass incarceration is under attack. By contrast, if we take crime trends into account, we find that the criminal legal response to crime continued to *intensify* through 2018 after incarceration rates peaked in 2007. The focus on (modestly falling) incarceration rates in isolation has obscured this fact.

The intensification of the criminal legal system response to crime in recent years stems from two important dynamics.[64] First, the share of felony arrests that resulted in a prison admission has continued to increase since mass incarceration's peak in the mid-2000s. The proportion of arrests for drug or property crimes that resulted in prison admission grew modestly, while the proportion of arrests for public order and violent offenses that resulted in prison admission rose substantially.[65] In addition, average sentence length and time served actually *increased* for all offense types during this so-called reform era.[66]

While these shifts have not been very large in (average) individual cases, they have worked in the aggregate to boost incarceration rates and to offset the decarcerative impact of dramatically falling crime rates.[67] By the end of 2018, the imprisonment rate had fallen by just 15 percent since its peak, despite much larger drops in crime.[68] Even after decades of plummeting crime rates, the United States remains home to the largest prison population the world has ever known. Many prisons and some jails continued to operate well over capacity heading into the pandemic, and conditions of confinement, including the use of solitary confinement, remain troubling.[69] Outside of prisons and jails, more than 4 million people live under correctional supervision, where a punitive system of surveillance, sanctions, and control prevails. This punitive logic has spread even to ostensibly nonpenal institutions. Some welfare programs, for instance, now rely on the disciplinary sanctioning regimes associated with penal institutions, while many public schools employ police, metal detectors, surveillance, and expulsion to keep young people in line.[70] Mass incarceration—and the carceral logic and punitive practices upon which it rests—is alive and well.

The Prospects and Realities of Reform

The first part of this book seeks to explain how and why recent criminal legal reforms have *not* led to reductions in the intensity of the system's response to crime or made a meaningful dent in mass incarceration. In the second part, I identify more transformational changes that, if enacted, *would* notably reduce the reach and power of the penal system while also ameliorating the harm associated with violence, racial inequality, substance abuse, and extreme poverty.

One popular explanation of the persistence of mass incarceration emphasizes that most of the reforms enacted to date target the "low-hanging fruit," or what political scientist Marie Gottschalk calls the "nons": nonserious, nonviolent, and nonsexual crimes.[71] The legislative analyses presented in this book support this supposition. While many states have passed or modified sentencing laws in an attempt to reduce prison populations, these reforms have been limited to comparatively minor offenses, especially drug law violations.[72] Even within the drug law reform category, most decarcerative reforms focus only on drug possession. In fact, in recent years, lawmakers are more likely to have *enhanced* penalties for drug distribution than to have lessened them. As a result, the vast majority of the draconian sentencing laws that contributed so much to the prison buildup remain on the books and continue to ensure long prison stays for many.[73]

Noting that most enacted reforms have focused on the least serious offenses does not imply that we should not pursue reforms aimed at less serious crimes. We *should* eliminate confinement sanctions for minor offenses such as drug possession, for several reasons. First, the routine imposition of harsh penalties for low-level crimes does contribute to mass incarceration and mass criminalization, does involve the imposition of entirely avoidable pain and suffering, and does contribute to the reproduction of racial and socioeconomic inequality. Second, relying on confinement sentences in such cases does not protect public safety. And third, it seems unlikely that lawmakers will be willing to tackle long sentences for violent and other comparatively serious crimes if they have not already weaned themselves from reliance on confinement in cases involving more minor offenses.

At the same time, if the goal is far-reaching and transformative change, reforms aimed at reducing or eliminating penalties for minor offenses must be carefully and thoughtfully pursued. As analysts have pointed out, reforms, especially those aimed at making fundamentally problematic practices more procedurally fair,[74] sometimes create the perception but not the reality of change, thus pacifying critics, entrenching carceral state power, and making more transformative change more difficult.[75] Moreover, in some cases, political actors justify their support of very modest reforms in terms of the increased capacity those reforms will generate to more severely punish other people. As Senator Ted Cruz explained when announcing his (initial) support for the Smart Sentencing Act, his support for that particular drug reform measure was *not* indicative of a new way of responding to violence: "All of us agree, if you have violent criminals, if you have criminals who are using guns, who are using violence, who are dealing drugs to children, the criminal justice system should come down on them like a ton of bricks."[76] In "pro-reform" statements like these, the current approach to violence, and the belief that dealing harshly with people "works," is legitimized and reinforced.

Another danger associated with reform initiatives that focus solely on minor offenses is that supporters sometimes exaggerate the capacity of those reforms to meaningfully reduce mass incarceration and criminalization. Some drug policy reform advocates, for example, simply ignore the fact that the majority of the nation's prisoners were convicted of a violent crime and the related fact that the United States imposes far longer sentences in such cases than other democratic countries.[77] While drug policy reform is clearly needed, it is also important to recognize that the United States would continue to boast the largest prison population in the world even if all prisoners serving time for a drug crime were released tomorrow. This does not mean that drug policy reform is unimportant, but it does mean that it will need to be accompanied by broader changes that create and support alternative ways of responding to both substance abuse and violence, reduce the number of drug *and* non-drug cases processed by the system, and end the excessive sentences that are now routinely imposed, mainly in cases involving violence.

Ending Mass Incarceration

While some believe that the era of mass incarceration is coming to a close, I argue throughout this book that transformative change in penal policy and practice remains elusive. In part I, I seek to explain how and why the kinds of reforms that have been adopted to date have not produced transformative change. In part II, I identify some of the most important cultural, institutional, and policy shifts that are needed to reduce the harm caused by mass incarceration *and* the social problems to which it is a (misguided) response. Throughout, I analyze a number of types of evidence, including data regarding prison admissions, sentences, and time served; legislative records; news media stories about crime, punishment, and reform; case studies of local reform efforts; and conversations with incarcerated people serving long and life sentences.

The chapters in part I identify some of the less well understood dynamics that are working to sustain exceptionally high incarceration rates and mass supervision. These dynamics include the extraordinarily challenging politics surrounding the issue of violence, the changing geography of punishment, and the limits of mainstream drug policy reforms, including drug courts. The chapters in part II identify the cultural, institutional, and policy shifts that are needed to bring about truly meaningful change both in the criminal legal system and in society more generally. These changes include comprehensive sentencing reform aimed at radically reducing reliance on incarceration generally, and on long and life sentences in particular; the development and expansion of alternative, restorative responses to violence that hold people accountable for the harm they cause without relying on prison; and harm-reduction-oriented alternative responses to problems such as substance use that keep people out of the criminal legal system while also providing long-term care and support.

In making the case for these changes, I focus on solutions that are receiving comparatively little attention. For example, I do not focus extensively on the need for cash bail reform; many other analysts and activists have helpfully drawn attention to that issue, and significant progress is underway.[78] I do focus extensively on the politics of violence, in part because research shows that the excessive sentences imposed in cases involving interpersonal violence are a key driver of mass incarceration, yet virtually all lawmakers (with the possible exception of Senator Cory Booker) are reluctant to engage in this challenging conversation. Similarly, my recommendation that we rely less on drug courts' coercive treatment model and more on harm-reduction-oriented frameworks that operate outside of the criminal legal system reflects my belief that drug courts' limitations are not widely appreciated and that harm-reduction-oriented approaches have far more potential to reduce the scale and scope of the criminal legal system while also improving the quality of life of the most marginalized members of our society.

My recommendations are also informed by a number of normative commitments, including antiracism and social justice. As Michelle

Alexander, historian Khalil Gibran Muhammad, and others have noted, mass incarceration cannot be understood without reference to the long history of racial injustice, especially the enslavement and subjugation of Black people throughout U.S. history.[79] Moreover, the criminal legal system continues to be rife with bias and unfairness and now reproduces racial inequality in communities that are also struggling with poverty and numerous forms of violence.[80] Efforts to reverse mass incarceration must, I believe, treat equity, fairness, and remediation of past and current injustices as primary objectives. From this perspective, replacing racially disparate mass incarceration with racially disparate mass supervision would not represent meaningful change, as it would do nothing to redress racial inequality and little to reduce the harm that is disproportionately imposed by the criminal legal system on communities of color.

Similarly, my belief in the import of social justice means that changes pursued by reform advocates should seek not only to reduce the power of the carceral state but also, wherever possible, to address other sources of harm that disproportionately impact the socially disadvantaged. The concept of social justice has been articulated and theorized in numerous ways. At its core, it involves a commitment to redressing social inequality and promoting "the capacity to flourish."[81] This value underlies my preference for, and focus on, changes that reduce the harm caused by the criminal legal system as well as by social ills such as unmanaged addiction and interpersonal violence that disproportionately impact people of color and people contending with poverty.

Finally, my commitment to universal human rights shapes my arguments about what needs to be done to redress mass incarceration. The idea that all humans are entitled to certain inalienable rights, including the right to hope and to dignity,[82] has a long history in the United States and elsewhere, but it has been denied in practice far too often. The belief in the inherent value of all people, including those who live at the margins of society or have been convicted of terrible crimes, is sometimes expressed as the idea that "no one is disposable." This value underlies my recommendations and my view that everyone should be accorded the right to dignity and hope.

In short, I focus in part II on solutions that have the potential to significantly reduce both the scope of punishment as well as the underlying problems—such as untreated addiction and interpersonal violence, which are in turn rooted in poverty and inequality—that also cause suffering. Not all critics of the carceral state prioritize these broader issues. As Maya Schenwar and Victoria Law point out in their recent book, *Prison by Any Other Name*, many conservative and mainstream reform advocates are motivated mainly by the desire to reduce public spending on the criminal legal system but accept the dominant cultural assumption that responsibility for all lawbreaking falls solely within flawed individuals. Combined, these normative commitments lead some mainstream reform advocates to call for technological solutions such as electronic home monitoring that provide control and surveillance in a cost-effective manner but do nothing to address the social conditions that fuel addiction and violence.

Some progressives also seek to reduce incarceration without necessarily addressing problems such as substance abuse and interpersonal violence. As Gottschalk points out, large-scale decarceration in Finland and other countries happened as a result of "comprehensive changes in penal policy over the short term, not sustained attacks on structural problems and the root causes of crime."[83] Based on this observation, she warns that "Americans need to be careful about not stepping into the abyss: the idea that ending mass incarceration must be predicated on tackling the root causes of crimes such as unemployment, poverty, and unconscionable levels of social and economic inequality stratified by race and ethnicity." From this perspective, an insistence on tackling poverty, addiction, and violence may delay or even derail efforts to scale back the carceral state.

While this is a valid concern, it is also true that levels of poverty, addiction, social and racial inequality, and homicide in the contemporary United States are unique among wealthy countries.[84] I agree that tackling these social conditions is even more complex and difficult than reversing mass incarceration and that there are relatively straightforward things we can and should do—such as ending cash bail, sending far fewer people to jail and prison, and confining people for shorter amounts of time when we do—in the short term to reduce incarceration.

At the same time, the values associated with racial equity, social justice, and human rights suggest that, wherever possible, we should seek more transformative changes that address the harm caused by poverty, homelessness, systemic racism, unmanaged substance use disorders, mental illness, and other social ills. These social ills overwhelmingly impact people who experience multiple forms of disadvantage. Although the carceral state is neither a humane nor an efficacious response to these social problems, simply scaling back the carceral state in and of itself will not meaningfully reduce the suffering these problems cause. Better, I believe, to pursue broader changes that reduce the reach and power of the criminal legal system while *also* addressing the suffering associated with social issues such as addiction.

I have chosen to emphasize solutions that reduce the reach of the penal system and address the issues to which it is ostensibly a response for a more pragmatic reason as well. Some reform organizations seek to cut the incarceration rate by 50 percent in the next decade.[85] While this would still leave the United States with a far higher incarceration rate than comparable countries, it is still an ambitious objective. But such a massive reduction in the size of our prisons and jail populations could very well trigger an intense political backlash if not also accompanied by changes that ameliorate untreated mental illness, addiction, crime, housing instability, and related issues. The United States is characterized by unusually high levels of poverty-related problems, and these have become increasingly pronounced in recent decades.[86] Moreover, these issues generate many 911 calls for service, which lead, in some cases, to criminal legal involvement.[87] It is one thing to reduce a (comparatively small) prison and jail population by half in a country with a robust safety net, universal healthcare, sufficient affordable housing, and low levels of serious crime. It is quite another to do so in a country with extraordinarily high levels of extreme poverty, homelessness, addiction, healthcare uninsuredness, and lethal violence.

My emphasis on the importance of addressing both criminal legal power and the social conditions to which it is an ill-advised response is consistent with the ideas that animated the original call for Justice Reinvestment. As the authors who popularized this term explain:

> The destructive effects of mass incarceration and harsh punishment are visited disproportionately upon individuals and communities of color. Justice Reinvestment was conceived as part of the solution to this problem. The intent was to reduce corrections populations and budgets, thereby generating savings for the purpose of reinvesting in high incarceration communities to make them safer, stronger, more prosperous and equitable.[88]

Advocates of Justice Reinvestment thus emphasized that efforts to reverse mass incarceration should also seek to redress racial and ethnic inequities, restore the safety net, and shift resources in ways that allow for communities to meet their needs for healing and public safety, broadly defined. Many Black Lives Matter activists also give expression to this theme in calls to defund or divest from the police and invest instead in social services and community-based organizations.

The recommendations I offer here are also, I believe, consistent with the abolitionist call for *transformative* reforms. As abolitionist writers Dan Berger, Miriame Kaba, and David Stein point out, "Abolitionists are not naïve dreamers. They're organizing for concrete reforms, animated by a radical critique of state violence."[89] In this context, many prison abolitionists differentiate between "reformist" and "nonreformist" reforms. Reformist reforms create the illusion of change but do not fundamentally reduce the power to punish.[90] By contrast, nonreformist reforms include "measures that reduce the power of an oppressive system while illuminating the system's inability to solve the crises it creates."[91] Abolitionists also emphasize the importance of tying nonreformist reforms to "a broader vision of liberation."[92] These criteria for identifying transformative reforms are similar to those I derive from the values of antiracism, social justice, and universal human rights: each of my recommended reforms involves reducing the size, power, and scope of the criminal legal system and racial inequities in it while also reallocating resources toward housing, the safety net, and community-based organizations that work to promote public safety and well-being in their communities.

In some instances, however, the insistence that criminal legal reforms shift resources away from the penal system can be a difficult position to maintain. Gottschalk points out, for example, that efforts to improve prison conditions may require *increased* spending on prisons.[93] In such cases, I believe it is necessary to make case-by-case decisions based on evaluation of the degree of the danger and harm involved. As legal scholar Paul Butler suggests in explaining his (ambivalent and reluctant) support of Department of Justice "pattern and practice" investigations of local police departments, "Federal investigations work, some of the time, to reduce police violence and to improve community perceptions about the police. They are expensive and the benefits may be only short term. But, in the jurisdictions where the federal intervention is successful, fewer people are killed or beat up by the police, and that is a good thing."[94] For Butler, then, the fact that *more people will die* absent these imperfect and limited reforms matters. Moreover, even imperfect reforms can sometimes be used as "ratchets," to use Butler's terminology, to call attention to pervasive problems such as policy brutality even when they fail to produce radical transformation. In some cases, these "ratchets," inadequate as they are, can save lives.

In short, in weighing the advantages and disadvantages of various reform options, their consequences—and the consequences of alternative paths forward and of inaction—must be considered. These caveats and complexities notwithstanding, the ideas and recommendations offered in part II of this book are informed by the values of antiracism, social justice, and human rights, which generally require a reallocation of resources from criminal legal institutions to communities, housing, and appropriate social services wherever possible. In the following sections, I provide a more detailed summary of the ideas and arguments presented in each chapter.

Part I: Understanding the Persistence of Mass Incarceration

The chapters in the first part of the book identify three dynamics that help to explain the persistence of mass incarceration despite dramatically falling crime rates and the widespread enactment of ostensibly decarcerative reforms. Chapter 2 focuses on the politics surrounding violence and argues that our collective failure to question widespread assumptions about the nature and causes of violence constitutes a crucial and, so far, insurmountable barrier to meaningful reform. Analysis of recent legislative measures shows that the vast majority of these reforms have been limited to the least serious nonviolent offenses. This "bifurcated" approach to criminal legal reform draws a sharp but misleading line between those who are involved with drugs (or who commit other low-level offenses, such as theft) and those who have been convicted of a violent act. It also ignores the fact that the proliferation of long and life sentences, which are mainly imposed in cases involving more serious crimes, has been an important driver of mass incarceration.

I argue that the widespread imposition of long and life sentences in cases involving violence rests on the myth of monstrosity, which erroneously assigns sole responsibility for interpersonal violence to the allegedly unredeemable souls who commit it at one point in their lives. This popular mythology, which social psychologist Craig Haney calls "the crime master narrative,"[95] stands in sharp contrast to research findings on these topics.[96] For example, a wide body of psychological and sociological research shows that this myth rests on an overly narrow conception of violence, obscures the social underpinnings of violence, and ignores the human capacity for maturation and growth.[97] Moreover, researchers have amassed a mountain of evidence showing that people who were convicted of violent crimes, and prisoners in general, have frequently been the targets of assaults, often throughout their entire lives. Although abundant, such evidence of trauma and victimization in the lives of the condemned does not square with racist images of ostensibly remorseless and irredeemable perpetrators of violence, and is often ignored or swept aside as a result. As socio-legal scholar Steve Herbert shows in *Too Easy to Keep*, many lifers work hard to make amends and transform their lives in meaningful ways. Nevertheless, the myth of monstrosity, and the politics of violence it engenders, prevails and constitutes an important obstacle to transformative change.

In chapter 3, I describe recent changes in the geography of punishment that help explain the persistence of mass incarceration. This chapter draws on analyses of crime, arrest, and imprisonment trends, and shows that criminal

legal outcomes in urban and nonurban counties have been increasingly divergent. Specifically, while many urban prosecutors are rethinking the drug war
and the overuse of incarceration (especially for nonviolent crimes), the criminal legal response to all types of crime has continued to intensify in nonurban
areas. Political and cultural dynamics in nonurban counties are thus working
to bolster mass incarceration. Although these findings underscore the consequential nature of the discretion that county-level actors such as prosecutors
and judges exercise, this chapter shows that sentencing law fuels mass incarceration by enabling zealous prosecutors and judges to impose excessively
long sentences.

The analyses presented in chapter 3 identify the county characteristics, including social disadvantage, political conservatism, and the size of the Black
population (especially in smaller counties), that are associated with the
greater use of prisons. While efforts to curb the propensity to punish in nonurban areas will necessarily involve the replacement of statutory minimums
with statutory maximums, they will also require addressing the intensification of social disadvantage in suburban and rural areas and the unhelpful
ways that authorities in politically conservative jurisdictions are responding
to that trend.

Chapter 4 explores the limits of mainstream drug policy reforms. While
drug reform is important and necessary, many of the policies and programs
that have been enacted in its name do not fundamentally challenge the dominant approach to addiction and drug markets in ways that truly reduce harm.
Nor do these reforms notably diminish the role of criminal legal institutions
in the lives of those who are ensnared by addiction, for several reasons. First,
most current reforms are aimed at those who use, but do not distribute, drugs.
Just as some reform advocates draw a sharp but misleading line between
drug use and violent crime, others cleave drug use from drug distribution
in ways that obscure their interconnectedness. Even if working as intended,
such reforms would not have much of an impact on prison populations and
would have a comparatively minor effect on jail and probation populations.[98]
Moreover, in recent years, such reforms have been accompanied by calls to
treat drug selling as a violent crime and a notable uptick in prosecutions for
drug-induced homicide. This trend threatens to further limit the impact of
recent drug policy reforms.

Drug courts have been one of the most common ways cities and counties
have responded to the failures of the drug war. Yet the capacity of therapeutic
courts in general, and drug courts specifically, to actually keep people out of
jail and prison is limited. In fact, studies indicate that drug courts *increase* drug
arrests and that, as a group, people who are diverted to drug court may end up

spending more time in prison than they would have otherwise.[99] Moreover, these courts often rest on an outdated and ineffective approach to addiction, subject many participants to extended and intensive court supervision, and return many of those who are unable to abstain to jail or prison. Effective drug reforms that meaningfully reduce legal system involvement while also addressing the harm caused by unmanaged addiction, an unregulated drug supply, and illicit drug markets that generate a great deal of violence, are desperately needed. Sadly, it appears that drug and other therapeutic courts fail to achieve these ends.

Part II: Toward Transformative Change

Together, then, the chapters in part I identify the main institutional and political dynamics that help to explain the persistence of mass incarceration. The chapters in part II identify some of the cultural, political, and policy shifts that are needed in order to bring about transformative change that would reduce the size and scope of the carceral state and racial inequities in it while also enhancing the well-being of the most marginalized people.

Chapter 5 focuses on the need to end excessive sentencing, which in turn requires tackling the myth of monstrosity. Incarcerating people who have committed interpersonal violence—people who are often from disadvantaged, high-crime neighborhoods and have themselves experienced violence—for decades in degrading and traumatizing conditions is neither an effective nor a humane response to the problem of violence. Like capital punishment, the widespread imposition of long and life sentences sets the United States apart from comparable countries.[100] Life sentences—and especially life without the possibility of parole—are now routine in the United States but are nonexistent or very rare in most other democratic countries. In fact, the United States, one in seven prisoners, and one in five Black prisoners, is serving a life sentence.[101] I argue that comprehensive sentencing reform is needed to create the possibility for more humane and viable approaches to violence. While this may seem obvious, the argument that sentencing reform is not needed, and would not reduce mass incarceration, has received notable publicity in recent years.[102] In chapter 5, I show why this argument is mistaken and explain how the adoption of a twenty-year maximum sentence *would* help to reduce mass incarceration—especially the incarceration of the elderly. Redressing the harm caused by the proliferation of long and life sentences also requires the creation and expansion of postconviction review processes in which long-term prisoners have the opportunity to show that they are safe to release. Such policy reforms would enable the reallocation of resources away from prisons and toward pro-social investments in communities and social supports such as subsidized child care and housing. Some of these resources should also be redirected toward survivors of crime and violence, whose needs are often unaddressed in the current policy regime.

Securing the passage of these policy changes will require undermining the myth of monstrosity, which has had a stranglehold on public policy. Toward the end of this chapter, I offer some ideas about how advocates might undermine the myth of monstrosity in order to facilitate comprehensive sentencing reform. There, I also summarize the life histories of five men (Christopher Blackwell, Jeff Foxx, Ray Williams, Anthony Wright, and Eugene Youngblood) who were serving very long or life prison sentences in Washington State through 2020.[103] Their stories bring to life many of the themes developed in this chapter, and powerfully underscore the need for policies that recognize the remarkable capacity for maturation and growth that many incarcerated people exhibit despite their history of abuse and confinement in dehumanizing institutions.

Chapter 6 advocates for the expansion of restorative justice principles and practices, especially in cases that involve direct interpersonal harm. As Howard Zehr writes, restorative justice principles "involve, to the extent possible, those who have a stake in a specific offense to collectively identify and address harms, needs and obligations, in order to heal and put things as right as possible."[104] Increased awareness of the problems associated with mass incarceration and the inability of current criminal legal practices to address victims' needs have led some to consider restorative justice as an alternative or supplement to the traditional criminal legal process. However, most of the programs that exist in the United States exclude cases involving violence, and few divert people who have caused harm from the criminal legal system.

I argue that this pattern should be reversed, for several reasons. First, studies show that restorative justice interventions can both reduce violence and facilitate victim-healing in cases involving violent trauma.[105] Second, as author and restorative justice practitioner Danielle Sered notes, people who are convicted of violent crimes have often been a victim of violence in the past.[106] In such cases, addressing the trauma of those who went on to cause harm is crucial. Finally, insofar as the majority of people in prisons have been convicted of a violent crime, diversionary, restorative approaches that include cases involving violence have the potential to meaningfully reduce reliance on prisons. In the long run, the development of alternative, nonviolent ways of holding people who harm others accountable for the harm they cause— while also enabling them to address the conditions that fueled their harmful actions—will reduce the violence associated with both interpersonal aggression and mass incarceration.

Chapter 7 emphasizes the importance of expanding harm-reduction and community-based response frameworks for responding to less serious crimes, especially drug law violations. These frameworks represent an alternative to drug and other therapeutic courts that have spread across the country. While therapeutic courts help some people, they also expand the reach and power of the criminal legal system, exacerbate racial inequities in it, and connect receipt of social services to forfeiture of legal rights. For these and other reasons, I argue instead for the expansion of harm-reduction-inspired alternatives such as LEAD (Let Everyone Advance with Dignity) and JustCARE in Seattle. Unlike therapeutic courts, these community-based frameworks steer people who live unsheltered and contend with behavioral health challenges *away* from police, courts, and jail, and toward harm-reduction-oriented services, care, and opportunities.

I draw on my research on LEAD and its most recent incarnation, JustCARE, to show how and why alternative response frameworks guided by harm-reduction principles and trauma-informed practice offers a more meaningful opportunity to reduce incarceration and other forms of suffering than drug courts or even decriminalization of drug possession alone. I also show why the long-term success and viability of such frameworks will depend on increased investments in low-income housing, behavioral health, and expanded substance abuse treatment, especially medication-assisted treatment, which has been shown to improve health and well-being while reducing drug poisonings and overdose deaths. Radically expanding this approach has the potential to shrink illicit and hence unregulated drug markets and to reduce the violence that often accompanies them. In short, while alternative response frameworks based on harm-reduction principles are highly promising, significant additional investments in housing, drug treatment, and social services would enhance the efficacy of these alternative response models enormously.

Chapter 8 highlights the need to reimagine public safety to include anti-poverty measures and social and racial equity. This concluding chapter also briefly summarizes the book's main themes and underscores the need for meaningful changes that reduce all forms of harm and violence, including those perpetrated by the state and under cover of law.

PART I
UNDERSTANDING THE PERSISTENCE
OF MASS INCARCERATION

2
The Politics of Violence

> If violent crime is the product of monstrous offenders, then our only
> responsibility is to find and eliminate them. On the other hand, social
> histories—because they connect individual violent behavior to the vi-
> olence of social conditions—implicate us all in the crime problem.
> —**Craig Haney, "The Social Context of Capital Murder"**

In recent years, some observers have suggested that the era of tough sentencing and mass incarceration is over. For example, the editors of the *National
Journal* opined in 2014, "After three decades where Republicans could reli-
ably win elections by posturing on crime, the trend has reversed and the momentum for sentencing reform has reached its zenith thanks to the influx of
conservative support."[1] Political scientists David Dagan and Stephen Telles
similarly argue that "the political momentum is turning against our over-
reliance on cuffs and cages" largely as a result of falling crime rates and the
willingness of conservatives to take a more critical look at our prison system.[2]
Criminologists Joan Petersilia and Francis Cullen went even further, arguing
that the hegemony of the old way of thinking about crime and punishment
has been "shattered" and replaced by a broad consensus that prisons must be
downsized: "virtually everyone" is "trumpeting the need for downsizing, as
though they had not previously fully embraced prison expansion."[3]

As I discussed in chapter 1, the idea that the era of mass incarceration has
come to an end captures some very real and important changes. Increasing
numbers of elected officials, including some prominent conservatives, now
openly express concern about mass incarceration and recognize the need for
change. Media discourse has also shifted, and the costs of mass incarceration
are receiving far greater attention than in the past. Against this backdrop, virtually all states have enacted measures intended to reduce the size of their
prison population and the incarceration rate has dropped a bit.

Yet an exclusive focus on these hopeful developments obscures the difficult and seemingly intractable politics surrounding the issue of violence. I argue in this chapter that the political and cultural challenges associated with the issue of violence pose a significant obstacle to transformative criminal legal reform, one that is even more difficult to surmount than the opposition of vested interests that often work to block reform. Although the opposition of these interest groups is real and challenging, advocates of change have not found it to be consistently insurmountable. In fact, virtually all states have adopted at least some decarcerative reforms (often against the opposition of vested interest groups such as prison guard unions or prosecutor associations).

By contrast, the politics surrounding the issue of violence represent a profound and enduring obstacle to change, one that has thus far prevented transformative criminal legal reform from being enacted—or, perhaps, even seriously considered. As political scientist Marie Gottschalk observes, most of the reforms that have been enacted benefit only the "nons"—people convicted of nonserious, nonviolent, and nonsexual crimes.[4] Moreover, many reform advocates explain their support of these quite modest reforms in terms of the increased capacity they will generate to punish people convicted of more serious offenses even more harshly.[5]

This pattern reflects deeply rooted and widely shared images of people who have committed an act of violence at one point in their lives as monstrous and irredeemable others. This chapter critiques these popular understandings. I show that this mythology is deeply rooted in racist tropes and stereotypes. It is also in tension with a substantial body of research showing that people who have been convicted of more and less serious crimes do not comprise two distinct moral or social categories, and that extreme poverty, trauma, instability, and/or violent victimization typically precipitate acts of interpersonal violence. Evidence of extensive victimization among people who subsequently commit an act of violence not only challenges popular understandings of criminal behavior, but also casts doubt on the widespread assumption that people who commit and people who survive acts of violence are two distinct groups with opposing interests.

I also argue that the myth of monstrosity rests on an overly narrow conception of violence, one that disregards and discounts the racial and structural violence that pervade our history and our society. This structural violence—including extreme poverty, racial oppression and discrimination, housing precarity, and untreated addiction and mental illness—helps explain unacceptably high levels of interpersonal violence in some U.S. neighborhoods. Acknowledging the many forms violence takes is necessary if we are to develop responses that reduce rather than compound it.

Together, the evidence presented in this chapter suggests that the hegemony regarding the need for tough punishment has not been shattered, as some analysts allege. Instead, recent shifts in the criminal legal landscape are indicative of a comparatively minor adjustment of the symbolic boundaries that ostensibly delineate "real criminals" who deserve harsh penalties from more sympathetic others who have been deemed worthy of reform. Unfortunately, our collective unwillingness to reconsider the wisdom and efficacy of the routine imposition of long and life sentences, mainly in cases involving violence, will prevent us from making a significant dent in mass incarceration.

Institutional Barriers to Reform: The Role of Interest Groups

Social scientists have long recognized that institutional developments such as mass incarceration tend to be reproduced over time, in part because they generate vested interests that often work to maintain the status quo. The term "path dependence" captures this dynamic and refers to the tendency for courses of political or social development to "generate self-reinforcing processes"[6] that frustrate efforts to change direction. Researchers emphasizing the challenge of path dependence in the context of mass incarceration point to a range of (increasingly large and powerful) interest groups that have benefited from penal expansion and regularly endeavor to block criminal legal reform.

These groups are diverse and include a range of public and private actors seeking to protect jobs, political influence, leverage, and revenue.[7] For example, private corporations that own and operate prisons (or profit from contracts with them), correctional officers unions, the bail industry, and even county clerks who depend on the collection of fees and fines often seek to prevent decarcerative criminal legal reforms from being enacted.[8] Similarly, legislators from rural communities that house prisons constitute an important voting block that often seeks to obstruct the adoption of reform measures in state legislatures.[9] As legal scholars Rachel Barkow and Angela Davis emphasize, prosecutorial associations have been especially staunch opponents of reform and enjoy a good deal of access to, and credibility in, legislative bodies.[10]

It is true that some reform initiatives falter in the face of opposition from organized groups that benefit from mass incarceration and tough sentencing laws. Prison officers unions, for example, represent a powerful vested interest group that actively works to resist the closure of prisons and the laying off of correctional staff in some states. As sociologist Joshua Page has shown, the uniquely powerful California prison guards union, the California

Correctional Peace Officers Association, served for many years as an effective obstacle to legislative reform.[11] More recently, local prosecutors in Louisiana effectively blocked a bill that would have reduced (extremely harsh) penalties for marijuana possession.[12]

Yet it is also true that these interest groups are not consistently able to block reform. In fact, a significant number of such measures have been enacted, and prison downsizing has occurred in a number of states, over and against the opposition of correctional officer unions.[13] In New York State, for example, the recent closure of nine prisons was staunchly opposed by the prison officers union.[14] Nationally, "at least 22 states have closed or announced closures for 94 state prisons and juvenile facilities, resulting in the elimination of over 48,000 state prison beds and an estimated cost savings of over $345 million" since 2011.[15] Nearly all of these closures have been opposed by correctional unions. Although some of these facilities have been reopened or repurposed to serve alternative carceral purposes, many have not.

Vested opponents of penal reform have lost other battles as well. In 2016, for example, California voters adopted Proposition 57, which renders people serving time for nonviolent offenses eligible for parole, despite the opposition of most law enforcement groups, district attorneys, and the California Correctional Peace Officers Association. Large majorities of California voters have backed other major reform initiatives since that time, despite the organized opposition of prosecutor associations and other interest groups. In Maryland, New York, and New Jersey, bail reform advocates have made significant progress on eliminating cash bail for many defendants, the opposition of the bail bond industry and law enforcement groups notwithstanding.[16] In 2013, Congress enacted the Smarter Sentencing Act despite the strong opposition of the National Association of Assistant U.S. Attorneys, which made clear that it opposed the act because it would reduce their capacity to gain concessions in plea negotiations.[17] In Nebraska, lawmakers enacted a significant sentencing reform measure in 2015 over and against the opposition of prosecutors.[18] And although legislators from rural communities that house prisons often seek to obstruct proposed reforms, many such reforms have nevertheless been enacted. As noted previously, at least forty-eight states and the District of Columbia have undertaken some type of progressive criminal justice reform aimed at reducing reliance upon incarceration; more than half of U.S. states adopted significant drug law reforms.[19]

In short, although mass incarceration has expanded and empowered vested penal interests that often attempt to block decarcerative reform measures, these entities sometimes lose political battles over criminal legal policy.

Against this backdrop, I argue that the political and cultural dynamics surrounding the issue of violence pose an even more challenging constraint on the capacity of advocates to end mass incarceration.

The Politics of Violence

As many social theorists have emphasized, criminal law and punishment are emotionally and normatively charged topics. The morally expressive dimension of penal rituals and the intense condemnation of people convicted of crimes mean that public discussions of penal practices are necessarily fraught and morally loaded.[20] And as cultural sociologists point out, all societies juxtapose insiders—those who are entitled to the full range of rights and opportunities—with outsiders, including criminals, who are vilified and depicted as undeserving of rights and opportunities.

In the United States and elsewhere, these processes have been, and continue to be, highly racialized. Although in recent years some U.S. political actors (especially those associated with the Trump administration) have identified immigrants as the primary criminal threat, U.S.-born racialized minorities, especially Black people, have been vilified in this manner throughout American history. Historian Khalil Gibran Muhammad shows that dominant ideas about Black criminality have long emphasized the allegedly pathological nature of Black violence, in part because the alternative requires recognizing structural racism and violence.[21] The deep historical roots of these racialized images help explain the results of recent experimental studies by social psychologist Jennifer Eberhardt, which show that people generally associate Blackness with violence and violence with Blackness.[22]

Discussions of crime and punishment, then, are intensely emotional and normative phenomena; crime-talk generally, and reassertions of the need to punish "real criminals" and "predators," are highly subject to symbolic and racial politics.[23] For these reasons, policymakers often feel compelled to reassert the moral boundaries that differentiate ostensibly deserving citizens from criminal "predators" and to reassure the public that they remain committed to the idea that "real criminals" must be aggressively punished—even as they make the case for certain (limited) criminal legal reforms. In recent years, some reform advocates have juxtaposed the comparatively sympathetic target of their efforts—usually "nonviolent drug users"—with "serious and violent" criminals.[24] Particularly in the context of the opiate crisis, which has disproportionately killed White drug users, the racial subtext of this cultural distinction is difficult to miss.

Sociologist Christopher Seeds argues that the tendency to juxtapose the (comparatively sympathetic) people who commit relatively minor crimes such as drug possession against the (decidedly less sympathetic) people who have been convicted of violent crimes is a fundamental characteristic of "late mass incarceration."[25] According to Seeds, this logic of bifurcation—which holds that the response to nonviolent crime should be fundamentally different from the response to violent crime—has become the guiding principle of the mainstream reform movement led by bipartisan elites and technocratic reformers. Seeds supports his argument by showing that many states have continued to expand life-without-parole statutes (which authorize the imposition of life- and death-in-prison sentences) even as they enacted decarcerative reforms pertaining to drug and other low-level, nonviolent offenses.[26] In what follows, I provide additional evidence that legislatures are willing to embrace reform for certain low-level offenses but are quite reluctant to reconsider harsh sentencing policies that impact people convicted of more serious offenses.

Legislative Reforms

In this section I describe the results of an analysis of legislative trends during a recent period characterized by significant reform efforts. This analysis involved compilation of information about new sentencing laws enacted from 2007 to 2016 in all fifty states and recorded by the National Conference of State Legislatures. The goal of the analysis is to identify provisions that were intended to reduce or enhance criminal sentences or time served in prison. Measures intended to alter the length of sentence imposed upon conviction were classified as "front-end" reforms; provisions intended to alter the amount of time prisoners served by, for example, enabling prisoners to earn good-time credits that would shorten their prison stay, were classified as "back-end" reforms.[27] (See appendix A for more information about the data and methods used in this analysis.)

The findings from this analysis confirm that decarcerative reforms intended to reduce prison sentences and time served outnumbered incarcerative measures intended to do the opposite by a substantial margin. Specifically, a total of 502 decarcerative and 177 incarcerative provisions were enacted during the period under investigation, the former outnumbering the latter by a ratio of roughly 3 to 1. Moreover, this pattern was fairly consistent across the fifty states. It thus appears that state legislatures have undertaken significant efforts to reduce their prison populations since incarceration rates peaked in 2007, over and against the opposition of vested groups such as prosecutorial associations and prison guard unions.

However, the findings also indicate that a clear majority of the decarcerative reforms were limited to nonviolent offenses; very few states adopted measures intended to reduce sentences or prison stays for people convicted of violent or other serious crimes. Figure 2.1 shows the number of front-end sentencing provisions enacted by type and offense category. As this figure reveals, states enacted far more decarcerative legislative provisions aimed at reducing prison sentences for drug, property, or other "nonserious" offenses[28] than measures aimed at shortening sentences for people convicted of violent (including sex) or public order (many of which involve weapons violations) crimes. Thus, very few reform measures targeted more serious offenses that carry relatively long prison sentences, and some states continue to pass legislation that *increases* the sentences imposed in such cases.

A similar—and even more pronounced—pattern can be discerned when we analyze back-end reforms that seek to alter the amount of time people spend behind bars. Figure 2.2 shows that state efforts to reduce the amount of time served by prisoners by facilitating early release and/or reducing prison admissions for technical parole violations (such as failure to show up to an appointment) have been quite popular—and vastly outnumber measures intended to do the opposite. However, *none* of these decarcerative measures was aimed at people convicted of violent and other serious crimes.

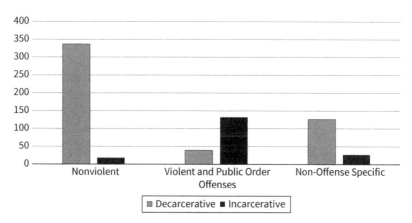

Figure 2.1 Front-end sentencing reforms by type and offense category, 2007–2016.
Source: Katherine Beckett, Lindsey Beach, Anna Reosti, and Emily Knaphus, "U.S. Criminal Justice Policy and Practice in the 21st Century: Toward the End of Mass Incarceration?," *Law & Policy* 40, no. 4 (2018): 321–45 and additional analysis of 2015 and 2016 National Conference of State Legislatures records by the author.

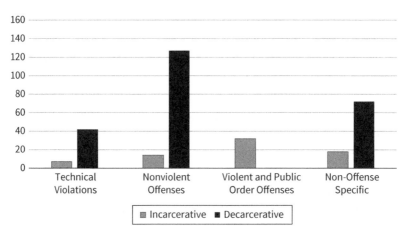

Figure 2.2 Back-end release reforms by type and offense category, 2007–2016.
Source: Katherine Beckett, Lindsey Beach, Anna Reosti and Emily Knaphus, "U.S. Criminal Justice Policy and Practice in the 21st Century: Toward the End of Mass Incarceration?," *Law & Policy* 40, no. 4 (2018): 321–45 and additional analysis of 2015 and 2016 National Conference of State Legislatures records by the author.

In sum, although these legislative findings indicate a clear shift in favor of decarcerative reforms, they also provide support for the claim that most recent reform measures are largely limited to people convicted of nonviolent, nonserious offenses. This means that few of the draconian sentencing laws that contributed so significantly to the prison buildup, many of which pertained to violent offenses, have been repealed; in some cases, these measures have actually been enhanced.[29] These findings are consistent with Seeds's bifurcation hypothesis: legislatures generally limit decarcerative reforms to drug, property, and other "nonserious" offenses.[30]

In a related analysis, my colleagues and I analyzed news stories about criminal legal reform in order to discover how advocates justified reforms and who was featured in the news media as their main supporter.[31] The sample includes newspaper articles that were retrieved by a ProQuest Newsstand search containing the following terms: "United States," "criminal justice," "prison," and "reform." Overall, the findings from this analysis indicate that Republican officials were most prominently featured in the news media as reform advocates. In and of itself, this finding might seem to indicate that the involvement of conservatives in the criminal justice reform movement has enabled widespread recognition of the need for comprehensive sentencing and prison reform. Yet our other findings do not provide much support for this interpretation. For example, the most common argument for reform concerned the fiscal costs associated with mass incarceration. By contrast, discussions of the human costs of mass incarceration were mentioned far less frequently in news coverage of reform efforts.

Moreover, reform advocates quoted in the news often work hard to reassure public audiences that the reforms for which they advocated would *not* benefit people who are undeserving, particularly those convicted of violent crimes: "The research showed that our prisons were being overwhelmed by those who could receive treatment rather than incarceration and therefore preserve our resources for the dangerous violent offender. . . . 'The key is getting the right person in treatment, not the violent offenders.'"[32] Even Senator Jim Webb, a Democrat from Virginia who has taken a leading role in highlighting the need for reform in Congress, apparently felt compelled to reassure the public that his interest in criminal justice reform was not broadly applicable: "Every statement I've ever made on this, every forum I've had, I've said we want to put those who perpetrate violence, those who commit crime as a way of life . . . we want those people to go to jail."[33]

These examples show that reform advocates typically go to great lengths to distinguish between deserving and undeserving reform recipients and to make it clear that their interest in reform extends only to those they believe are comparatively deserving. A somewhat stronger version of this logic asserts that the resources and energies of the criminal justice system, including those resources preserved by progressive criminal justice reforms, should be used to focus on undeserving offenders:

> The courts are one facet of Georgia's criminal justice reform initiative that seeks to divert nonviolent offenders to treatment, so expensive prison beds can be reserved for the most dangerous criminals.[34]

> Gov. Mark Sanford threw his support Wednesday behind a proposed law to shift future nonviolent offenders to alternative sentences as a way to free up more than 2,400 prison beds for violent criminals and avoid the $300 million-plus expense of building a new prison.[35]

The strongest version of this line of argument asserts that decarcerative reforms aimed at deserving offenders need to be coupled with enhanced punishment for undeserving lawbreakers:

> The chief justice of the state Supreme Court has called on lawmakers to keep violent offenders in prison longer and devise alternatives to incarceration for nonviolent offenders. And the attorney general has suggested a similar plan—no parole for violent criminals and non-prison punishments for others.[36]

Proponents say the new law will ensure there is prison space for high-risk, violent criminals, who will serve longer prison terms.[37]

Other articles similarly featured officials touting their "tough" credentials and commitment to harsh punishment for violent offenders alongside their calls for decarcerative reforms. John Kasich, former governor of Ohio, explained that his endorsement of a measure benefiting nonviolent offenders should not be taken as evidence that he and his colleagues have become soft on *serious* crime:

"House Bill 86 is focused on keeping dangerous and violent offenders behind bars and rehabilitates inmates who are first time, non-violent offenders. . . . I don't want anyone to think we've lost discipline," Kasich said. "You do bad . . . we're locking you up. But for someone that wants to do better, we're giving you a chance."[38]

Politicians' reiteration of their commitment to harshly punishing "the truly heinous" stems, at least in part, from a strategic effort to limit the political cost associated with endorsement of any reform measures. For example, in the following statement, a county commissioner in Colorado refers to her proposal to curtail sentences for nonviolent drug offenders and explains that the proposal will be more politically palatable if it is coupled with a new punitive, truth-in-sentencing measure: "Maybe what we're going to do is make more space available so we keep those violent offenders in longer," she said. "I don't think this will end up being a politically risky thing to do when we do our job well."[39]

In short, calls for, and justifications of, criminal legal reform commonly distinguish between more and less sympathetic groups of lawbreakers, and sometimes suggest the importance of redirecting criminal justice resources toward enhancing the punishment of those in the latter category. While the data on which these conclusions rest cover the 2007–14 period, there is reason to believe that this dynamic has not changed. As social psychologist Craig Haney notes, the "master crime narrative" that emphasizes the centrality of the (evil) individual continues to serve as the bedrock of American jurisprudence.[40] The pattern just described reflects the depth and tenacity of the myth of monstrosity—the idea that people who commit an act of violence at one point in their lives are fundamentally depraved and brutal people who cannot be redeemed. This myth, and all that it obscures, is explored next.

The Myth of Monstrosity

Arthur Longworth is currently serving a sentence of life without the possibility of parole (LWOP) in Washington State. Art committed murder at the age of twenty. Now in his mid-fifties, he has become a teacher, an activist, and an award-winning writer.[41] Several years ago, he had the opportunity to have his clemency petition considered. His attorney emphasized two main themes: the first concerned Art's remarkable maturation and development since his conviction; the second involved the horrific abuse Art experienced as a child at the hands of his parents—and again after the state placed him in a group home for boys, where physical and sexual abuse were common.

During the hearing, Art's sister, Dawn, described the abuse they experienced as young children: "My brother and I were tied up, locked up, stripped of our clothes, beaten till we would bleed and pass out. This was normal life for us." She went on to recount a pattern of starvation and shockingly brutal abuse that persisted for years, despite the fact that she and Art regularly arrived at school malnourished and visibly injured. When Art was eleven and Dawn was nine, their parents abandoned them. The state took custody of and immediately separated the two children. Eventually, state officials placed Dawn in a home with a relatively stable and caring family.[42] Unfortunately, they placed Art in a group home for boys where residents suffered regular physical and sexual abuse.[43] By age sixteen, Art had been discharged from state custody and was living on the streets, committing a variety of crimes in order to survive. Tragically, Art's downward spiral eventually culminated in his murder of a twenty-five-year-old acquaintance, Cynthia Nelson, and his receipt of an LWOP sentence.

In most countries, such sentences do not exist or are imposed exceedingly rarely. This is not the case in the United States, where more than 200,000 people, two-thirds of whom are people of color, are serving some form of life sentence.[44] In fact, one in seven prisoners, and one in five Black prisoners, is serving a life sentence.[45] The routine imposition of extreme sentences, mainly in cases involving violent crime, stems from widespread acceptance of the myth of monstrosity, which assigns sole responsibility for violence to the allegedly unredeemable souls who commit interpersonal violence at one point in their lives. The impact of this myth extends far beyond the prison walls.[46] It also limits our ability to develop an effective and humane solution to the problem of violence and to develop meaningful alternatives to the policies that made the United States the world's leading jailer.

The myth of monstrosity has deep roots in American history and racial subjugation. Under slavery, the predominant image of Blackness foregrounded the alleged docility of Black people. This imagery served an important role in maintaining and rationalizing slavery. As museum curator David Pilgrim explains:

> These portrayals were pragmatic and instrumental. Proponents of slavery created and promoted images of blacks that justified slavery and soothed white consciences. If slaves were childlike, for example, then a paternalistic institution where masters acted as quasi-parents to their slaves was humane, even morally right. More importantly, slaves were rarely depicted as brutes because that portrayal might have become a self-fulfilling prophecy.[47]

However, the cultural association of Blackness with docility quickly ended after the American Civil War, as newly free Black people began to obtain social, economic, and political rights. As many have observed, this growth in Black power challenged White supremacy and intensified White fear of Black mobility and freedom. In this context, many southern towns and states adopted Black codes, vagrancy laws, convict leasing systems, and other legal mechanisms aimed at reasserting White supremacy.[48]

It was during this time that images of Black people as savage and brute monsters with a propensity toward violence became ubiquitous.[49] Much of this imagery centered on the alleged threat that Black men posed to White women.[50] Muhammad shows that these cultural depictions were reinforced by "expert" knowledge about the alleged association between Blackness, crime, and violence.[51] Black men were also reported to possess superhuman strength, particularly when under the influence of certain drugs. This claim was the basis of the adoption of more powerful weaponry by local police departments, ostensibly needed to stop Black violence.[52] (Similar claims are often made today by police seeking to justify the excessive use of force against Black men.) The spread of these racist images and tropes was bound up with, and served to rationalize, the Jim Crow system and the lynchings that helped to maintain it.

These tropes remain salient today. Studies indicate that the issue of violence is racially coded and that the mere presence of Black people, especially men, increases fear and perceptions of dangerousness among Whites. In fact, the relationship between race and violence is bidirectional: Black people are associated with violence, and violence is associated with Blackness.[53] In the United States, then, the demonization and dehumanization of people who have been convicted of violent offenses has deep historical, cultural, and racial roots, whatever the racial identity of particular defendants may be. These historical roots mean that the myth of monstrosity is deeply culturally embedded and largely taken for granted, and therefore especially difficult to disrupt.

The Empirical Fallacies of the Myth of Monstrosity

The idea that violence stems from the monstrous nature of the people who commit it is deeply empirically flawed. As Haney notes, "There is still a curious and highly problematic disconnect between what we know as researchers and mental health practitioners and what the larger society and institutions of justice routinely—and sometimes stubbornly—assume about these issues."[54]

In the first place, the myth of monstrosity and the idea that we can and should draw a bright line between people who commit minor crimes and those who commit an act of violence rest on the demonstrably false idea that people who have contact with the criminal justice system can be neatly divided into two distinct moral and social categories. By contrast, criminological research shows that the vast majority of people who engage in crime are "generalists" rather than "specialists," meaning they tend to engage in multiple kinds of crime, often to generate money to purchase drugs.[55] For example, many of the people who have been ensnared by addiction are also involved in drug distribution, have lengthy rap sheets that include property offenses, and have long lived in close proximity to violence, often as its victims and witnesses, sometimes as its perpetrators.[56] In fact, illicit drug markets are characterized by high levels of violence, and the people involved in them often use violence as a means of protecting themselves and for other, less salutary purposes.[57] Conversely, people convicted of sex offenses[58] and homicide have, on average, less extensive criminal histories and some of the *lowest* rates of recidivism upon their release.[59] Thus, in some ways, the people who are convicted of the most serious offenses are least likely to fulfill the stereotype of persistent pathology and depravity. Moral matters are thus far murkier than the neat violent/nonviolent distinction allows.

The myth of monstrosity rests on another empirical fallacy: that survivors of violence and those who perpetrate it are fundamentally different groups with opposed interests. In fact, a substantial body of research shows that the same disadvantaged people and communities that are harmed by mass incarceration also experience high levels of interpersonal violence. While rates of crime fell in the United States from the early 1990s through the late 2010s, the risk of violent victimization is quite uneven and profoundly shaped by race and ethnicity. Rates of violent victimization are highest for Black and

Native American adolescents and young adults.[60] Among men age fifteen to thirty-four, violent injury is the leading cause of death for African American men, the second leading cause of death for Latino men, and the fifth leading cause of death for White men.[61] Social class also matters: on average, the rate of violent victimization for members of poor households is more than double the rate for people living in high-income households.[62] People with mental and physical disabilities are also twice as likely as others to experience violent victimization.[63] In short, the risk of violent victimization is much higher for people of color, people living in poverty, and the disabled.

Sadly, the experience of violence often has long-term and adverse emotional, health, and social consequences, and these consequences contribute to inequality. For example, violent victimization is highly correlated with negative mental health and social outcomes such as posttraumatic stress disorder (PTSD) and socioemotional distress, presumably as a result of the often long-lasting trauma associated with violent assault.[64] People who experience violent victimization are also at increased risk for physical illness.[65] Because violence is associated with socioemotional distress, PTSD, poor physical health, and reduced quality of life, the experience of violence by young people may have a significant impact on their transition to adulthood and life course trajectory.

The negative consequences of violent victimization are especially acute for survivors who live in communities that are disproportionately impacted by both violence and mass incarceration. Like violence, mass incarceration disproportionately impacts the young, poor people, and disabled people,[66] particularly those of color. And like violence, criminal punishment is overwhelmingly concentrated in poor neighborhoods.[67] An estimated 30 percent of all adult Black men have been convicted of a felony offense,[68] and nearly 60 percent of young Black men without a high school degree have spent time behind bars.[69]

It is thus clear that violence and mass incarceration disproportionately affect the same marginalized and racialized communities. This connection also exists at the individual level. In fact, a history of violent victimization is the norm in the biographies of those serving time.[70] Children who experience repeated trauma and abuse are far more likely to end up behind bars than children who do not. This association between prior victimization and subsequent justice involvement persists after risk factors such as poverty are taken into account.[71] For example, a recent study found that Black Americans who had experienced four or more traumatic/violent events were more than four times more likely to be arrested or imprisoned, and more than five times more likely to be jailed, than those who had not experienced comparable levels of trauma (after controlling for other risk factors).[72]

The erasure of the violence that so often precipitates criminal conviction is a truly remarkable feat. In *Just Mercy*, attorney and author Bryan Stevenson shows how the violence visited upon young people who subsequently become system-involved is so handily expunged when prosecutors, judges, and juries hold children as young as thirteen—almost all of whom have suffered unfathomable abuse—criminally responsible for their harmful acts. In such cases, the (allegedly monstrous) child is deemed solely responsible for his or her violent behavior, while the rest of society is found innocent. With all complicating realities erased, the idea that violence is a consequence of the monstrosity of the condemned lives on. The alternative view—that interpersonal violence is the expression of the historical, structural, and social violence that permeates society and of our collective failure to address poverty, ensure equality, and protect the vulnerable—recedes with each condemnation of the "monsters" who fill our prisons.

The juxtaposition of nonviolent and violent offenses (and people) also obscures the fact that "violent" and "nonviolent" are socially constructed categories, the meaning of which changes over time. Historically, most U.S. states have defined violent crimes in terms of the use of physical force and/or infliction of bodily harm, injury, or death. In recent years, some domestic violence activists have pushed for expanded definitions of violence that include behaviors such as stalking in order to underscore the harm associated with those behaviors.[73] For very different reasons, conservatives also often favor expanded definitions of violence. For example, in 2018 House Republicans introduced and passed H.R. 6691, The Community Safety and Security Act of 2018, which would reclassify dozens of federal offenses, including fleeing and coercion through fraud, as violent—and therefore deportable—offenses.[74] The classification of certain acts as violent or not violent is thus not fixed and is often subject to political debate.

The changing and varied legal status of burglary illustrates this point well. Although the FBI classifies burglary as a property crime, at least a dozen states and the federal government consider burglary—entering a dwelling that is not your own without permission and with the intent to commit a crime—to be a violent offense.[75] This categorization of burglary as a violent crime is not supported by research. Although burglary can be extremely distressing to those who experience it, research suggests that it rarely results in physical harm or injury to the victim:

Except in a small minority of cases, burglary is not a crime of violence. The majority of burglaries (about 73%) occur when household members are not present. As indicated by prior research, burglars go to great lengths to learn the patterns of their victims, ostensibly to avoid them. . . . When violence is disaggregated by type (threat vs. attack), the argument that burglary is physically violent . . . becomes even more tenuous. While a small minority of burglary victims do experience a physical attack (4.3%), an even smaller minority reports physical injuries. Victims reported being injured in 2.5% of all burglaries, with half of those who were injured reporting only cuts and bruises.[76]

Nevertheless, Congress elected to classify burglary as a violent crime for sentencing purposes under the Federal Comprehensive Crime Control Act of 1984. The U.S. Supreme Court has, on numerous occasions, upheld this classification, including in cases in which neither physical force nor injury was involved.[77] Snatching a purse, manufacture of methamphetamines, and theft of controlled substances are also classified as violent offenses in a number of states.[78] In fact, based on his inventory of sentencing laws in all fifty states, Marshall Project journalist Eli Hager found:

In Kentucky, committing "Possession of Anhydrous Ammonia in an Unapproved Container with Intent to Manufacture Methamphetamine" a second time puts you in a "violent" category under the law—and you'll face 20 to 50 years in prison. In Minnesota, aiding an attempted suicide is listed as violent, as is marijuana possession (depending on the amount). In North Carolina, trafficking a stolen identity and selling drugs within 1,000 feet of a school or playground are both violent crimes, according to the state's "habitual violent offender" statute. And in New York, it's deemed a violent felony to simply possess a loaded gun illegally—with "loaded" defined as simply being in possession of bullets. These crimes differ from ones like accidental vehicular homicide or "felony murder," in which the perpetrator never intended to hurt or kill someone but still did, or participated in doing so. . . . Those classifications aren't just semantics: When a crime is described as "violent," there are all kinds of consequences for incarcerated people. Anyone convicted of such offenses can face longer mandatory-minimum sentences, the triggering of "three-strikes-you're-out" and "habitual violent offender" penalties and, in immigration cases, are at risk of deportation. They can also be disenfranchised at the ballot box: Some states let certain nonviolent ex-prisoners vote, but not violent ones. And they are often placed in different housing behind bars, according to their supposed violence level.[79]

There is, then, evidence that definitions of violent crime are subject to political influence and that the range of offenses deemed violent has increased in recent years. This trend has expanded the scope and intensity of criminal punishment.

Race and racial attitudes also affect whether behaviors are categorized as violent. Research shows, for example, that White people with higher levels of racial prejudice are more likely to perceive police violence against Black suspects as justifiable (that is, as not violence) than White people with lower levels of bias.[80] Moreover, experimental studies indicate that observers are more likely to identify an ambiguously shaped object as a gun when the person holding the object is Black.[81] Perceptions of behaviors and situations as violent or not violent are thus shaped by racial bias.

The Erasure of Structural Violence

Thus far, I have argued that the idea that system-involved people can be neatly sorted into two moral and social categories is false. I have also emphasized that violent victimization and abuse often precipitate justice system involvement, and that crime victims and the convicted are best understood as overlapping groups with shared interests. Nevertheless, people who have been convicted of a crime that is considered violent are routinely condemned as brutal and irredeemable monsters whose wrongdoing is an expression of flawed character rather than social circumstances combined with immaturity or youthful impulsiveness.

The vigor with which this myth of monstrosity leads us to demonize and punish people convicted of violent crimes stands in sharp contrast to our collective failure to acknowledge the violence upon which our nation was founded. In his introduction to *American Violence: A Documentary History*, historian Richard Hofstader wrote, "What is impressive to one who begins to learn about American violence is its extraordinary frequency, its sheer commonplaceness in our history, its persistence into very recent and contemporary times, and its rather abrupt contrast with our pretensions to singular national virtue."[82] American violence has included everything from the forceful subjugation and genocide of indigenous peoples, slavery and other forms of racial violence, imperial wars, lynchings, and mob violence to innumerable forms of interpersonal violence. Of these, war has been the preferred subject of historians, many of whom have focused narrowly on battlefield tactics and strategies, often valorizing and sanitizing the use of lethal violence in the process. Government officials have also been reluctant to draw attention to the centrality of violence in U.S. history. For example, there has been little public recognition and memorialization of the transatlantic trade in human beings that led to the enslavement of 12 million Africans and African Americans or to the role of violence in sustaining White supremacy throughout Jim Crow and beyond, although Black Lives Matter activists have done much to connect police violence to these issues.[83] Awareness and acknowledgment of the genocide of Native Americans and its devastating aftermath also remain inadequate.[84]

At first glance, it appears that society has been comparatively willing to acknowledge and address family violence. In fact, the laws governing domestic tyranny have evolved considerably. Violence directed at partners and children is now statutorily recognized as serious criminal behavior in all fifty states. Yet intimate partner violence (experienced by one in four women and nearly one in ten men)[85] and child abuse remain pervasive.[86] Children living in poverty are five times more likely to experience abuse or neglect than children living in more fortunate circumstances.[87] Sadly, the state's failure to provide safe haven for adults and children living in abusive situations often compounds the injuries associated with family violence.[88] Tens of thousands of people (mostly women) contending with domestic violence need, but are unable to secure, housing every day and their requests for services often go unmet.[89] Similarly, the abject failure of the U.S. child welfare and foster care system to provide safe and nurturing environments for children—more than half of whom are children of color—itself constitutes a form of structural violence.[90]

Truly reckoning with violence in the United States requires considering structural as well as interpersonal forms of violence. The term "structural violence" refers to the harm and suffering that occur when social structures and institutions prevent people from meeting their basic needs, including the need for security.[91] The United States has been, and continues to be, an outlier among wealthy nations in terms of the degree of structural violence it enacts. Inequality, poverty, incarceration rates, and lethal violence are notably more pronounced in the United States than in other wealthy countries.[92] In fact, the United States has higher poverty rates and greater levels of inequality than all but a handful of other countries with membership in the Organisation for Economic Cooperation and Development (OECD).[93] Child poverty rates are especially high in the contemporary United States.[94]

Moreover, racism and its institutional legacies continue to shape not only the distribution of poverty but also its consequences. Highly segregated urban neighborhoods with concentrated poverty are uniquely damaging. Indeed, sociological research shows that "broad patterns of segregation, isolation, and discrimination" in disadvantaged urban neighborhoods lead to "concentrated problems of poverty, crime and violence."[95] As a result of these social conditions, rates of lethal violence are five to seven times higher in the United States compared to other high-income countries.[96] Comparatively high rates of serious violence, and its uneven distribution, are thus an expression of racial and socioeconomic inequality (as well as the ubiquity of firearms) in the United States.[97]

In short, our enthusiasm for getting "justice" by condemning and punishing people convicted of a violent act is not matched by a passion for making amends for, or even acknowledging, the centuries of racial violence that pervade our national history and continue to shape the distribution of both violence and opportunity. Nor is our collective desire to condemn those convicted of violent crimes accompanied by an equally zealous effort to address the interpersonal and structural violence that so frequently precipitate the crimes we rush to denounce. With all complicating realities erased, the idea that violence is a consequence of the monstrosity of the condemned lives on. The alternative view—that high rates of interpersonal violence are the expression of the historical, structural, and social violence that permeates society, and of our collective failure to ensure equality and protect the vulnerable—recedes with each condemnation of the "monsters" who fill our prisons.

Excessive Sentencing, Violence, and Mass Incarceration

The unprecedented popularity of Michelle Alexander's best-selling book, *The New Jim Crow*, did much to underscore the tenacity and depth of the problem of racial inequality in our criminal legal system, the weakening of many constitutional protections in the name of fighting drugs, and the harm caused by the drug war itself. Unfortunately, the book also led many to conclude that mass incarceration is mainly the result of the drug war.[98] While the nation's most recent drug war has drawn far too many people into the criminal legal system and amplified racial disparities in it, it is not the primary cause of mass incarceration, as many other researchers have pointed out.[99] In fact, recent data indicate that more than half—54 percent—of those in state prisons are behind bars as a result of a violent offense, while only 15 percent are confined as a result of a drug conviction. Moreover, only a small fraction of the latter—just 3 percent—are incarcerated because they were convicted of drug possession.[100] Reforms that target drug possession alone will thus have a small impact on the size of state prison populations.[101]

However, these figures do not include local jails or federal prisons or probation, where the share of people who are being punished for drug law violations or other nonviolent offenses is greater. Against this backdrop, analysts disagree about whether reforming practices and policies pertaining only to nonviolent and nonserious crimes will make a significant dent in mass incarceration. On the one hand, Dagan and Telles argue that "while major decarceration will ultimately require reformers to face tough questions about shortening the sentences of serious offenders, there is much that can be achieved through less controversial changes—what critics might call 'tinkering' with the carceral state."[102] Dagan and Telles buttress this claim by pointing out that roughly 60 percent of people in prison or jail were convicted of a nonviolent offense.

Although this is correct,[103] people convicted of violent crimes spend far longer than others behind bars. For example, in 2009 PEW estimated that state prisoners convicted of drug and property crimes will spend an average of two to three years behind bars, whereas those convicted of violent crimes will spend on average more than seven years in prison.[104] People convicted of violent crimes therefore have a disproportionate impact on the size of prison populations. Moreover, most long and life sentences are imposed in cases involving a crime that is classified as violent. It is for these reasons that many scholars have concluded that significantly reducing levels of incarceration will require eliminating the very tough mandatory sentencing laws that are mainly imposed in cases involving violent crime. (This issue is explored in more depth in chapter 5.)

Yet the problem is not only that we focus on drug reform and ignore long and life sentences. In addition, recent reforms have most frequently authorized diversion and/or shorter sentences for people convicted of only *the least serious* drug and property crimes. For example, reform measures have mainly targeted drug possession rather than drug distribution, theft rather than burglary. In fact, the argument that drug dealing is an inherently violent crime poses a major barrier to reform, and many states have heightened sanctions imposed on people convicted of selling drugs.[105] At this point, then, sentencing reform remains elusive even for many drug and property crimes as well as for violent, sex, and public order offenses.

In short, measures that reduce confinement for only the least serious nonviolent crimes, especially drug possession, have the potential to affect only a very small proportion of people in prison, although they may have a slightly larger impact on jail and probation populations. Some argue that limiting reform to minor crimes not only renders those reforms largely toothless but may also constrain future reform options. Gottschalk, for example, argues that reform rhetoric that sharply distinguishes people convicted of violent offenses from the "nons" reinforces the widespread assumption that the former are depraved and undeserving of second chances. From her perspective, the enactment of reforms that target the lowest-hanging fruit may make it more difficult to enact more ambitious reforms in the future.

The findings presented earlier in this chapter regarding the juxtaposition of people convicted of nonviolent with those convicted of violent offenses in legislation and news stories provide some support for this idea, as they show that even modest reform efforts are often accompanied by language that reinforces the idea that people who have been convicted of a violent crime are not deserving of reform. It thus appears conceivable that by reinforcing popular myths about violence, and the racist images that help to maintain them, mainstream advocates of drug and other more minor reforms make it *more* difficult to enact more transformative reforms. However, this hypothesis does not appear to have been empirically tested to date. It is possible that the opposite is true: reducing penalties for less serious offenses may pave the way for more ambitious sentencing reforms that include people convicted of violent crime by showing that alternatives to incarceration exist and that public safety is not imperiled when penalties are reduced.

In short, while arguments for reform that draw a sharp moral and social distinction between people convicted of minor versus violent offenses, and between crime survivors and system-involved people, are empirically problematic, it is not clear whether the enactment of low-level reforms renders the subsequent enactment of more transformative measures more or less likely. What is clear is that reinvesting criminal legal system savings that accrue from minor reforms back into the criminal legal system diverges importantly from the original vision of justice reinvestment and the more recent call to divest in police and prisons and redirect those monies toward housing, communities, and social services that improve public health and public safety without relying on confinement.

Summary

Significant obstacles to meaningful transformation of the criminal legal system exist. Although interest groups that benefit financially or politically from mass incarceration are sometimes able to block reform, the evidence presented here shows that many states have adopted numerous decarcerative reforms despite the opposition of such groups. By contrast, very few states have reduced penalties imposed in cases involving more serious, and especially violent, crimes. It therefore appears that cultural and political dynamics surrounding the issue of violence continue to constrain the kinds of reform lawmakers and advocates are willing to adopt—and even discuss.

This chapter also showed that the myth of monstrosity, and the bifurcated approach to criminal legal system reform it supports, are in tension with key empirical findings related to the issue of violence. In particular, the fact that the search for drug monies (in the context of criminalization) motivates many harmful acts and evidence of low recidivism rates among people convicted of the most serious offenses cast doubt on the idea that people convicted of crimes can be neatly divided into two distinct moral categories. The myth of monstrosity also obscures the fact that many people who are serving time for a violent act experienced violent victimization and trauma, often repeatedly, prior to (and often during) their incarceration. Crime survivors and the justice-involved are thus not two distinct groups with opposed interests, as many politicians assume. Finally, our cultural fixation on ostensibly evil criminals obscures the extent of the structural violence and inequality that exist in the contemporary United States and the fact that these harms and inequities fuel interpersonal violence.

The continued challenge posed by the politics of violence and the myth of monstrosity suggests that "old" hegemony regarding the need for tough punishment has *not* been shattered. Instead, while some policymakers are willing to reconsider harsh punishments for low-level crimes, the dominant assumption that interpersonal violence must be countered with long and life sentences endures and, at least in the policy arena, remains largely unquestioned. Whatever their empirical weaknesses, the cultural and political constraints that prevent reconsideration of our response to violence are deep and tenacious and constitute an important obstacle to dismantling mass incarceration. Sadly, our unwillingness to reexamine our reliance on long and life sentences does not make us more safe—and works to sustain the largest prison population the world has ever known.

It did not take long for the Washington State Clemency and Pardons Board to unanimously deny Arthur Longworth's clemency petition. One board member explained their decision to Art this way: "Some people grow up in similar circumstances but don't grow up in a life of crime. . . . You make your choice and pay the price." Art's sister's suggestion that their parents and the state that failed to protect Art also bear some responsibility for his crime fell on deaf ears. Evidence regarding Art's dramatic maturation and development in recent decades was similarly dismissed as irrelevant.

We will never know what would have happened if the clemency board had fully considered these points. But its apparent refusal to deeply reflect on them is indicative of our impoverished way of thinking about violence. As long as we continue to ignore the historical and structural violence that has shaped and continues to plague our country, to deny our collective responsibility for it, to insist that the sole cause of violence is the monstrosity of the convicted, and to ignore ample evidence of the capacity of people who have been convicted of a serious violent crime to mature, we will never develop a more capacious, humane, and effective approach to violence. Nor will we ever make a significant dent in mass incarceration. Tinkering with the line that separates comparatively innocent drug law violators from the allegedly monstrous will do little to address this problem. Neither will coming down on people convicted of violent crimes "like a ton of bricks." Instead, a comprehensive reexamination of our history, our criminal legal system, and our collective response to violence is in order.

3
The Place of Punishment

The United States incarcerates a larger share of its population than any other country and has done so for many years.[1] Although still remarkably high by international standards, the U.S. incarceration rate dropped by roughly 15 percent between mass incarceration's peak in 2007 and 2018.[2] This modest decline in the use of confinement has been attributed to a number of factors, including the widespread adoption of state sentencing reforms aimed at reducing prison populations. Yet, as I discussed in chapter 1, the recent drop in incarceration has been notably smaller than the decline in crime rates. In fact, the number of index crimes fell by more than three times as much as the number of people who are incarcerated in recent years.[3] The fact that the decline in incarceration has been far more modest than the fall in crime rates is puzzling given the ubiquity of state legislative reforms aimed at reducing prison populations.

In the previous chapter, I identified one dynamic that helps explain the perpetuation of mass incarceration: the politics surrounding the issue of violence, which have prevented the enactment of meaningful sentencing reforms that would reduce long and life sentences. In fact, the imposition of long and life sentences continues apace, and the number of middle-aged and elderly people behind bars continues to rise.[4] In this chapter, I explore a second dynamic that is also helping to sustain historically high incarceration rates. Specifically, I show that the continued reliance on prisons and jails at high levels in rural and suburban areas helps to explain why the decline in incarceration has been more modest than the drop in crime rates. I also present findings that help explain why some rural and suburban counties continue to rely heavily on prisons even as many large urban counties reduce their reliance on incarceration, at least for less serious offenses.

The election of Larry Krasner, a former defense attorney and strong proponent of criminal legal reform, as Philadelphia's top prosecutor in 2017 marked the beginning of a new tactic in efforts to dismantle mass incarceration. Since that time, numerous candidates for district attorney have run and been elected on their reform credentials.[5] Most of these "progressive prosecutors" have been elected in large urban counties,[6] a pattern that suggests significant geographic variation in the degree to which progressive criminal justice platforms appeal to voters. The analyses presented in this chapter show that differences in the political environments of urban and nonurban counties are significant and predate the fairly recent election of "progressive prosecutors." In fact, the criminal legal response to all types of crime was comparatively punitive in nonurban areas even prior to the Great Recession, and this geographic difference was even greater a decade later. Consistent with this pattern, recent studies show that jail expansion has mainly taken place in less populated areas, and that nonurban counties are sending more and more people to prison even as urban counties send fewer.[7]

While suggestive, these studies did not factor in crime patterns or identify which criminal case processing decisions led to greater use of confinement in nonurban areas. In this context, some have speculated that geographic differences in the use of prison pertain mainly to drug offenses.[8] The first analysis presented in this chapter builds on this research by taking the distribution of crime into account and by identifying where in the criminal legal process, and for which types of offenses, these geographic differences exist. The results show that while urban counties have far higher crime rates than nonurban areas, criminal legal authorities in suburban and especially rural counties send a notably greater share of the people who are arrested on felony charges to prison. In fact, prison admission rates are highest in rural counties, despite the fact that those counties have far lower crime rates than large urban counties. Moreover, the heightened propensity to imprison in suburban and rural counties exists for all kinds of cases—drug, property, public order, and violent. It thus appears that the criminal justice reform movement has not reached a receptive audience outside of large urban areas.

This chapter also explores the role of state law in explaining this variation in penal intensity within states. This analysis aims, in part, to address the claim that tough sentencing laws do not contribute importantly to mass incarceration.[9] By contrast, I show that both legal discretion (exercised by judges and prosecutors) and sentencing law are highly consequential. In fact, the juxtaposition of these is misleading, as sentencing law and legal discretion are best understood as intertwined rather than as separate and distinct.

The evidence shows that legal actors in urban and rural counties located in the same state, and therefore governed by the same sentencing laws, are responding differently to felony arrests. As expected, urban authorities are sending far fewer people to prison than nonurban officials operating in the same state policy environment. Taken alone, such evidence might be interpreted to mean that the exercise of discretion by prosecutors and judges is more consequential than state sentencing law. Such a conclusion would be inaccurate. Research shows that criminal sentencing law also profoundly influences the distribution of power in the courtroom and, often, the intensity of the penal response to crime. Moreover, while the propensity of prosecutors, judges, and other legal actors to punish may vary across localities, tough state sentencing laws create what sociolegal scholar Mona Lynch calls "statutory hammers"[10] that authorize the imposition of very long sentences and provide powerful tools to zealous prosecutors and judges. Such laws also alter the balance of power in the criminal legal process and influence outcomes. This is true even where local legal cultures are characterized by some restraint. And in jurisdictions where such restraint is absent, prosecutors and judges readily invoke tough sentencing laws to impose the harshest penalties possible.

The analyses presented in this chapter thus show that variation in the propensity to employ statutory hammers increasingly falls along urban/nonurban lines but is made possible by the existence of tough sentencing laws that enable zealous prosecutors and judges to impose severe penalties. The argument that changes in the exercise of discretion are the sole cause of the prison buildup ignore the ways in which changes in sentencing policy facilitated these shifts.

Finally, this chapter identifies the county characteristics that are associated with the greater use of prisons and estimates the real-world impact of existing geographic differences in the propensity to punish. These findings indicate that counties with higher levels of social disadvantage, more conservative electorates, and larger Black populations have higher prison admission rates after controlling for crime-related problems. Even after taking all of these factors into account, however, geography still matters: rural and suburban counties are characterized by significantly higher prison admission rates. This variation in the use of prison across county types has significant consequences. If rural and suburban counties matched urban counties in terms of their use of prison sentences, the number of prison admissions would have been an estimated 33 percent lower.

Together, these findings indicate that the reform movement has not yet influenced policy conversations about crime and punishment outside of urban areas. Resistance to reform and commitment to the punitive practices that fueled the prison buildup outside urban areas thus constitutes another important obstacle in the effort to dismantle mass incarceration.

The Penal Divide in Twenty-First-Century America

In this section I compare criminal case outcomes, especially the use of prisons, in rural, suburban, and urban counties. I also assess whether geographic variation in the use of prisons varies by offense type and where in the criminal legal process differences exist. To accomplish these goals, a colleague and I constructed and analyzed an original county-level data set.[11] The analysis presented here relies on these data and focuses specifically on admissions to state prisons, where the majority of U.S. inmates reside.[12] Because many felony convictions result in a probation sentence or jail time rather than a prison admission, the proportion of felony arrests that result in a prison sentence is widely treated as an indicator of the strength of punishment in the relevant locale. Given the focus on county-level differences, the data include only prison admissions over which county officials have influence.[13]

To assess geographic differences in penal intensity, we compared several case processing outcomes across rural, suburban, and urban counties. First, we calculated the punishment rate—that is, the ratio of prison admissions to index crimes—to generate a broad measure of the strength of the criminal legal response to crime at the county level. We also calculated two more specific outcomes to identify *where* in the decision-making process geographic differences exist: arrest-to-crime ratios and prison admission-to-arrest ratios. Comparatively high arrest-to-crime ratios indicate that a relatively large share of reported felony crimes result in an arrest. Relatively high admission-to-arrest ratios indicate that a larger share of arrests result in prison admission.[14] This approach enables us to assess whether differences in policing or in case processing explain county-level differences in the use of prisons.

Table 3.1 shows the results of this analysis. Unsurprisingly, the data show that crime and arrest rates are far higher in urban counties than in suburban and rural counties. These differences are not small. For example, in the later time period, the average violent crime rate in urban counties was more than twice as high as the average violent crime rate in suburban counties, and more than three times higher than the average violent crime rate in rural counties. Differences in property crime rates are similar in direction but somewhat smaller in magnitude. Drug arrest rates are also notably higher in urban than in nonurban counties.

By contrast, prison admission rates are higher in suburban and rural than in urban counties in the later time period. Clearly, then, higher prison admission rates in nonurban counties were not primarily a function of crime rates. In theory, the greater use of prison in nonurban counties could result from greater police efficacy and/or differences in case processing. The findings

Table 3.1 Crime Rate and Criminal Case Processing Outcomes in Urban, Suburban, and Rural U.S. Counties, 2001–2003 and 2011–2013

	Urban Counties		Suburban Counties		Rural Counties	
All Felony Offenses	2001–3	2011–13	2001–3	2011–13	2001–3	2011–13
Crime Rate	5,856	4,345	3,364	2,792	2,557	2,228
Arrest Rate	1,357	1,301	682	759	385	433
Arrest/Crime	.232	.282	.202	.271	.15	.194
Admission Rate	142	120	117	130	119	133
Admission/Crime	.024	.027	.035	.047	.047	.046
Admission/Arrest	.104	.092	.172	.171	.31	.31
Violent Offenses						
Crime Rate	882	706	313	268	247	213
Arrest Rate	291	265	129	114	118	103
Arrest/Crime	.33	.375	.41	.43	.476	.482
Admission Rate	45	42	31	33	30	33
Admission/Crime	.051	.059	.10	.124	.123	.154
Admission/Arrest	.154	.157	.243	.291	.258	.320
Property Offenses						
Crime Rate	4,974	3,640	3,051	2,524	2,310	2,014
Arrest Rate	484	573	328	420	267	330
Arrest/Crime	.097	.157	.107	.166	.116	.164
Admission Rate	34	29	34	40	36	40
Admission/Crime	.007	.008	.011	.016	.016	.020
Admission/Arrest	.07	.051	.095	.135	.135	.121
Drug Offenses						
Arrest Rate	502	387	192	196	163	174
Admission Rate	50	28	33	33	34	36
Admission/Arrest	.10	.073	.173	.166	.212	.205
Population (in thousands)	58,751	63,763	119,249	134,314	35,515	38,324

Sources: Author's analysis of National Corrections Reporting Program and Uniform Crime Report data. See also Beckett and Beach, "The Place of Punishment."

Note: Crimes include the eight index crimes that are most likely to trigger a prison sentence, but do not include drug law or weapons violations. Felony arrests include arrests for index crimes as well as drug violations (other than marijuana possession, which rarely triggers prison admission) and weapons violations. Prison admissions include admissions of inmates with confinement sentences of twelve or more months stemming from new convictions and those resulting from probation violations. Rates are calculated per 100,000 residents. Population figures are rounded to the nearest thousand.

presented in Table 3.1 indicate that the latter largely explain the greater use of prison in nonurban areas. In fact, detailed analysis reveals that geographic differences in the use of prisons stem almost entirely from variation in the likelihood of imprisonment given arrest rather than from differences in the efficacy of policing. That is, the ratio of felony arrests–to–index crimes is similar across rural, suburban, and urban counties (except for violent crimes). By contrast, the admission-to-arrest ratio is far higher in suburban and rural than in urban counties, for both time periods and for all offense categories. In the later time period, the share of arrestees who were sent to prison in suburban counties (17.1 percent) is nearly twice as high as in urban counties (9.2 percent). The rural/urban contrast is even more dramatic: the proportion of arrestees sent to prison in rural counties (21 percent) is more than twice as great as in urban counties. In short, the chances that imprisonment will occur following an arrest for an index crime are much greater in suburban and especially rural counties than in urban counties.

Interestingly, the greater use of prisons in nonurban counties does not pertain only to drug law violations, as some have speculated.[15] Instead, the findings shown in Table 3.1 indicate that the share of arrests that trigger a prison admission is greater in nonurban counties *for all types of offenses*. Using the data shown in Table 3.1, we calculate that the rural admission-to-arrest ratio is 2 times higher for violent crimes, 2.4 times higher for property crimes, and 2.8 times higher for drug offenses than in large urban counties. Differences in the use of prisons across counties thus appear to be widespread rather than offense-specific.

In short, the greater use of prisons in suburban and rural counties does not stem primarily from more efficacious or aggressive policing. Nor does it stem solely from a differential response to drug offenses specifically. Rather, this geographic difference in the use of prisons is the result of decisions and processes that occur after people are arrested for all kinds of offenses. These processes may include prosecutorial charging decision-making, the plea-bargaining process, and, in rare cases that are adjudicated at trial, judicial and jury decision-making.

State Sentencing Law and Local Discretion: Intertwined and Interactive

Taken alone, evidence of this county-level variation in the use of prisons might be interpreted to mean that institutional practice, especially the exercise of prosecutorial discretion, is more impactful than sentencing law. After all, authorities in rural counties send a much larger share of people arrested on felony charges to prison than officials in urban counties do. This is true even *within* states.

The argument that discretion (and especially prosecutorial discretion) is far more consequential than sentencing law has been most strongly advanced by legal scholar John Pfaff. In his analysis of the causes of the prison buildup, Pfaff contends that shifts in sentencing policy did *not* cause an increase in time served in prison and therefore did not contribute to mass incarceration. Instead, he argues, "the only thing that really grew over time was the rate at which prosecutors filed felony charges against arrestees."[16] Based on this analysis, Pfaff claims that efforts to enact sentencing reform are misguided and will not have an appreciable impact on the scale of punishment in the United States.[17]

Pfaff's emphasis on informal decision-making (i.e., discretion) over and above sentencing law is in some ways consistent with sociolegal scholarship, which emphasizes that the exercise of legal discretion helps explain why "law in action" often bears little resemblance to "law on the books."[18] Indeed, discretion is ubiquitous throughout the criminal legal process. Scholars have long noted, for example, that prosecutorial discretion is enormously consequential. Prosecutors significantly impact criminal legal outcomes by altering their charging practices or modifying their standards for plea bargains.[19] Similarly, in states with indeterminate sentencing systems, parole boards exercise substantial discretion that greatly impacts the amount of time inmates spend in prison.[20] In short, it is true that the often-substantial gap between the "law on the books" and the "law in action" in the criminal legal context results in large part from the exercise of discretion by criminal legal actors.[21]

However, implicit in Pfaff's argument is the idea that the exercise of discretion and sentencing law itself are separate and distinct rather than intertwined and interrelated. While research does highlight the importance of informal discretion, it also shows that local practices are powerfully influenced by the nature of the legal tools that are available to variously situated actors. Mona Lynch's illuminating analysis of the prosecution of drug cases in the federal courts, for example, shows that the federal Sentencing Reform Act of 1984 and other tough drug sentencing laws shifted discretionary power to prosecutors, whose leverage in plea negotiations expanded dramatically and whose charging decisions became even more consequential for sentencing outcomes.[22] This redistribution of the power to punish had a number of important effects on prosecutorial filing practices, the power of the federal law enforcement apparatus, the capacity of federal defendants to assert their rights, the conviction rate, and sentencing outcomes across jurisdictions. Thus, while local norms and practices matter, tough sentencing laws alter courtroom dynamics and dramatically increase sentence length, albeit unevenly.

Research on California's three-strikes law similarly shows that tough sentencing laws matter. Although use of this law varies across counties, it and other harsh sentencing laws shift the balance of power in the courtroom and enable zealous legal actors to impose very severe sentences. In California, for example, state courts sent more than 80,000 second-strikers and 7,500 third-strikers to prison between 1994 and 2004.[23] By the end of 2004, strikers made up more than one-quarter—26 percent—of the California prison population; the fact that they were sentenced under the three-strikes law often added many years, and often decades, to their sentences. Although there is significant geographic variation in the use of the state's three-strikes law across counties, and this variation is likely due at least in part to prosecutorial discretion,[24] it is clear that its enactment enhanced the scope and severity of punishment in California. Many prosecutors also avail themselves of other statutory hammers where they exist. For example, the number of prisoners serving life-without-parole (LWOP) sentences has skyrocketed as states expanded their LWOP statutes.[25]

Studies thus show that although some prosecutors in some locales avoid triggering tough sentences even where the law allows them, many others eagerly use any and all such statutory hammers where they are available. Harsh sentencing laws also have important indirect effects, such as enhancing prosecutorial power and leverage, even if the majority of defendants do not receive the maximum allowable sentence.[26] The research on truth-in-sentencing laws illustrates this point well: the mere existence of these laws encourages guilty pleas and increases sentences *even when defendants plead guilty to lesser crimes that are not subject to truth-in-sentencing laws.*[27] Lynch's analysis of courtroom dynamics illuminates why this is the case: even if prosecutors refrain from charging defendants under harsh sentencing statutes, the existence of those statutes enhances prosecutorial power in plea negotiations, which yields longer average sentences.

The fact that both informal discretion and sentencing law impact case outcomes is illustrated in Table 3.2, which compares the punishment rate (that is, the share of index crimes that results in a prison sentence) in counties in the ten most and least punitive states. If state policy environments were irrelevant, as Pfaff contends, we would expect that the use of prison would vary across rural, suburban, and urban counties but that variation across states would be minimal. Table 3.2 shows that this is not the case. Instead, differences in the use of imprisonment are associated with both the state policy environment and the urbanness of the county. In nearly all states, rural and suburban

Table 3.2 Punishment Rates (Prison Admission-to-Crime Ratio) in Urban, Suburban, and Rural Counties in Most and Less Punitive States, 2011–2013

	Urban Counties	Suburban Counties	Rural Counties	Suburban/ Urban Ratio	Rural/ Urban Ratio
Most Punitive States	.04	.06	.09	1.7	2.5
Least Punitive States	.02	.02	.03	1.3	1.7

Sources: Author's analysis of National Corrections Reporting Program data and Uniform Crime Report data. See also Beckett and Beach, "The Place of Punishment."

Notes: Figures include prison admissions involving inmates with confinement sentences of twelve or more months stemming from new convictions/court commitments and from probation violations. Crimes include the eight, Part I "index" crimes that are most likely to trigger a prison sentence.

counties do have higher punishment rates than urban counties.[28] But the punishment rate in urban counties located in more punitive states is twice as high as the punishment rate found in urban counties in less punitive states. Similarly, punishment rates in suburban and rural counties located in more punitive states are three times higher than those found in less punitive states.

In sum, while rural counties are more punitive than urban counties in the vast majority of states, the use of prisons across rural, suburban, and urban counties also depends a great deal on the state sentencing policy environment. In fact, urban counties located in more punitive states boast higher punishment rates than rural counties in less punitive states. These findings suggest that both county type and state policy environments have an important impact on the use of prisons across the United States. This conclusion is consistent with the results of regression-based analyses, which find that state-level factors explain roughly half of variation in incarceration rates that is observed across counties after controlling for crime and other relevant factors.[29]

Elsewhere, my coauthor Lindsey Beach and I present comparative case studies of a highly punitive state (Kentucky) and a less punitive state (Washington) to further explore how state law shapes penal outcomes.[30] While prior studies examine how tough sentencing laws are differentially employed by actors operating within the same legal system, our comparative approach shows how decision-makers can be both enabled and constrained by state sentencing law. In both Kentucky and Washington, the availability of statutory hammers empowers local criminal legal actors who are motivated by ideological or other reasons to impose tough sentences. In Washington, however, such hammers are limited to people convicted of more serious offenses, as the state sentencing grid places caps on the severity of the sentences that can be imposed in cases involving property or drug crimes. In Washington, then, the required use of a determinate sentencing grid that specifies comparatively moderate sentences for drug and property offenses in most cases means that zealous prosecutors and judges simply cannot send as many drug or property law violators to prison or for as long as they can in states like Kentucky.

In short, state policies that expand the number and range of statutory hammers give tough prosecutors and judges the tools they need to fill prisons and, in some cases, local jails as well. Conversely, limits on maximum sentence length effectively constrain enthusiastic prosecutors and judges located in punitive (mainly nonurban) counties and reduce the impact of their zeal. These findings provide additional support for the argument that both formal sentencing policy and informal discretion are consequential and that they are best understood as intertwined rather than separate and distinct.

Disadvantage, Politics, and the Geography of Punishment in Twenty-First-Century America

The evidence provided so far indicates that on average, suburban and especially rural counties are characterized by higher prison admission rates than large urban counties, despite the fact that urban counties have far higher crime rates. Tough prosecutors and judges, increasingly concentrated in nonurban areas, continue to employ existing statutory hammers to impose comparatively severe penalties, whereas criminal legal actors in more urban counties are more likely to refrain from doing so. These findings are complemented by a number of reports issued by researchers affiliated with the Vera Institute, which show that jails and jail populations have also been expanding mainly in nonurban areas. This body of research suggests that the growth of jails and jail populations outside of large urban areas is fueled, at least in part, by county officials' quest for the state and federal subsidies that are provided to counties for housing state prisoners and immigrant detainees.[31]

Recent developments suggest the potential import of both economic and political factors that help to explain continued, heavy reliance on jails and prisons outside of large cities. Whereas urban areas have largely recovered from the economic downturn of the mid-2000s, this is not true of rural communities, many of which are also grappling with the effects of the opioid crisis.[32] Poverty and attendant problems are also worsening in some suburban locales, a pattern sociologists refer to as "the suburbanization of poverty."[33] At the same time, the chasm between the political orientations of rural and urban areas has continued to grow, reaching record levels.[34] That is, urban areas are increasingly dominated by Democratic voters, and the opposite is true in rural communities. Apparent shifts in the geography of punishment are thus unfolding as the economic fates and political orientations of urban and non-urban areas move in different directions. The simultaneity of these penal, economic, and political developments suggests that they may be connected. In what follows, I explore how and why this may be the case.

Social Disadvantage and Punishment

One body of sociological theory and research emphasizes the link between socioeconomic disadvantage, crime, and incarceration. This framework suggests that the spatial concentration of disadvantage (which includes high levels of poverty, unemployment, family disruption, and spatial segregation) fuels violence and involvement in illicit markets, which increases incarceration rates, which in turn exacerbates crime and disadvantage.[35] From this perspective, incarceration is both a reflection and a cause of concentrated disadvantage.[36]

Research emphasizing the role of concentrated disadvantage as a determinant of "incarceration hot spots" within cities provides support for this perspective. These empirical studies of intra-urban variation in incarceration show a high degree of correlation between crime and disadvantage, but also between disadvantage and incarceration (after taking crime rates into account). In Chicago, for example, some neighborhoods with high levels of disadvantage have incarceration rates that are more than three times higher than other communities with similar crime rates but lower levels of disadvantage.[37] While most of this research focuses on urban neighborhoods, sociologist Jessica Simes also finds that concentrated disadvantage is significantly and positively correlated with incarceration rates, over and above its association with crime, at the census-tract level across the state of Massachusetts.[38]

There is, then, a body of research that suggests disadvantage and incarceration tend to go hand in hand and that this association persists even after crime rates are taken into account. Thus far, researchers have not explained the independent correlation of social disadvantage and incarceration (beyond the association of the former with crime). Still, these findings suggest that increased penal severity in rural and suburban areas in the twenty-first century may reflect changes in the spatial distribution of social disadvantage.

In fact, there is evidence that the geography of poverty and marginality has changed in recent years, as disadvantage has deepened in rural America in both absolute and relative terms.[39] For example, the proportion of rural counties experiencing high rates of poverty and inequality in the aftermath of the Great Recession is more than twice as high as the share of large metropolitan counties characterized by these twin markers of disadvantage (44 percent vs. 21 percent).[40] The number of nonmetropolitan communities with poverty rates of 30 percent or higher increased by 50 percent during and after the Recession.[41] Whereas employment in metropolitan areas is now significantly higher than it was prior to the Recession, employment remains well below its pre-Recession rate in nonmetropolitan areas.[42] The rural-urban gap in both poverty and child poverty rates has also grown in recent years. By 2012, the rural child poverty rate had climbed to 26.7 percent (compared to the urban child poverty rate of 21 percent).[43] Similarly, rates of deep poverty (defined as having cash income that is less than half of the poverty threshold) have historically been comparable in rural and urban areas, hovering around 5 percent for much of the 1980s and 1990s. In the aftermath of the Great Recession, however, more than 12 percent of all rural children lived in deep poverty, compared to fewer than 9 percent of urban children.[44]

Sociologists have identified a number of related socioeconomic trends that increasingly characterize the "new rural America."[45] Many such communities have experienced population loss, especially among young adults, as the geographically mobile increasingly relocate to metropolitan areas in search of employment and other opportunities.[46] At the same time, rising male joblessness and increasing levels of female employment have fueled a notable rise in single-parent households in these communities.[47] The health and well-being of many rural residents has declined in this context,[48] and the injury-related mortality rate is now higher in rural than in urban areas.[49]

Many suburban areas are also undergoing significant transformation. The number of suburbanites living in poverty grew by 57 percent from 2000 to 2015.[50] By 2010, 55 percent of the nation's poor were concentrated in the suburbs.[51] This "suburbanization of poverty" is driven by the relocation of poor urban residents fleeing gentrification, as well as by the implementation of HOPE IV, a federal government program that integrates low-income housing voucher recipients in mixed-income communities.[52] The geographic dispersal of employment opportunities, especially low-paid jobs, outside of central cities also fueled suburban growth and poverty.[53] Relatedly, some analysts highlight the recent dispersal of drug-trafficking organizations to rural, suburban, and fringe metropolitan communities as well as the intensification of human suffering due to substance misuse in these communities.[54]

In short, the spatial distribution of disadvantage has shifted in recent years, as poverty and related problems have become more pronounced in nonurban areas. Research that highlights the relationship between disadvantage and incarceration suggests that counties with greater disadvantage will also send significantly more people to prison after crime and other relevant factors are taken into account. These associations may help explain the geographic variation in the use of prisons in twenty-first-century America.

Politics and Punishment
in Twenty-First-Century America

While the impact of concentrated disadvantage on incarceration has been empirically established, it is unclear how and why the severity of poverty-related problems affects the use of prisons beyond their association with crime. Social control perspectives emphasize the impact of politics and racial dynamics on penal discourse and outcomes and suggest one way of explaining the association of disadvantage and incarceration (independent of crime rates).

Broadly speaking, this framework rests on the idea that punishment is an inherently political phenomenon and a key component of state strategies for governing the poor.[55] From this perspective, as punishment scholar David Garland writes, punishment should be seen "not in the narrow terms of the 'crime problem' but instead as one of the mechanisms for managing the underclass. . . . In this broader view, criminal penal measures are shaped not just by patterns of criminality, but primarily by governmental perceptions of the poor as social problems and the preferred strategies for their treatment."[56] Consistent with this approach, social control theorists focusing on the contemporary United States highlight the utility of the crime issue in conservative governance strategies developed in response to the civil and welfare rights movements and associated changes in the electoral landscape.[57] This literature suggests that the crime issue was an especially useful means of attracting and building political coalitions that support harsh criminal punishment, welfare retrenchment, and other "tough" approaches to poverty-related problems, particularly for conservatives seeking to mobilize and attract White voters alienated from the Democratic Party's embrace of the civil rights cause.[58] In fact, rhetoric regarding the alleged breakdown of law and order was designed to, and did in fact, appeal to White voters with higher levels of implicit and explicit bias.[59] From this perspective, the politicization of the crime issue and the embrace of "law and order" rhetoric and tough anticrime policies in the aftermath of the 1960s were not only a response to the civil and welfare rights movements and part of an effort to attract disaffected voters, but were also part of a conservative effort to enhance the state's social control capacity while weakening its commitment to social welfare.[60]

Consistent with this line of thought, studies analyzing state-level variation in punishment rates have found that the strength of the Republican Party and/or conservative values were significant predictors of incarceration rates and spending on social control in the 1980s, 1990s and 2000s. Specifically, there is evidence that conservative citizen ideology predicts higher incarceration rates after controlling for crime-related problems, presumably because conservatives tend to emphasize the individual rather than social determinants of behavior and are more likely to believe that more severe penalties will deter potential law violators.[61] Similarly, studies have found that the strength of the Republican Party predicted heightened penalty at the state and local levels in recent decades.[62]

This body of research demonstrates the centrality of politics to the distribution of punishment and suggests that the shift in the geography of punishment in the United States may be bound up with recent changes in the political landscape. Whereas political divisions in the United states historically fell along state and regional lines, "the new political divide is a stark division between cities and what remains of the countryside."[63] This split has been growing for some time: an increasing number of America's major cities have voted Democrat each year over the past several decades. For example, only four large cities (Phoenix, Oklahoma City, Fort Worth, and Salt Lake City) voted Republican in the 2012 presidential election; all others—including those located in famously Red states such as Texas—voted Democrat. This pattern was even more pronounced in the 2016 presidential election.[64] These shifts in the political landscape have implications for the ideological orientation of criminal legal officials, as the vast majority of prosecutors and judges in the United States are elected.

There are additional theoretical grounds for anticipating that conservatism, race, and disadvantage help to explain why prison admission rates are comparatively high in nonurban counties. Recent research shows that animus toward the poor (measured mainly in terms of opposition to welfare) is an important predictor of punitive attitudes regarding criminal punishment.[65] This research also indicates that anti-Black affect, animus toward the poor, and support for harsh criminal penalties tend to cluster. Thus, support for conservative penal policies and racial animus are associated with opposition to welfare spending and other policies aimed at leveling the playing field. Consistent with these findings, there is evidence that Black defendants receive longer sentences than similarly situated others in more conservative counties, suggesting that bias is more pronounced (or at least more likely to be expressed in criminal sentences) in more conservative jurisdictions.[66] Together, this literature points to the possible role of political ideology and racial dynamics in the distribution of punishment.

In sum, social control theorists see punishment as a key component of state strategies for managing the poor, the racialized, and the marginalized, and therefore emphasize the role of politics and political ideology as a determinant of penal outcomes. To date, this body of literature has been largely distinct from research emphasizing the impact of concentrated disadvantage on incarceration-related outcomes. Insofar as punishment is a component of state strategies for governing the poor, this separation appears to be unwarranted. In fact, there are theoretical grounds for expecting that conservatism, disadvantage, and race significantly predict prison admissions in twenty-first-century America.

Findings

The analysis presented next is designed to explore the impact of a variety of county characteristics such as social disadvantage on prison admissions in the post-Recession context. Hierarchical linear modeling (HLM) was used to conduct this multilevel regression analysis, which identifies the factors that predict admissions to state prisons, where the majority of U.S. inmates reside, in 2,333 counties located in thirty-eight states.[67] For more information about the data and methods used and the descriptive statistics associated with the sample, see appendix B.[68]

The results of the HLM analysis identify a number of county characteristics that help explain why suburban and rural counties have higher prison admission rates (see Table 3.3; for a more complete presentation of the findings, see appendix C). As would be expected, a number of control variables, including the crime and drug arrest rates, are significantly and positively associated with prison admission rates. In addition, social disadvantage (measured here as an index that includes information about the share of the population that lives under the poverty line, the proportion of the population that has not completed high school, the percentage of households that are female-headed, the proportion of the labor force that is unemployed, and the age-adjusted premature mortality rate) is positively and significantly associated with prison admissions. That is, counties with comparatively high levels of disadvantage send a relatively large number of people to prison, holding all else, including crime and drug arrests, constant. In fact, a one standard deviation increase in the concentrated disadvantage index is associated with an increase of more than 21 percent in prison admissions. Relatedly, the opioid prescription rate is positively and significantly associated with prison admissions.

Table 3.3 County-Level Determinants of Prison Admission Rates, 2013

	Effect on Prison Admissions	
	Size of Effect	Significance
County Type Effects (Compared to Urban)		
Rural	17.1%	*
Suburban	17.2%	*
Crime and Policing Effects		
1 standard deviation increase in the crime rate	11.9%	***
1 standard deviation rise in the logged drug arrest rate	8.6%	***
1 standard deviation increase in the arrest-to-offense ratio	1.8%	
Disadvantage Effects		
1 standard deviation increase in concentrated disadvantage	21%	***
1 standard deviation increase in the logged drug death rate	−.03%	
1 standard deviation increase in opioid prescribing rate	7.0%	***
Demographics Effects		
1 standard deviation decrease in the White population	−.9%	
1 standard deviation increase in the Black population	8.5%	*
1 standard deviation increase in the Black population, squared	−13.5%	***
Conservatism Effects		
1 standard deviation increase in support for Romney in 2012	9.9%	***

p-values: *** < .001, ** <.01, * <.05

Source: Beckett and Beach, "Understanding the Place of Punishment," table 2.

Notes: The sample includes 2,333 counties located in thirty-eight states. All predictors are lagged by one or more years. Size of effect captures the impact of a one standard deviation increase in the predictor on the prison admission rate.

The share of the electorate that voted for the Republican candidate in the most recent presidential election is also a significant predictor of prison admissions. In other words, the more conservative a county's electorate, the higher the prison admission rate (after controlling for crime and other relevant factors). For the average county, an increase of one standard deviation in the share of the population that voted for Mitt Romney in 2012 was associated with a 9.9 percent increase in prison admissions; a one standard deviation increase in both concentrated disadvantage and support for Romney would result in a greater than 30 percent increase in the prison admission rate. Thus, disadvantage and conservative political ideology are essential to explaining contemporary patterns of incarceration.

Also consistent with social control perspectives, the size of the Black population is a significant predictor of prison admissions, though this relationship is nonlinear. An increase of one standard deviation in the percentage of the county population that is Black results in an 8.5 percent increase in the logged prison admission rate, after controlling for other factors. The non-linear measure of the Black population– captured by the squared percentage of the county population that is Black—is also significant, albeit negative. This indicates that the effect of the size of the Black population on prison admissions diminishes as the Black population increases in a county. Put differently, the size of the Black population matters more in counties with comparatively small Black populations than in (mainly urban) counties with larger Black populations. This finding is consistent with prior studies finding that the size of the Black population matters less in jurisdictions with very large Black populations, presumably because Black communities are able to secure a greater degree of political power where they comprise a comparatively large share of the population. This finding is also consistent with the observation that prosecutors and other officials in large urban counties that are generally home to comparatively large Black populations appear to be more enthusiastically embracing the criminal justice reform cause than their counterparts in less urban counties. (See appendix C for presentation of the results obtained when the various predictors are added to the model in a stepwise fashion.)

In sum, comparatively high levels of disadvantage in many nonurban counties, along with the rural/urban political divide and the size of the Black population, help to explain why suburban and rural counties have lower crime rates but higher prison admission rates than their urban counterparts. Interestingly, though, even after these and other relevant factors are taken into account, ruralness and suburbanness continue to have their own, independent effect on prison admissions.

The Impact of Heightened Punishment in Nonurban Areas

The findings just presented indicate, among other things, that the use of prisons is notably greater in nonurban counties than in large urban ones. Next, I show the results of a counterfactual analysis designed to assess the real-world impact of the comparatively high punishment rate in suburban and rural areas. I seek to quantify how much it matters that the punishment rate in nonurban counties is higher than in urban counties. How many fewer prison admissions would there be if the share of reported crimes that resulted in a prison admission in rural and suburban counties matched the proportion that trigger prison admission in urban counties?

In this analysis, crime and admission data are pooled within each county type. This method allows more populous counties within each category to have a greater impact on outcomes, as they do in the real world. Using this methodology, the results indicate that the punishment rate—that is, the ratio of prison admissions to index crimes—increased by 12 percent in urban counties between the pre- and post-Recession periods (mainly as a result of an increase in the arrest-to-crime ratio), but by 27 and 26 percent in suburban and rural counties, respectively. In the latter time period, the admission-to-crime ratio was .027 in large urban counties, but .047 in suburban and .46 in rural counties.

The results of the counterfactual analysis indicate that the impact of these geographic differences on prison admissions in the post-Recession time period is substantial (see Table 3.4).[69] In this hypothetical scenario, 87,889 prison admissions from suburban counties and 53,432 from rural counties would have been avoided in 2014 if the ratio of crimes to prison admissions in nonurban counties matched the ratio observed in urban counties. In both rural and suburban counties, admissions would have been reduced by more than 40 percent. Overall, the number of prison admissions that would have

Table 3.4. Impact of Geographic Differences in Punishment Rate, 2014

	Urban Counties	Suburban Counties	Rural Counties	All Counties
Actual Admissions				
Index Crimes	118,295	132,320	103,344	353,959
Drug Violations	27,237	56,360	16,687	100,284
All Offenses	*145,532*	*188,680*	*120,031*	*454,253*
Hypothetical Admissions				
Index Crimes	118,295	76,014	60,658	254,967
Drug Violations	27,237	24,777	5,940	57,946
All Offenses	*145,532*	*100,790*	*66,599*	*312,912*
Absolute Difference (All Offenses)	0	87,889	53,432	141,330
Percentage Difference (All Offenses)	0	−46.6	−44.5	−31.1

Sources: Author's analysis of National Corrections Reporting Program data and Uniform Crime Report data.

Notes: Absolute numbers reflect data from counties included in the sample. Prison admissions involving inmates with confinement sentences of twelve or more months stemming from new convictions/court commitments and from probation violations are included. Crimes include the eight, Part I "index" crimes that are most likely to trigger a prison sentence. Drug violations are measured in terms of arrests for drug violations other than marijuana possession.

taken place in 2014 would have been 31.1 percent lower than it actually was if the punishment rate—the proportion of felony crimes and drug arrests that resulted in a prison sentence—in rural and suburban counties matched that observed in urban counties in our sample. These findings indicate that the significantly higher punishment rate in nonurban counties has a substantial impact on the number of people sent to prison each year.

Summary

Prison admissions were higher in rural and suburban counties in the aftermath of the Great Recession despite the fact that urban counties contend with far higher crime rates. In addition, the majority of jail growth that has taken place in recent years has occurred outside of large, urban areas.[70] A number of county-level characteristics have a significant impact on prison admissions in twenty-first-century America and help to explain comparatively high prison admission rates in nonurban counties. These include concentrated social disadvantage (including poverty-related measures as well as the opioid prescription rate), political conservatism, and the size of the Black population (which matters more in counties with smaller Black populations). That is, counties with higher levels of poverty-related problems, more conservative electorates, and larger Black populations (except in counties with especially large Black populations) send comparatively large numbers of people to prison, after taking crime and other relevant factors into account. Even after controlling for all of these factors, though, both ruralness and suburbanness are associated with the greater use of prison. County officials outside of large metropolitan areas appear to retain a high degree of faith in the use of prisons and jails to address the many social problems with which their communities contend.

When it comes to explaining the persistence of mass incarceration, social disadvantage, conservatism, race, and geography all matter. These findings support both theories of concentrated disadvantage (which highlight the impact of disadvantage and poverty-related problems on penal outcomes) and social control perspectives, which emphasize the importance of political and racial dynamics. They also suggest that geography is an increasingly salient driver of penal outcomes. Together, these findings indicate that embrace of the criminal justice and drug policy reform cause by an increasing number of urban residents, judges, and prosecutors—and the apparent rejection of this cause in many suburban and rural areas—is altering the spatial distribution of punishment in the contemporary United States and helping to sustain mass incarceration.

In the previous chapter, I argued that the politics surrounding the issue of violence, and the reluctance of most policymakers to question the wisdom of relying on very long and life sentences as our primary public safety strategy, is working to block meaningful sentencing reform, thereby bolstering mass incarceration. The evidence presented in this chapter identifies a second dynamic that is also sustaining mass incarceration: the war on crime and drugs is alive and well outside of large, urban counties. This geographic pattern helps to explain why reform measures enacted by states have not made a more significant dent in mass incarceration. These reforms target only the lowest-level crimes and leave prosecutors and judges with ample tools for continuing to send many people to prison (and jail), often for long periods of time. In the absence of comprehensive sentencing reform, zealous prosecutors and judges can, and do, rely heavily on confinement sanctions. These findings suggest the need to address both the intensification of social disadvantage and the counterproductive ways in which local authorities in nonurban areas are turning to the criminal legal system to address a range of social problems in their communities.

4

The Limits of Recent Drug Policy Reforms

The use of consciousness-altering substances has been the subject of intense governmental regulation for over a century. Yet the most recent war on drugs, which began its dramatic escalation after President Ronald Reagan assumed office in 1981, has been characterized by an unprecedented number of arrests, record levels of incarceration, and massive racial disparities.[1] Researchers have identified numerous dynamics that help to explain the unparalleled intensity of law enforcement's most recent crackdown on those who use and/ or distribute (certain) drugs.[2] Although the intensity of the nation's most recent drug war has many drivers, the centrality of race may be its most notable feature.

Numerous studies show that the discourse through which the drug issue was framed in the 1980s and 1990s in particular was highly racialized. This racialization took many forms: the proliferation of media images of Black crack cocaine users in handcuffs and under the (ostensibly necessary) control of law enforcement; the absence of any serious discussion of the need for treatment and the possibility of recovery; the lack of attention to the structural conditions that fueled the spread of crack cocaine; misleading stories about the allegedly permanent damage caused to babies as a result of in-utero exposure to crack; and repeated assertions of the need for heightened law enforcement to control the spread of crack in particular.[3] Policy developments mirrored this unforgiving rhetoric, as lawmakers at the federal level and in many states ratcheted up criminal sanctions for those who possessed or sold drugs, especially crack.[4] At the same time, the police and prosecutorial focus on people alleged to have possessed or distributed crack amplified racial disparities in drug arrests and convictions.[5]

In this context, the number of drug arrests taking place in the United States nearly quadrupled—from just over a half a million in 1981 to a peak of nearly 1.9 million in 2006. Black, Native, and Latinx people bore the brunt of law enforcement's intensified campaign to punish those who used and/or sold controlled substances. Between 1980 and 2006, for example, the national

Black drug arrest rate increased from roughly 5 to 15.9 per 1,000 persons, while the (much lower) White drug arrest rate increased more modestly, from approximately 2.2 to 5.[6]

Commitment to the national war on drugs was unwavering through the mid-2000s. In more recent years, however, the wisdom of this approach has been called into question. In addition, today it is the increased use and abuse of opiates—a trend that has disproportionately impacted White people and led to an unprecedented number of overdose deaths—that has gripped America's imagination.[7] Contemporary opiate users tend to be portrayed through a lens that emphasizes the possibility of recovery and humanizes those struggling with addiction.[8] The contrast between this rhetoric and the ways in which people associated with crack cocaine were portrayed in the 1980s and 1990s is especially sharp.

Some researchers argue that the apparent Whiteness of the current drug crisis has precipitated a change not just in media representations but also in drug policy and drug law enforcement.[9] It is true that some public health–oriented measures, such as medication-assisted treatment and the distribution of naloxone (used to reverse overdose), have expanded in some places in the context of the opiate crisis, although the pace of reform has arguably been slow.[10] It is also true, as I will show later in this chapter, that states across the country have enacted many drug policy reforms intended to reduce the use of confinement in drug possession cases. Many states have also legalized marijuana for recreational as well as medicinal use.

And yet the drug war trundles on. Nationally, drug arrests did decline after 2006, falling from roughly 1.9 million to 1.45 million in 2015, but rose again after 2015, reaching 1.65 million in 2018 (see Figure 4.1). Judging by historical standards, it appears that the drug war is alive and well.

Similarly, while the number of people serving time in prison for a drug offense has declined, this drop has been fairly modest. The total number of people in state or federal prison as a result of a drug conviction fell by 32.3 percent from 2007 to 2017.[11] While this shift is nontrivial, the incarceration of drug law violators in the mid-2000s had reached unprecedented levels. Recent declines in the imprisonment[12] of people who were convicted of drug charges thus do not signal a clear and unequivocal rejection of the drug war but rather a return the very high enforcement level of the late 1990s rather than the super-high level of the mid-2000s.[13]

There are many reasons to expect that the impact of recent drug policy reforms might have been greater than it has been. As noted previously, representations of (mainly White) people struggling with (mainly opioid) addiction are comparatively sympathetic. Perhaps relatedly, elected officials on

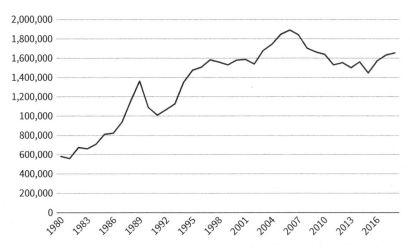

Figure 4.1 Number of drug arrests in the United States, 1980–2018
Source: FBI, Uniform Crime Reports, 1980–2018.

both sides of the aisle now question the wisdom of the drug war; virtually all states have enacted one or more drug policy reforms intended to reduce drug penalties;[14] and many states have legalized some or most of the marijuana market. Given all of these developments, the persistence of relatively high drug arrest rates and the continued use of confinement to punish drug law violators at historically high levels is surprising.[15]

This chapter explores why recent drug policy reforms have had such a modest impact on drug arrests and incarceration. The first and most obvious reason is this: state lawmakers have focused overwhelmingly on reducing penalties for drug possession, but people who were convicted of this specific offense comprise a very small share (3.5 percent) of the state prison population. By contrast, more than 50 percent of all state prisoners are locked up because they were convicted of a violent offense.[16] Reforms that target drug possession alone will thus have a very small impact on the size of state prison populations. Although such reforms will likely do more to reduce jail and probation populations, their potential remains limited.[17] Yet the findings presented in this chapter show that the vast majority of recent drug reforms enacted by state legislatures focus exclusively on drug possession rather than distribution.

Second, while reducing the use of confinement in cases involving drug distribution could have a more meaningful impact on the scale of incarceration, the policy zeitgeist is moving in the opposite direction. Sentencing laws enacted by states in recent years are more likely to have shifted penalties for drug distribution in a punitive direction than to have reduced those sentences.

At the same time, the argument that drug distribution is, and should be treated as, a violent crime is increasingly widely accepted, with more states enacting drug homicide laws and more prosecutors charging people who provide or share drugs with overdose victims with homicide.[18]

Third, the ongoing commitment to drug war practices in rural and suburban areas is sustaining high drug arrest rates and incarceration. As was shown in chapter 3, people who are arrested for all kinds of felony offenses are more likely to receive a prison sentence if they are arrested in a suburban or rural county rather than a large urban county. This geographic difference is especially pronounced in drug cases. In fact, the drug war continues to be fought with vigor by prosecutors and judges in many nonurban areas across the United States. Because many recent reforms allow, but do not require, diversion, prosecutors, judges, and other legal authorities in many states are still able to throw the book at people arrested on drug charges if they are so inclined.

Fourth, drug courts are the most common type of "reform" but are likely increasing rather than reducing drug arrests and incarceration and enhancing racial disparities in drug case outcomes. Many drug court participants are unable to comply with abstinence-oriented treatment requirements and end up back behind bars. Even when drug court participants are able to "graduate" from drug court, they are subjected to extended periods of court supervision as well as compulsory treatment programs that entail much humiliation, significant hardships, and limited treatment options.

In short, recently enacted drug policy reforms have not meaningfully reduced the scale of punishment or the harm the criminal legal system inflicts on people who struggle with substance use disorders. Recent popular reforms also fail to address the property crime and interpersonal violence generated by untreated addiction in the context of an illegal drug market. Studies show that many property crimes are motivated by the quest for monies and goods that can be used to purchase drugs.[19] Moreover, illicit drug markets are unregulatable and hence characterized by comparatively high levels of violence.[20] Even if drug courts and other diversion programs achieved all of their intended effects, and had no unintended ones, their limited scope means that the size and unregulated nature of the drug market would remain essentially unchanged, and the crime and violence associated with drug markets would be unaffected.

The remainder of this chapter supports and illustrates these claims. In chapter 7, I identify some alternative approaches to the problem of substance misuse and to illicit drug markets that have been shown to reduce a wider range of the drug-related harms as well as the damage caused by the criminal legal system itself.

Recent Drug Policy Reforms

Many states have enacted drug policy reforms in recent years. In this section, I describe these changes. This analysis includes state-level drug-sentencing statutes adopted between 2010 and 2016. These legislative reforms were identified through the National Council of State Legislatures (NCSL) database of Statewide Sentencing and Corrections Legislation. This list was then cross-checked against databases compiled by researchers at the Vera Institute of Justice, the Drug Policy Alliance, Vox journalist German Lopez, and the NCSL's own reports on drug sentencing trends. After compiling and refining this comprehensive database, the relevant provisions of each law were coded to reflect whether each provision shifted drug penalties in a lenient, punitive, or mixed direction.[21] Laws that reduced confinement time were coded as lenient, while those that increased confinement sentences were coded as punitive. In a small number of cases, legislative provisions modified sentencing rules in a way that reduced confinement time in cases involving relatively small quantities of drugs but increased penalties for cases involving larger amounts of the same substances. These reforms were coded as "mixed." For more information about the methods used to identify and code these legislative records, please see appendix A, part 2.

Toward Reform—For Drug Possession Only

Many states have decreased criminal penalties for drug possession (see Figure 4.2). These measures generally reduce penalties and/or authorize (but do not require) judges to divert certain drug possession cases to drug courts and other diversionary treatment programs. Our findings indicate that these new laws are not focused on or limited to those who use opioids, as some have speculated, but rather pertain to all types of drugs. However, the majority of new laws affecting penalties for drug distribution actually *enhanced* rather than reduced sentences. That is, legislation that shifts drug-sentencing policy in a more lenient direction overwhelmingly reduced penalties for drug possession as opposed to drug distribution or manufacture. By contrast, those that address sentences for drug distribution or manufacture are decidedly more mixed and tilt toward the punitive end of the spectrum (see Figure 4.2).

In short, state legislatures have reduced penalties and/or authorized diversion in cases involving all types of drugs. However, lawmakers have intensified penalties for drug distribution more often than they have

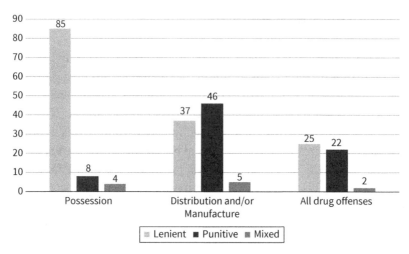

Figure 4.2 Nature of state sentencing policies enacted by type of drug offense, 2010–2016

Source: Author's analysis of legislative records taken from the National Council of State Legislatures database on Statewide Sentencing and Corrections Legislation. See also Beckett and Brydolf-Horwitz, "A Kinder, Gentler Drug War?"

reduced those penalties. In addition, many states have tinkered with the rules that govern eligibility for, and the requirements of, drug courts and other court-supervised treatment programs in an effort to increase the diversion of people arrested for drug possession to court-supervised treatment. Between 2010 and 2016, states enacted thirty-four provisions aimed at expanding drug courts or eligibility to participate in drug court or other diversionary treatment programs; only four provisions restricted eligibility. Similarly, states enacted thirty-eight provisions that modified conditions to enable or require drug treatment or supervision; nine provisions expanded the circumstances under which judges may elect *not* to revoke court-ordered treatment or probation; and another thirteen did both of these things. Clearly, then, states are attempting to increase access to drug courts and other diversionary programs that involve court-supervised treatment for people arrested on drug possession charges.[22] (Later in this chapter, I describe research that helps explain why the expansion of drug courts and similar programs does not reduce the punishment and surveillance of people who use drugs.) More generally, the fact that lawmakers have reduced penalties for drug possession while also increasing, in many instances, sentences for drug distribution means that recent reforms have a limited impact on state prison populations.[23]

Drug Distribution as Violent Crime

These findings suggest that policy and practice pertaining to drug possession and distribution have been moving in very different directions: while state legislatures have endeavored to reduce the use of confinement as a sanction for drug possession, they have more often increased penalties for drug distribution than reduced them. The increased prosecution of people on homicide charges who provide drugs to another person who subsequently dies of an overdose further illustrates this point. Beginning in 2016, in the face of increased conservative support for federal drug law reform, some opponents began to argue that selling drugs is an inherently violent act. As William Bennett and John Walters put it, "The Sentencing Reform and Corrections Act now before Congress is based on a lie—that drug dealing is not a violent crime. Americans have been told this lie for years even as we witness the violence and death caused by drug dealers in our communities. Now, this lie is propelling legislation through Congress that will destroy more lives."[24] Observers have long noted that illicit drug markets are often associated with violence because illegal markets cannot be regulated and are not subject to conventional dispute-resolution mechanisms such as small claims court. However, the argument that drug distribution *constitutes* violence is a different and much bolder claim, one that appears to have gained traction in some conservative circles.

In this context, the number of states defining drug distribution that results in an overdose death as homicide has increased sharply. The Drug Policy Institute has conducted one of the most comprehensive studies of this subject[25] and reports that fourteen states enacted drug homicide laws during the height of the drug war (i.e., in the 1980s and 1990s). After holding steady for some time, this number began to climb once again. As of 2016, twenty states had drug-induced homicide laws on the books, with six having been adopted since 2000. In 2017, legislators in Connecticut, Idaho, Illinois, Maine, Maryland, Massachusetts, New Hampshire, New York, Ohio, South Carolina, Tennessee, Virginia, and West Virginia all introduced bills to create or increase penalties for drug-induced homicide.[26] By 2019, nearly half (twenty-four) of all U.S. states had such laws on the books.[27] Even in states without such statutes, prosecutors still charge the offense of drug delivery resulting in death under various felony-murder, depraved heart, or manslaughter laws. West Virginia provides one extreme example. There, prosecutors charge drug-induced homicide under first-degree murder provisions, which is punishable by life in prison and possibly the death penalty.[28]

The number of people charged with homicide after providing drugs to or sharing drugs with someone who overdosed has increased in this context. Although data regarding prosecutions under drug-homicide laws are not systematically available, analysts have been tracking media coverage of such cases to get a sense of the trend. The results show that media stories about drug-induced homicide prosecutions have risen notably. For example, in 2011, there were 363 news articles about individuals charged with drug-induced homicide. By 2016, that number had grown by over 300 percent, to 1,178.[29] The Health in Justice Action Lab at Northeastern Law School reports similarly dramatic increases in the number of news stories about drug-related homicide prosecutions.[30] Interestingly, analyses by the Lab also indicate that using media coverage as a measure of the prevalence of drug-induced homicide cases almost certainly dramatically underestimates their actual prevalence. For example, in 2016 the news media in Pennsylvania covered seven such cases, but eighty-nine drug-induced homicide prosecutions appear in Pennsylvania's state records for that year.[31] Analyses that rely on media coverage of drug-induced homicide cases as a proxy for the number of prosecutions thus almost certainly underestimate their prevalence by a significant margin.

Although it is unclear whether the stories covered by the media are representative, qualitative analysis of these stories suggests some interesting patterns. In the cases covered by the news media, roughly half of those who have been charged with drug-related homicide were friends or relations who shared drugs with the deceased.[32] While some defendants in these cases were traditional drug dealers (as opposed to family members or friends of the deceased), the vast majority of these "dealers" were people who use drugs and who sometimes worked at the lowest levels of the drug market in order to access them. Moreover, among the cases covered by the media in which the race of the parties could be identified, roughly half involved White buyers and dealers of color.[33] On the basis of such findings, researchers concluded, "These laws and prosecutions have proliferated despite the absence of any evidence of their effectiveness in reducing drug use or sales or preventing overdose deaths. In fact . . . these efforts exacerbate the very problem they seek to remediate by discouraging people who use drugs from seeking help and assistance."[34] At the very least, the proliferation of laws and prosecutions that treat people who share drugs or sell small amounts of drugs to other people as violent criminals reflects an ongoing reluctance to meaningfully challenge the logic of the drug war.

It appears that state lawmakers are drawing a sharp distinction between the comparatively sympathetic figure of the drug user/addict and those who distribute or manufacture drugs. This distinction has a long and racialized history in American culture and politics.[35] Its intensification as reflected in recent legislative trends is also consistent with the "bifurcating" discourse discussed in chapter 2. That is, many reform advocates juxtapose comparatively innocent lawbreakers with (often racialized) others who are depicted as highly culpable, morally depraved, predatory, and beyond redemption.[36] In conversations about drug policy, it appears that drug users and addicts are compared favorably to those who sell or distribute drugs. While the distinction between users and dealers thus appears to be quite meaningful to state lawmakers, empirical research shows that there is significant overlap between these groups, as many users serve as brokers, "mules," or dealers in order to gain access to the drugs they seek.[37] Whatever its empirical errors, this crackdown on people who share or distribute drugs is offsetting any reductions in confinement stemming from reforms aimed at drug possession.

The (Changing) Geography of the Drug War

As was discussed in the previous chapter, the criminal justice response to all types of crime is comparatively intense in nonurban areas. While these geographic differences are not new, they increased somewhat in the aftermath of the Great Recession as poverty-related problems have worsened in nonurban areas and the urban/nonurban political divide has intensified.[38] In this context, urban prosecutors are increasingly embracing criminal justice reform, at least for offenses they consider to be less serious. At the leading edge of this trend are the "progressive prosecutors" who run for office and are elected based on their commitment to criminal justice reform. But even some urban prosecutors who were formerly known for their "tough on crime" credentials now question the wisdom of the drug war and embrace alternatives to it.

The history of the drug war in King County, Washington, exemplifies this pattern. As in most states, Washington's war on drugs was, in earlier years, a disproportionately urban affair. In fact, the share of the state's drug arrests that took place in the largest county, King County, in which Seattle is located, increased from 22 percent in 1985 to 34 percent in 2000. The practices adopted by the King County prosecutor's office during this period exacerbated the effect of the aggressive law enforcement approach. In 2001, "King County was the outlier, convicting a far higher percentage of drug offenders of drug dealing offenses, who thus received prison sentences, than did the other counties."[39]

King County remained an outlier a decade later, but in the opposite direction. In 2000, more than one-third (33.9 percent) of the state's drug arrests took place in King County; in 2015, that figure was 15.8 percent. Felony drug convictions declined even more dramatically, and on a per capita basis are now far lower than anywhere else in the state.[40] This dramatic shift in drug enforcement policy in King County reflects, in large part, a series of decisions made by Prosecuting Attorney Dan Satterberg, who assumed office in the early 2000s and faced unprecedented budget cuts in 2008:

> Satterberg managed the reduction in prosecutorial resources not by across-the-board cuts but by reordering his priorities. Many less serious drug cases that earlier would have been prosecuted as felonies were classified as "expedited crimes," which resulted in a gross misdemeanor conviction or were diverted to drug court. This combination of an evolution in drug sentencing policy and resource constraints reduced felony drug convictions from 1,427 in 2007 to 373 in fiscal year 2010.[41]

Shortly thereafter, Satterberg and other city and county officials announced the creation of the LEAD program, which initially stood for the Law Enforcement Assisted Diversion Program. LEAD began as a prebooking diversion approach aimed at reducing the neighborhood- and individual-level harm associated with outdoor drug and sex markets—as well as the criminal justice expenditures and human injury associated with conventional enforcement practices—by diverting low-level drug and sex offenders into intensive, community-based social services guided by harm-reduction principles.[42] LEAD's creation was a result of pressure on local officials from community members concerned about aggressive law enforcement practices, stunningly high levels of racial disparity in Seattle's drug arrests, and the harm associated with unregulated drug markets.[43] New and modified versions of LEAD now exist across much of Seattle and King County and have been implemented or are in the process of being developed, in roughly one hundred locales across the country.[44]

The shift in drug enforcement philosophy and practice in King County has been especially dramatic, but nevertheless provides insight into the larger political dynamics that are leading many urban prosecutors to reject at least some of the practices associated with the drug war. Like all but a few large urban counties, King County is now solidly Democratic. In the age of mass incarceration, elected officials in increasingly liberal urban areas are finding that the politics of law and order no longer serve them well. In this context, (comparatively) progressive prosecutors have campaigned and been elected on the basis of criminal justice reform agendas with a particular focus on drug policy reform.[45]

By contrast, the drug war continues to be waged with enthusiasm in many suburban and especially rural areas, and recent reform efforts by state officials have done little to curb the impact of this zeal. In Kentucky, for example, prison and jail populations continued to explode throughout the 2000s. In fact, in the decade ending in 2009, Kentucky had one of the fastest growing prison populations in the country, growing by 45 percent (compared to a national increase of 13 percent).[46] Alarmed by this trend and the associated fiscal costs, the state legislature enacted the Public Safety and Offender Accountability Act in 2011. This legislation sought to reverse rising incarceration rates. Toward this end, the act reduces maximum penalties for drug possession, prevents some drug possession convictions from triggering the Persistent Felony Offender statute, and revises the drug-free school zone sentencing provision to cover offenses that occurred within one thousand feet (rather than one thousand yards) of a school building. Despite these reform measures, Kentucky prison and jail populations have continued to grow steadily throughout the 2010s.[47] In fact, according to analysts with the Vera Institute of Justice, the entire state population will be incarcerated in 113 years if incarceration rates continue to grow as they have since 2000.[48]

It is thus clear that Kentucky's (quite modest) drug reform measures failed to achieve their intended effects. It is also clear that the drug war is being fought with unique intensity in Kentucky's rural areas, and that the schism between rural and urban Kentucky's response to drug arrests may be growing.[49] Probation officers in rural counties regularly send to prison people on probation who are unable to comply with the requirements of abstinence-oriented treatment programs. Moreover, prosecutors in rural counties generally do not utilize the deferred prosecution option authorized by the 2011 legislative reform, and request—and often obtain—sentences for drug offenses that would be considered "extremely harsh and not just" in comparatively urban Louisville.[50]

As was discussed in the previous chapter, this pattern is playing out nationally. The data shown Table 4.1 focus specifically on drug arrests and drug case processing outcomes to highlight the magnitude of the difference in the way drug cases are unfolding in urban, suburban, and rural counties. As these data make plain, drug arrest rates (like crime rates) are highest in urban counties, but rural counties send 2.8 times as many of the people they arrest on drug charges to prison as urban counties do (20.5 vs. 7.3 percent).

The continued embrace of the war on drugs in many nonurban areas thus helps to explain why the national response to drug law violations was even tougher nearly a decade after drug arrests peaked in 2007. Specifically, while drug arrests fell modestly after 2007, the proportion of those arrests that

Table 4.1 Drug Arrests and Case Processing Outcomes in Urban, Suburban and Rural Counties

	Urban Counties	Suburban Counties	Rural Counties
Drug Arrest Rate	387	196	174
Drug Admission Rate	28	33	36
Admission/Arrest	.073	.166	.205

Sources: Author's analysis of National Corrections Reporting Program and Uniform Crime Report data. Data are for 2011–13.

Note: Drug arrests include arrests for all narcotics violations other than marijuana possession. Rates are calculated per 100,000 residents.

triggered a prison sentence, the average sentenced imposed, and expected time served for those sent to prison on a drug charge increased slightly during this time period.[51] Notably, these increases pertain to both drug possession and drug distribution cases. In addition to often ratcheting up penalties for drug distribution, state-level reforms often allow but do not require judges to divert drug possession cases. Such reforms have not prevented prosecutors and judges in nonurban areas from continuing to wage a war on drugs and on those whose lives are entangled with them.

In summary, I have identified three limits of recent drug policy reforms that help explain why drug arrests and drug-related incarceration persist at historically high levels. First, drug reforms have been largely limited to drug possession cases, and when such measures are passed, diversion is often optional. Second, penalties for drug distribution offenses have been enhanced in many cases, and prosecutions for drug-induced hom-icide are on the rise. Third, legal authorities in suburban and especially rural counties continue to send comparatively large proportions of people who were arrested on drug charges to prison. Finally, reliance on drug courts has failed to curb the punishment of people whose lives involve il-licit substances.

The Limits of Therapeutic Courts

In recent decades, many jurisdictions across the United States have created "therapeutic" or "problem-solving" courts such as drug courts, mental health courts, and community courts.[52] The underlying idea is that by focusing on the root causes of a person's situation and offering treatment to cure those ills, problem-solving courts may help reduce crime more than incarceration does.

When prosecutors and/or judges believe that defendants' behavior originates in a condition such as substance use disorder, they can offer those defendants (at least defendants who are deemed eligible and are willing to plead guilty) an opportunity to have their case diverted to a therapeutic court. Participants are then required to engage with service and treatment providers and to meet court requirements in order to "graduate" and avoid reincarceration. For example, sobriety and having a full-time job are graduation requirements in many drug courts.[53] People who are unable to comply with such requirements may be unable to graduate from the court program and are often required to serve the original confinement sentence.

The first drug court in the United States was created in 1989, and they have proliferated since that time. By 2014, an estimated 2,800 such courts existed in the fifty U.S. states and territories; at least half of all U.S. counties now have at least one drug court.[54] Yet drug courts represent the "tip of the iceberg" that is court-mandated treatment, as criminal courts also require many people sentenced to probation to participate in court-authorized treatment programs.[55] As a result, drug courts and probation and parole departments now generate the majority of all referrals to publicly funded drug treatment programs.[56] These programs tend to be based on the therapeutic community model, which typically involves residential stays, cognitive and behavioral modification, and intensive monitoring by staff, criminal legal authorities, and other residents.[57]

Although drug courts differ in their particulars and vary across jurisdictions, they are organized around a core set of principles. The first is an emphasis on treatment, which requires that the court attempt to connect a defendant with relevant service providers and thereby address the underlying issues. This means that the approach is "defendant-based" rather than "case-based": courtroom encounters are used to work with the defendant to craft a treatment plan and to monitor compliance with that plan.[58] To accomplish this, problem-solving courts require defendants to surrender many of the due process rights they ordinarily possess.[59] This approach also assumes that treatment is necessary and, often, sufficient to change behavior. Second, drug and other therapeutic courts use a team approach, whereby all the actors—including judges and both prosecuting and defense attorneys—seek to minimize the adversarial nature of the courtroom. Finally, staff are tasked not only with crafting a treatment plan but also with monitoring defendants' compliance with that plan and determining when sanctions should be imposed and which defendants should be "failed" from the program and returned to jail.[60]

While recognizing that law violations are often rooted in medical and behavioral health issues, advocates of therapeutic courts also believe that having a judge who may impose sanctions for noncompliance is a necessary "stick" needed to compel the reluctant and hard-to-treat to stay on track. Implicitly, this approach assumes that the root of the problem is not inadequate or culturally inappropriate treatment programs, insufficient social services, unresolved trauma, a lack of affordable housing, or the flaws associated with abstinence-only approaches, but rather "treatment resistance" among people struggling with chemical dependency (and other) issues. Sociologist Rebecca Tiger memorably refers to this approach as "enlightened coercion."[61] Similarly, sociologist Forrest Stuart calls police efforts to strong-arm arrestees into abstinence-oriented treatment programs "coercive benevolence."[62]

Studies conducted in the 1990s and early 2000s focused mainly on the efficacy of drug courts, which was typically measured in terms of those courts' capacity to reduce recidivism. Many of these studies evaluated specific drug courts and were not peer-reviewed. In recent years, however, researchers have conducted meta-analyses of these studies in an effort to assess the efficacy of drug courts more generally. The findings generally indicate that drug court participation reduces recidivism by between 8 and 20 percent.[63] Drug court supporters have read this evidence as overwhelmingly positive and recommend expanding the drug court model on the basis of it. For example, analyst Michael Rempel and colleagues conclude:

> As a starting point, since drug courts are effective on average, they should seek to enroll more offenders. One recent analysis found that adult drug courts now serve less than 4 percent of the potentially eligible defendant pool nationwide, while another estimates that less than 1 percent enter a drug court. Accordingly, expanded eligibility—especially for high-risk defendants—and implementation of more effective screening and referral protocols at the outset of any court case, may comprise particularly fruitful policymaking avenues.[64]

By contrast, other analysts emphasize that the evaluations upon which most meta-analyses of drug courts are based are characterized by significant methodological flaws, including non-random selection, non-equivalent comparison groups, the inability to control for many relevant variables, confidence intervals that include null effects, and highly variable outcome measures.[65] To take just one example of a troubling methodological issue: a number of researchers contend that assessments of the impact of drug courts on recidivism are inflated because participants are often "cherry-picked." The argument is that courts often screen out people with more serious substance abuse problems but include many low-risk participants, namely, people who use drugs recreationally and may not need treatment or heightened supervision. As Drug Policy Alliance analysts put it:

As a result of cherry-picking, people who suffer from more serious drug problems
are often denied access to drug court. This, in turn, gives rise to misleading data
because it yields drug court participants who are, on the whole, more likely to succeed than a comparison group of conventionally sentenced people who meet drug
court eligibility criteria but who are not accepted into the drug court.[66]

Recent studies support this argument. For example, a 2009 study found that
about one-third of drug court participants did not have serious substance use
issues. These "optimal performers" were significantly more likely to graduate
from drug court than those with more serious challenges.[67] Another study
found that participants with low composite drug use scores were significantly
more likely to graduate than those with mid- and high-level scores, leading
the authors to suggest that "some participants are able to successfully complete the program because of a low substance use severity at baseline."[68] To the
extent that it occurs, then, cherry-picking yields higher completion rates and
greater reductions in recidivism than would otherwise occur.

Recent studies also call attention to a host of important dynamics that were
often overlooked in the past. First, there is reason to believe that drug courts
do not reduce, and may actually increase, both drug-related incarceration and
drug arrests relative to what would occur in their absence. For example, a recent study funded by the National Institute of Justice found no statistically significant differences between the amount of time spent behind bars by people
who entered drug court and by those who did not. In fact, the data suggest
that drug court participants may end up serving *more* time behind bars than
those whose cases are not diverted.[69] This counterintuitive finding appears
to reflect the fact that although successful drug court graduates may avoid
jail time, those who are unable to graduate from drug court often face even
more severe penalties than they would have if they had simply pled guilty to
the original charge.[70] This is particularly concerning given wide variation in
drug court completion rates, which range from 15 to 89 percent.[71] Similarly,
there is evidence that drug courts *increase* aggregate drug arrests, presumably
because their existence encourages police to make arrests and prosecutors to
file charges as a way of getting people into treatment. One recent study, for
example, found that cities that established drug courts experienced a nearly
17 percent *increase* in misdemeanor drug arrests per year.[72]

The evidence regarding drug courts' implications for racial equity are also
troubling. Research shows that cities with larger populations of color were
more likely to create drug courts, but once established, drug courts were associated with a higher arrest rate for Black—but not White—residents.[73] More
generally, studies indicate that drug courts enhance rather than alleviate racial inequality in drug-related incarceration. One recent study, for example,

found that sanctions are higher for drug court participants of color who violate the rules of the program.[74] For this and possibly other reasons, people of color, and Black people in particular, have lower graduation rates than White participants and are often therefore subject to longer confinement sentences than they would have if they had not been diverted to drug court.[75]

Another set of concerns has to do with the nature and quality of the treatment that drug courts provide—and require. In therapeutic courts, judges make healthcare decisions that they are not trained, and are often unprepared, to make. Moreover, the treatment programs in which drug court participants are required to participate are often not the most efficacious. Analysts with Physicians for Human Rights explain:

> Diagnosis and initial treatment plans for drug court participants were often developed by people with no medical training or oversight, at times resulting in mandated treatment that was directly at odds with medical knowledge and recommendations. The most egregious example of this was the refusal, delay, or curbing of medication-assisted treatment . . . (also known as substitution or replacement therapy) to people with opioid use disorders, despite evidence that treatment for such disorders in many cases requires long-term—sometimes permanent—medication.[76]

In addition to limiting access to the most efficacious kinds of treatment, drug courts arguably consume resources that might be devoted to broadening access to treatment and other services in the community. Nearly 90 percent of people with a substance abuse disorder who need treatment do not receive it.[77] Although there are many reasons for this, millions of Americans who want and need treatment are unable to access it. Moreover, investment in treatment in the community is more cost-effective and efficacious than using courts to mandate and supervise treatment.[78] Nevertheless, chemical dependency treatment programs remain underfunded, and many of those who need and would like to receive treatment are unable to access it outside of the court system.[79] Drug courts thus consume significant treatment beds and dollars that might be used to expand access to voluntary treatment in the community.

Even in cases in which incarceration is reduced or avoided, drug courts entail long-term court supervision and surveillance, and therefore arguably enhance carceral state power. Tiger's ethnographic study of the legal control of poor opiate users in rural Vermont vividly illustrates this. On the basis of her observations, Tiger argues that the proliferation of drug courts, and the medicalized approach they ostensibly represent, has done little to reduce the punishment of people who use drugs. This is because drug courts fuse medicalization and punishment and rest on the idea that people who use drugs can be "fixed" only through sobriety. At the same time, the idea that addiction is a chronic, relapsing disorder means that "fixedness" is never assured and that long-term surveillance and coercion are therefore required. In other words, medicalization and criminalization are not separate and incompatible but rather overlapping and mutually reinforcing methods of control to which poor people and people of color are increasingly subject.[80]

Elsewhere, sociologists Monica Bell, Forrest Stuart, and I raise yet another concern about drug courts. Specifically, we contend that key elements of drug court theory and practice are in tension with a dignitarian approach to law and justice.[81] Whereas the concept of dignity is recognized and legally protected in international human rights law, in the European context, and in the constitutions of some transitional regimes, dignity makes no appearance in the U.S. Constitution, although it is discussed in some recent case law.[82] Dignitarian principles and norms may provide a useful tool for bring U.S. criminal legal practices in line with human rights norms and may serve as an effective metric for assessing the degree to which proposed reforms actually diverge from the compliance-based culture of the American criminal legal system.

Drawing on ethnographic accounts of drug courts and the treatment programs with which they partner,[83] we argue that drug courts tend to engage in practices that violate three key elements of a dignitarian approach. First, drug court participants are routinely denied narrative autonomy: the right to tell their own story and identify their own needs and priorities.[84] Drug courts (and other court-mandated treatment programs) operate with two particular goals at the forefront: the replacement of addiction with sobriety and the cessation of illegal activities.[85] Ethnographic studies indicate that these foci lead drug courts to rely on treatment programs that require participants to accept and internalize their identity as addicts and treat rejections of this identity as evidence of "denial."[86] In fact, the pressure to adopt the addict identity is so great that some low-level drug dealers who manage to gain entry to drug court learn to present themselves as "addicted to the drug lifestyle" in order to satisfy this program requirement.[87]

Second, the ethnographic literature suggests that drug courts and other court-mandated treatment programs tend to violate participants' personal integrity, that is, their right to privacy and to not be humiliated. According to the National Association of Drug Court Professionals, the frequent monitoring of drug court participants' abstinence through the use of drug tests is a key component of a drug court, one that exists to serve the end of abstinence: "Frequent [alcohol and drug] testing is essential."[88] As a result, drug court participants are subject to frequent urine analysis tests, the results of which are often discussed in open court. Moreover, in these discussions, drug court participants seeking to contextualize those results are often treated as unreliable manipulators.[89]

Finally, drug court authorities generally communicate a sense of inequality and difference rather than equality and belonging. As was discussed previously, advocates of therapeutic courts believe that imposing sanctions (e.g., jail time) for noncompliance is a necessary stick needed to compel people arrested on drug charges to stay on track. Reliance on the threat of incarceration to compel compliance sends the strong message that participants do not belong on equal footing in the community; instead, participants inhabit a liminal state between confined and not confined, banished and belonging.

Even setting aside these and other concerns about net-widening, the amplification of racial inequities, the enhancement of carceral power, and violations of the right to dignity, the argument that modest reductions in recidivism warrant drug court expansion *assumes that drug courts and traditional drug war policies are the only available options.* This, of course, is untrue. As I discuss in chapter 7, harm reduction–oriented interventions that do not involve the criminal legal system and do not impose sanctions such as jail time when people continue to use drugs are quite promising.

In short, while drug courts may offer some benefits to *some* defendants relative to the conventional alternative (i.e., jail time), they continue to involve the justice system in the delivery and oversight of drug treatment and fail to meaningfully reduce reliance on prisons and jails in the aggregate. Moreover, there is evidence that they amplify racial disparities in the justice system; consume valuable resources that could be allocated to housing, behavioral health services, or treatment in the community; and consign many participants to long-term surveillance, coercive and undignified treatment, and repeated jail stints. If the choice were between drug courts and no drug courts, weighing their costs and benefits would be a difficult and complex task. But alternatives that reduce the role of the criminal legal system in the lives of people with chemical dependency issues while also improving their quality of life do in fact exist and are preferable, for reasons I explore in chapter 7.

Summary

Although the war on drugs is not the primary cause of mass incarceration,[90] it has drawn far too many people into the criminal legal system, is characterized by massive racial inequities, and has saddled millions with debilitating criminal records and legal debt. It has also exacerbated rather than alleviated the suffering associated with untreated substance use disorder. By continuing to criminalize many drugs and by failing to offer meaningful assistance to large numbers of people who use them in harmful ways, we have also lost an important opportunity to reduce the property and violent crimes that are associated with illicit drug markets.

Meaningful and efficacious drug policy reforms are clearly needed if we are to reduce the harm caused by the punishment of people who struggle with harmful forms of substance use, as well as the unregulated and hence dangerous nature of the illicit drug market. Most legislative reforms have merely tinkered with the penalties imposed on people who are arrested for possessing small quantities of drugs. In fact, lawmakers have drawn a bright but misleading line between those who use and those who distribute drugs, often subjecting the latter to even harsher penalties, despite the fact that many people who use drugs also share or distribute them and some engage in other crimes to secure access to drugs. Moreover, one of the most common types of reform, drug courts, appears not to reduce drug arrests or incarceration—or racial inequalities in these outcomes—relative to the conventional alternative.

We can, and we must, do better. Chapter 7 offers some suggestions regarding meaningful drug-related innovations that are doable in the short term and would ameliorate the suffering associated with untreated substance use disorders and reduce the scope and reach of the largest penal system the world has ever known.

PART II
TOWARD TRANSFORMATIONAL CHANGE

5

End Excessive Sentencing

The first part of this book identified three important dynamics that have been sustaining mass incarceration even as crime rates plummeted and states adopted measures intended to reduce reliance on incarceration. The chapters in the second part identify ways we can reduce incarceration while also addressing the social problems to which it is an often harmful and counterproductive response. I begin in this chapter by making the case for comprehensive sentencing reform that would dramatically reduce the number of people serving long and life sentences, create a more just sentencing system, and make possible more humane and effective approaches to violence prevention. To start, I show how changes in criminal sentencing policy and practice fueled penal expansion and distorted the criminal legal process in ways that undermine justice. I also synthesize research showing that these policy changes failed to ensure public safety. Against this backdrop, I argue for comprehensive sentencing reform that creates a twenty-year maximum sentence as well as postconviction review processes that enable prisoners who have served many years behind bars to show they are safe to release. Although the need for such changes is clear, the path to achieving it is difficult. The third section of the chapter therefore explores how advocates can undermine the myth of monstrosity in order to facilitate comprehensive sentencing reform that limits the power to punish—even in cases involving violence.

In the final section of this chapter, I summarize the life histories of five men (Christopher Blackwell, Jeff Foxx, Ray Williams, Anthony Wright, and Eugene Youngblood) who have spent much of their lives serving long or life prison sentences in Washington State. I developed these biographical accounts in collaboration with Chris, Jeff, Ray, Anthony, and Eugene over the course of my work as an instructor and volunteer in the Washington State Reformatory. These stories illustrate several themes that are central to this chapter. First, these men's life histories reveal how the violence they enacted as teenagers or young adults grew out of the difficult circumstances in which they lived as children and early adolescents. Second, their stories show how the threat of long and life sentences casts a long shadow over legal proceedings. Finally, their life histories show clearly and powerfully that, as several Washington

State Supreme Court justices recently wrote, "we know not a person's capacity to change" at the time of sentencing.[1] Their stories, like those of so many other people who are presumed by prosecutors and judges to be incapable of growth and maturation, remind us of the importance of retaining both humanity and humility when developing sentencing policies. In fact, there is abundant evidence that even people who experienced tremendous violence and abuse as children, commit acts of violence, and spend much of their adult life behind bars under traumatizing circumstances often seek and find ways to make amends and live lives of integrity and meaning.[2] We need policies that recognize the remarkable capacity for maturation and growth that so many people exhibit despite their history of abuse and confinement in dehumanizing institutions.

The Need for Comprehensive Sentencing Reform

Researchers agree that shifts in policy and practice rather than rising crime rates were the proximate driver of mass incarceration.[3] This conclusion is based on studies that decompose the criminal justice process into a series of decision-making points to assess how the criminal legal system's response to crime changed in recent decades. In theory, rising incarceration rates could stem from mounting crime rates. They could also reflect increases in the likelihood that reported crimes result in arrest and that arrests result in a confinement sentence (as opposed to probation or community service) and/or from increases in sentence length and time served.

Studies that analyze changes at each of these levels find that prison growth was the direct result of changes in policy and practice rather than of changes in crime rates. For example, on the basis of their comprehensive decompositions and simulations, economists Stephen Raphael and Michael Stoll conclude that "nearly all (if not all) of the growth of the state and federal prison populations can be attributed to tougher sentencing policy."[4] Similarly, sociologist Bruce Western's analysis of state and federal prison growth finds, "At every stage of criminal processing, from policing, to the court hearing, to parole, criminal justice officials decide on the disposition of offenders and these effects on the scale of imprisonment far overshadow fluctuations in the level of crime."[5]

These and other researchers have identified three main shifts in policy and practice that fueled mass incarceration. First, as a result of the war on drugs, narcotics arrests and the number of people sent to prison for drug law violations increased. Second, the odds that a felony arrest would result in a prison sentence grew after the early 1980s.[6] This shift likely stemmed in part from prosecutors' increased proclivity to file felony charges and is thus consistent with research that highlights prosecutors' vast—and unregulated—discretionary power, which includes the authority to decide whether to file charges, which charges to file, and which plea bargains to accept. Third, changes to sentencing policy that encourage the use of prison (rather than community service, probation, or jail) might also have increased the likelihood that a felony arrest would trigger prison admission.[7]

In addition, all but one of the researchers who have examined this topic conclude that the amount of time prisoners spend behind bars has been increasing.[8] The most straightforward way to measure time served is to record the amount of time people who leave prison spent behind bars. Although simple and intuitively appealing, this direct, observational method excludes a growing number of people who are serving long or life sentences—and who therefore do not leave prison—and therefore underestimates time served. In fact, this observational measure is the least accurate of the available options for assessing trends in time served.[9] Because the nature of the crimes people are imprisoned for changes over time, it is also important to analyze time served separately by offense type. Similarly, it is crucial to separate people sentenced to prison by courts from those who are returned to prison as a result of technical parole violations, who generally serve comparatively short stints in prison.[10]

Studies that take these and other methodological precautions consistently find that time served in prison increased notably in recent decades, especially for violent offenses. For example, Raphael and Stoll find that time served for murder and negligent manslaughter increased by 55 percent, for robbery by 44 percent and for burglary by 21 percent between 1984 and 2004.[11] Examining a slightly different time period, Western reports that time served increased by 61, 75, and 71 percent for violent, property, and drug offenses, respectively, from 1980 to 2000.[12] Jeremy Travis et al. report similar findings for the period 1980–2010.[13] My own research indicates that time served has continued to increase in more recent years as well.[14]

In sum, research using the most careful methods that include long-term prisoners in their analyses find that time served in prison has increased for many offense categories, and especially for violent crimes. These findings have important policy implications. In the first place, they suggest that the tough sentencing laws that many state legislatures passed in the 1980s and 1990s *did* increase time served. These changes include laws calling for tough mandatory minimums as well as restrictions on prisoners' ability to reduce their sentence by accumulating "good time" credits.[15] Increasingly cautious parole release decisions in states that have parole boards, and the abolition or contraction of parole in other states, have also enhanced time served.[16]

Studies indicating that time served in prison has increased notably imply the need to overhaul sentencing policy and to reduce sentences for violent crimes in particular. They also underscore the need to ensure that parole release occurs in states that have parole boards[17] and to reintroduce opportunities for postconviction review in states that have abolished it. In his recent book, legal scholar John Pfaff disagrees with this conclusion, arguing that tough sentencing laws did *not* impact time served and therefore that it is *not* necessary to repeal or modify them in order to reduce mass incarceration.[18] As he puts it, "the only thing that really grew over time was the rate at which prosecutors filed felony charges against arrestees."[19] Pfaff therefore does not believe that sentencing reform is needed in order to reduce mass incarceration.

Pfaff's argument stems in part from his apparently erroneous finding that time served in prison did not increase in recent decades.[20] It also derives from the problematic assertion that prosecutors do not actually invoke tough sentencing statutes even when they are available because they understand that to do so would increase state correctional costs to unacceptable levels.[21] Yet, as discussed previously, researchers using the most careful methods find that time served in prison has increased notably due, in large part, to the proliferation of tough sentencing statutes. In addition, there is a great deal of evidence that casts doubt on the claim that prosecutors do not invoke tough sentencing laws where they exist for fear of increasing state correctional costs.

First, it is clear that many prosecutors *do* invoke tough sentencing laws when they are available to them, although there is significant geographic variation in the degree to which this occurs.[22] In California, for example, courts sent more than 80,000 second-strikers and 7,500 third-strikers to prison between 1994 and 2004 alone.[23] By the end of 2004, three-strikers comprised more than one quarter, 26 percent, of the California prison population.[24] In the federal system, an estimated 46,000 of the roughly 100,000 federal prisoners—46 percent—serving time for a drug offense had been sentenced under mandatory minimum sentencing laws.[25] These sentences are often *very* long. For example, for a defendant with a felony record, a drug conviction might easily yield a sentence of ten years or longer. Similarly, the number of prisoners serving life sentences has skyrocketed as states have adopted and expanded the range of cases in which life sentences may be imposed. Today, over 200,000—one in seven prisoners, and one in five Black prisoners—are serving a life sentence.[26] Thus, although prosecutors in some jurisdictions do modify their charging practices to avoid triggering tough mandatory sentences, it is clear that many others eagerly utilize tough sentencing laws where they are available.

Second, the argument that prosecutors will refrain from using tough sentencing laws for fear of driving up state correctional costs makes little sense given the existing incentive structure. Insofar as the vast majority of prosecutors are elected in and funded by counties, they have had a clear political incentive to promote their tough-on-crime credentials in many parts of the country, but few or no incentives to reduce state costs. Indeed, the fact that local actors decide who to send to prison but do not incur the costs associated with that decision has been conceptualized by researchers as a "correctional free lunch" problem that has fueled the growth of prison populations.[27]

Third, truth-in-sentencing laws cannot be avoided by prosecutors, and they matter. Truth-in-sentencing laws mandate that prisoners serve a specified portion—usually 85 percent—of their sentence, thus reducing the capacity of parole boards to reward prisoners who earn "good time" credits by engaging in programming or avoiding infractions. Many states enacted such laws in the 1990s. By 1998, two-thirds of all people admitted to state prison had been sentenced under a truth-in-sentencing law,[28] and as legal scholar Michael Tonry shows, there is abundant evidence that the existence of these statutes increased both sentence length and prison populations.[29] Finally, even if prosecutors choose not to charge defendants under certain harsh sentencing statutes, the existence of those statutes enhances prosecutorial power in plea negotiations, which yields longer average sentences.[30]

For all of these reasons, it is clear that the adoption of punitive sentencing laws *has* increased time served and bolstered mass incarceration. The clear implication of all of this is that comprehensive sentencing reform will be needed if we are to meaningfully reduce our reliance on incarceration.

The (Contested) Role of Crime in the Development of Mass Incarceration

While it is clear that changes in policy and practice were the proximate cause of mass incarceration, some scholars have argued that crime trends mattered *indirectly* by impacting media coverage of, and public sentiment about, crime and punishment, which in turn fueled the enactment of policies and practices that led to mass incarceration.[31] While none of these authors contend that the incidence of crime or violence alone is sufficient to explain carceral expansion, each argues that rising levels of violence in the United States impacted the development of criminal legal policy and worked in concert with institutional, political, and/or cultural dynamics to produce mass incarceration.

In *The Myth of Mob Rule*, for example, political scientist Lisa Miller contends that rising levels of violence give rise to public concern about and media attention of crime (which she refers to as crime's public salience) as well as its political salience (that is, the amount of attention politicians pay to the issue). Miller argues that where rates of violence and the salience of the crime issue are high, and the capacity of "mass publics" to hold elected officials accountable for enacting effective policies is limited, the resulting "democracy deficits" lead to punitive policies that fuel penal expansion:

> When violent crime is rising rapidly or is relatively high for sustained periods of time democratic systems are likely to increase punitive rhetoric and policy, at least modestly. However, whether more arrests and harsher sentences are the exclusive response depends in part on whether democratic institutions facilitate or hinder the passage of comprehensive social policy in response to public concern.[32]

In *Incarceration Nation*, political scientist Peter Enns also emphasizes the importance of (ostensibly) rising crime rates, but offers a different account of how they matter. For Enns, rising crime rates triggered increased news coverage of crime, which in turn fueled punitiveness among the "mass public" to which politicians were then compelled to respond. To support this argument, Enns employs quantitative methods to identify the determinants of rising public punitiveness and to assess the impact of shifts in public opinion on national and state incarceration rates. Enns's results indicate that changes in crime rates closely correspond to changes in the volume of news coverage of crime, which in turn correspond to popular punitiveness. In addition, Enns finds that changes in punitiveness were a significant predictor of shifts in the incarceration rate. In substantive terms, Enns concludes that the U.S. incarceration rate would have been 20 percent lower if not for rising punitiveness.

This emphasis on the incidence of violence as an (indirect) driver of U.S. mass incarceration is intuitively plausible, as the United States is an outlier in terms of both lethal violence and incarceration rates. According to international victimization survey data, U.S. crime rates are similar to those found in other industrialized democracies,[33] with one important exception: homicide. Even after falling precipitously, the U.S. murder rate (now hovering around 5–6 per 100,000 residents) remains notably higher than that of comparable developed countries.[34] Within the United States, the prevalence of lethal violence varies dramatically by geography and demography. The homicide rate in Chicago's predominantly Black West Garfield Park neighborhood, for example, is more than twelve times higher than the national average, and twenty times greater than in nearby, predominantly White neighborhoods.[35]

Yet the argument that trends in violence significantly impacted public opinion and policy development, and thereby fueled mass incarceration, is in tension with studies that provide a more direct test of the idea that mass incarceration has been shaped to an important degree by levels of violence. In particular, researchers assessing the correlation between changes in violent crime and incarceration rates in the United States *in time periods that include some or much of the recent prison buildup* find little to no correlation between the two.[36]

Figure 5.1 depicts the trend in the homicide rate and shows why this is the case. (Homicide is seen as the most reliable indicator of trends in serious violence because nearly all cases are reported to, and recorded by, the police). As Figure 5.1 shows, after 1976 the homicide and incarceration rates were moving in the same direction for just a few years. After 1980, however, the homicide rate and the incarceration rate were moving in opposite directions. Thus, during the vast majority of the time in which incarceration rates were rising, homicide rates fell substantially.

A closer look at the distribution of the risk of violent victimization raises additional questions about the argument that rising levels of violent crime

Figure 5.1 Cumulative change in U.S. homicide and incarceration rates, 1976–2010

Sources: Bureau of Justice Statistics, Supplemental Homicide Data, provided by James Alan Fox, Northeastern University. Incarceration rate data compiled from Maguire 2013, tables 2.28.2012 and 6.14.2012; and Hindelang 1977. Jail incarceration rate figures were interpolated for missing years.

directly or indirectly fueled mass incarceration. When disaggregated by race, homicide data show that the White victimization rate increased very modestly in the 1970s and declined steadily thereafter (while incarceration rates shot up). The Black homicide victimization rate —which is six to eight times higher than the White homicide rate—rose in the 1970s, fluctuated in the 1980s, peaked in 1991, and declined notably thereafter 1990 (see Figure 5.2).

The upshot is that the vast majority of the growth in U.S. incarceration took place after 1980, when the overall homicide rate was dropping and the White homicide victimization rate was either steady or falling. The argument that trends in violent crime are a fundamental cause of penal expansion thus implies that any increases in the national political salience of the crime issue and in incarceration rates stemmed from the rise in the Black homicide victimization rate that took place between the early 1970s and the early 1990s.

The idea that the dramatic upsurge in attention and concern about crime stemmed solely from concern about high and (sometimes) rising levels of victimization among Black people strains credulity. While legal scholar James Forman Jr. persuasively argues in *Locking Up Our Own* that high levels of violence in Black communities did fuel support for punitive policies (as well as for other kinds of measures, such as social services and drug treatment) among some Black residents, it seems unlikely that the massive uptick in national attention to the crime issue that dominated the news

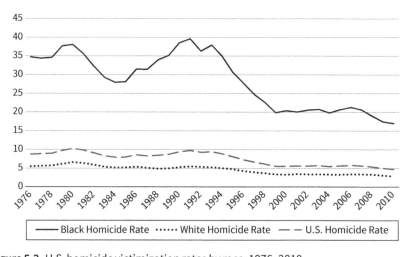

Figure 5.2 U.S. homicide victimization rates by race, 1976–2010

Source: Bureau of Justice Statistics, *Homicide Trends in the United States*, Supplementary Homicide Reports, provided by James Alan Fox, Northeastern University.

throughout the 1980s and 1990s stemmed solely from an increase in concern among the general population about rising rates of Black victimization. Certainly, the fact that the Black homicide victimization rate has been far higher than the White homicide rate throughout U.S. history had not previously generated similar levels of concern. Nor did the massive increase in the Black homicide rate that occurred between 1960 and 1970 engender an increase in incarceration rates that is comparable to what occurred in the 1980s, 1990s, and 2000s.[37] Including the time period in which incarceration rates rose the most and disaggregating the homicide rate by race complicate this story considerably.

The historical record also poses a challenge to the argument that rising rates of violence are a fundamental (if indirect) cause of penal growth in recent decades. It is true that violent crime (as measured by the homicide rate) increased in the 1970s and again in the 1980s, peaking at around 10 per 100,000 residents in the early 1980s and again in the early 1990s. But U.S. homicide rates also jumped dramatically in the late 1920s and early 1930s, very nearly matching the records set in 1980 and 1990.[38] While this dramatic increase in lethal violence during the Great Depression did trigger concern, incarceration rates rose quite modestly during this period and remained extremely low compared to the recent period of mass incarceration.[39] In other words, homicide rates were as high in the 1930s as they were in the 1980s and early 1990s, but incarceration rates were roughly five times higher in the latter period. Moreover, U.S. incarceration rates rose most dramatically in the 1990s through the mid-2000s—while rates of violence *plummeted*.[40]

This discussion has focused on whether changes in the national crime rate in recent decades help explain the dramatic rise in incarceration rates in the 1980s, 1990s, and 2000s. I have argued that there is little evidence for this proposition. Crime rates (at least as measured by the homicide rate) have been as high in the past as they were in the 1980s and 1990s and did not engender mass incarceration. Moreover, crime rates were actually falling for much of the time prison and jail populations exploded.

Other researchers interested in the relationship between crime and incarceration have approached the question differently. This body of research examines variation in incarceration across places rather than over time. These cross-sectional studies use statistical regression to analyze incarceration-related outcomes and include a host of social and political measures in their models in order to assess the relative importance of each. Such studies generally find that violent crime rates are positively correlated with incarceration rates at the state and county levels; they also show that a host of other social and political factors are significant predictors of incarceration rates across the states. In particular, the size of the Black population and the strength of the Republican Party have been significant predictors of prison population size.[41] Moreover, these studies indicate that a host of social and political factors explain more of the variation in incarceration rates across states and over time.[42] Still, the fact that violent crime and incarceration rates do tend to be correlated at the state and county levels within the United States—if not over time—suggests that they are not entirely independent of one another.

In short, it is difficult to make the case that changes in rates of violence have been correlated with changes in rates of incarceration *in the decades in which prison and jail populations grew most.* The absence of such a correlation casts doubt on the idea that rising levels of lethal violence were an important cause of mass incarceration. However, when we look at variation across places, we do tend to see such a correlation. One way to make sense of these mixed findings is as follows: perhaps comparatively high rates of lethal violence and mass incarceration reflect a certain tolerance for inequality that differentiates the United States from other democracies. From this perspective, our collective willingness to accept the structural and racial inequalities that generate comparatively high levels of interpersonal violence, and especially high rates of victimization among people of color, reflects a certain cultural orientation, one that also yields acceptance of the idea that incarcerating millions of people in small cages for many years is a reasonable way to address public safety. This idea is supported by a study by sociologists Bob Crutchfield and David Pettinicchio, which indicates that countries with a greater "taste for inequality" have more heterogeneous populations, greater income inequality, and larger prison populations. In short, high rates of lethal violence and high levels of incarceration may go hand in hand in the United States, and within its localities, not because fluctuations in crime rates necessarily drive criminal policy or incarceration rates but because both stem from a tolerance of inequality.

Yet, even if we assume that violence and incarceration rates are in some way connected, it is clear that the rise of mass incarceration was not an inevitable consequence of comparatively high levels of lethal victimization, especially among Black people. Instead, the growth of the prison (and jail) population was a direct result of changes in practice and policy, including the drug war, the increased proclivity of prosecutors to file felony charges, and changes in sentencing law and policy that dramatically increased time served, especially for violent crimes.[43] These proximate causes must be addressed in order to reduce mass incarceration, and for the reasons enumerated in the next section.

Harsh Sentencing Laws Undermine the Justice Process

Mandatory minimum and other tough sentencing laws have not only fueled prison growth; they also had profound implications for the quality of justice, for a number of reasons. First, the enactment of statutes that enable the imposition of long and life sentences dramatically reduced the proportion of cases that go to trial.[44] In the federal system, for example, the share of cases adjudicated at trial plummeted from about 20 percent in the 1980s to 3 percent in recent years.[45] A similar (if slightly less dramatic) shift has taken place at the state level.[46]

Tough sentencing laws reduce the share of cases that go to trial because they enable the state to plausibly threaten the imposition of extraordinarily long sentences when defendants exercise their right to a trial. That is, the enactment of mandatory minimum sentences has enabled prosecutors to compel many defendants to plead guilty rather than risk the potentially extreme consequences of being convicted at trial. There is some evidence that even people who are factually innocent are increasingly likely to plead guilty.[47] As one legal expert put it, the adoption of mandatory minimum and other tough sentencing laws creates a "prosecutor-dictated plea bargain system" characterized by "inordinate pressures to enter into plea bargains" that appears to have led a significant number of defendants to plead guilty to crimes they never actually committed.[48] Tough sentencing laws thus not only drive penal expansion; they also appear to be an important cause of the near-extinction of the criminal trial and may have exacerbated the problem of wrongful conviction.

At the same time, defendants who do exercise their right to a trial are subject to far longer sentences than was the case in the past. In Washington State, for example, the enactment of tough sentence laws in the 1990s and 2000s increased the difference between average sentences imposed via plea bargains and those imposed at trial, especially in cases involving violent crimes. In such cases, the gap between the average prison sentence adjudicated via a plea agreement versus trial was 64 months in 1986, but 174 months, or fourteen and a half years, in 2016. The "trial penalty" nearly tripled because average sentence length grew far more in cases adjudicated at trial than in those resolved through a plea agreement. In cases involving violent crimes, for example, average sentences reached via plea agreement increased by 30 percent, while those adjudicated at trial increased 111 percent from 1986 to 2016.[49] The growth of the trial penalty is thus also an important driver of long sentences and of mass incarceration.

Long and Life Sentences Are an Ineffective Approach to Violence

The widespread and continued reliance on very long and life sentences as the primary response to interpersonal violence ignores the fact that these sentences are expensive and do little to enhance public safety. As researchers at the National Research Council conclude:

> There is little convincing evidence that mandatory minimum sentencing, truth-in-sentencing, or life without possibility of parole laws had significant crime reduction effects. But there is substantial evidence that they shifted sentencing power from judges to prosecutors; provoked widespread circumvention; exacerbated racial disparities in imprisonment; and made sentences much longer, prison populations much larger, and incarceration rates much higher.[50]

Proponents of tough sentencing laws argue that long sentences protect society by deterring would-be criminals and by physically separating (i.e., incapacitating) people who have been convicted of a crime from those who have not, thereby protecting the latter. However, research provides little support for these claims. With respect to deterrence, "the evidence base demonstrates that lengthy prison sentences are ineffective as a crime control measure" because long prison sentences do not deter more than short ones.[51] This is because "the certainty of apprehension and not the severity of the legal consequences ensuing from apprehension is the more effective deterrent."[52] In other words, enhancing the certainty that punishment will occur could have some deterrent effect—but is very difficult to do. Increasing the severity of punishment is possible, but is not an effective deterrent.

Using long and life sentences to incapacitate people is an inefficient means of protecting the public for another reason as well: recidivism rates decline markedly with age.[53] Criminological research clearly shows that young people commit most crimes, with rates peaking in the late teenage years followed by rapid declines. Studies also show that the offending trajectories of *all* groups decline sharply with age.[54] Even those with the longest rap sheets desist from crime at relatively early ages, most commonly by their thirties.[55] As two prominent criminologists conclude, "crime declines with age even for active offenders."[56] Moreover, as the restorative justice advocate Danielle Sered points out, arguments about the incapacitative effects of incarceration ignore the violence that occurs inside prisons.[57] If these incidents were taken into account, it is entirely possible that we would find that imprisonment does not have any incapacitative effect at all.

For these and other reasons, researchers at the National Research Council recently concluded that "statutes mandating lengthy prison sentences cannot be justified on the basis of their effectiveness in preventing crime."[58] Their fuller explication of this finding reads as follows:

> The deterrent value of long sentences is minimal, as the decision to commit a crime is more likely influenced by the certainty and swiftness of punishment than by the severity of the criminal sanction. Research on criminal careers shows that recidivism rates decline markedly with age. Prisoners serving long sentences necessarily age as they serve their time and their risk of re-offending declines over time. Accordingly, unless sentencing judges can specifically target very high-rate or extremely dangerous offenders, imposing long prison sentences is an inefficient way to prevent crime. Finally, the evidence is clear that long prison sentences incur substantial costs to state and federal budgets and will likely add significant future costs as the prison population ages.[59]

Moreover, long sentences are not necessary to ensure public safety. Comparative research shows that many countries that rarely impose long and life sentences, and have far lower incarceration rates, have enjoyed recent crime declines akin to that which has occurred in the United States. In fact, crime rates fell as much in countries that did not implement harsh criminal policies in recent decades as in those that have done so.[60]

Similarly, studies of state variation within the United States show states that decreased their imprisonment rates the most have also enjoyed the *largest* drops in crime.[61] For example, New York State experienced the largest drop (24 percent) in imprisonment rates and also enjoyed the most substantial decline in the crime rate (54 percent) among the fifty U.S. states between 1994 and 2012. The state with the next largest decline in imprisonment rates (15 percent) was New Jersey, where crime rates fell by an impressive 50 percent, the second biggest drop in the country.[62] More generally, the ten states with the largest declines in imprisonment rates between 2009 and 2014 experienced a 16 percent drop in the overall crime rate, while those whose prison populations grew the most experienced a 13 percent decline.[63] Clearly, then, decarceration does not inevitably increase crime.

Long and Life Sentences Are an Inhumane Approach to Violence

The widespread imposition of long and life sentences also raises important ethical and human rights concerns. Like capital punishment, the widespread imposition of long and life sentences sets the United States apart from other democratic countries. As Tonry points out, sentences longer than ten years remain quite rare in other democratic countries; in the United States, they have become commonplace.[64] Similarly, life sentences, and especially life without the possibility of parole (LWOP) sentences, are now common in the United States but nonexistent or very rare in most other democratic countries.

In fact, only 20 percent of countries even allow for the imposition of LWOP sentences; those that do allow them use them quite rarely.[65] This is because LWOP sentences presume at the time of sentencing that a defendant will *never* mature and can *never* be safely returned to their communities. Because this presumption denies people the opportunity to demonstrate their maturation and transformation, leading authorities have determined that LWOP sentences deny people their right to dignity and are, therefore, a human rights violation.[66] Some countries, including Germany, France, and Italy, have also declared LWOP sentences unconstitutional for this reason.[67]

By contrast, forty-nine of the fifty U.S. states allow LWOP sentences to be imposed—and impose them frequently.[68] In fact, both the number and share of prisoners serving life continues to rise each year.[69] The widespread imposition of long and life sentences is a leading cause of the aging of the prison population. According to the Bureau of Justice Statistics, the number of U.S. prisoners age fifty-five or older increased by 400 percent from 1993 to 2013.[70] In 2013, one in ten U.S. prisoners was fifty-five or older. According to the National Institute of Corrections, prisoners fifty and older are likely to have a "physiological age" that is ten to fifteen years greater than their chronological age; this is because the stresses of life behind bars (including separation from family and friends, physical confinement, inadequate healthcare, poor diet, and the threat of victimization) combined with the lack of access to healthcare and healthy lifestyles before and during imprisonment accelerate the aging process.[71] Researchers have therefore concluded that these "prison boomers" are "important to consider as a distinct group from other incarcerated people because they experience rates of chronic illness and disability more typical of people chronologically much older. Consequently, most research in the area, corrections departments in many U.S. states, and many European countries consider incarcerated people "older" beginning around age fifty-five.[72] The costs associated with the care of older prisoners are two to four times greater than for younger prisoners, mainly due to the costs associated with the provision of healthcare behind bars.

The mass incarceration of the elderly raises a number of important concerns about the humanity of incarcerating older and often frail adults in circumstances that undermine mental and physical health—particularly when the people who are confined have not had the opportunity to show that they are safe to release. Yet the widespread and continued imposition of long and life sentences will further increase the number of elderly prisoners unless concerted action is taken to enable the release of people who have served substantial amounts of time behind bars. Diversion and reduced sentences for people convicted of drug and property offenses are clearly needed and may help prevent prison population growth to some degree. Yet meaningful and sustainable reductions in prison populations and in the number of elderly prisoners will occur only if fewer long and life sentences are imposed in the future and mechanisms are created to enable those who are serving such sentences to demonstrate that they are safe to be released.[73] These kinds of reforms have generally not been enacted. As a result, the current pace of change has been far too slow. In fact, Sentencing Project analyst Nazgol Ghandnoosh has concluded that it will take until 2085 to cut the prison population in half if states and the federal government maintain the current pace of decarceration.[74]

From a more philosophical perspective, it is clear that current U.S. sentencing practices are out of line with important normative principles. Retributive theories of punishment hold that penalties should serve the purpose of moral accountability rather than achieve particular ends. By contrast, consequentialist approaches treat punishment as a means to achieve certain ends, namely, protection of society. In theory, this protection could occur through rehabilitation, deterrence, or incapacitation. Some penal scholars blend retributive and consequentialist goals. This approach has been called "limited retributivism" or "modified just deserts."[75] The Model Penal Code calls it "utilitarianism within limits of proportionality."[76] From this perspective, prison sentences are justified only to incapacitate dangerous people and punish those who have committed such serious crimes that lesser sanctions would be "disproportionately lenient."[77] For limited retributivists, sentences that are longer than is necessary to incapacitate and signal the severity of the crime are unjustified.

Interestingly, both retributivists and consequentialists agree that two fundamental principles should govern penal policy.[78] The first is the principle of proportionality, namely, the idea that the penalties imposed should reflect the severity of the criminal conduct that occurred and the culpability of the person who engaged in it. Under this principle, the crime of homicide should be punished more severely than the crime of burglary, which should in turn carry a more severe penalty than theft. However, the principle of proportionality does not require any specific penalties for particular crimes. For example, under the principle of proportionality, neither the death penalty nor

LWOP sentences are necessary to achieve proportionality in cases involving homicide. Instead, according to the principle of proportionality, what matters is that the penalties imposed in homicide cases reflect the idea that this crime is more serious than offenses such as larceny.

The second principle upon which both retributivists and consequentialists agree is the principle of parsimony. According to this principle, punishment should never be more severe than is necessary to achieve retributive or public safety goals. This belief is based on the idea that the intentional infliction of suffering on other human beings (which incarceration necessarily entails) should be avoided as much as possible. For this reason, sentences should reflect only what is necessary to achieve valid penal goals—and no more.

As Tonry points out, the principle of proportionality has been reinterpreted to mean that penalties for serious crimes should be as severe as possible, while the principle of parsimony has been largely forgotten.[79] Sentences that compel people to spend the majority of their years behind bars have come to seem normal, even necessary, for justice. However, these beliefs are incompatible with widely accepted penal norms and practices, especially the principle of parsimony. In fact, the United States is now a global outlier as a result of both its continued use of the death penalty and its routine imposition of life sentences.

Reducing the number of long and life sentences imposed and expanding avenues for postconviction review will help bring the United States in line with democratic norms and reduce the human and fiscal costs associated with mass incarceration and the imprisonment of the elderly. Interestingly, for reasons that are discussed in detail in chapter 6, many crime survivors agree that current policies exacerbate rather than alleviate the problem of violence. Reducing violence and truly addressing survivors' needs will require developing a more thoughtful, preventative, and service-oriented approach in which long-term incarceration is the exception rather than the rule.

Toward Comprehensive Sentencing Reform

Across the country, many states have undertaken efforts to reduce their prison populations. In the vast majority of cases, these efforts have focused on reducing penalties for low-level offenses, mainly drug possession and theft.[80] Yet avoiding the costs associated with prison expansion will also require reconsidering the frequent imposition of long and very long sentences, which have a disproportionately large impact on prison populations.[81] The widespread imposition of long and life sentences is also an important driver of racial inequity in punishment.[82] As researchers affiliated with the Urban Institute explain, "States grappling with expanding prison populations must include those serving the longest prison terms in their efforts to curb mass incarceration."[83]

Lawmakers can influence time served in prison and reduce prison populations in two ways. First, on the front end, they can modify the sentences that are imposed upon conviction. In addition, legislators can change policies pertaining to postconviction review and release decision-making. (Parole is the most common type of postconviction review, but other, similar processes exist. These generally involve consideration of prisoners' records and activities during their incarceration to assess whether they are safe to release.) Policies that shorten sentences are sometimes called "front-end" reforms, while those that affect postconviction release decisions are called "back-end" reforms. Both types can significantly reduce the amount of time people spend in prison and should be enacted in order to dramatically lower the number of people serving long and life sentences.

Front-End Reform: Toward a Twenty-Year Maximum Sentence

In recent years, a number of experts, including Sentencing Project analysts Marc Mauer, Ashley Nellis, and Nazgol Ghandnoosh, have recommended a cap on maximum sentence length of twenty years. I endorse this recommendation. The idea of capping sentences at twenty years appears radical in the context of the contemporary United States, where very long and life sentences have become routine. While a twenty-year maximum would mean a significant change in the United States, such a policy would bring the country into line with the practices of other democratic countries. Such policies could be accompanied by the creation of mechanisms to evaluate the safety risk of people nearing the end of their term and, *in rare instances*, to extend the period of incarceration if such people are determined to pose a grave threat to public safety.[84] Many countries have similar policies and generally have far lower crime rates than those found in the United States.[85] Such a policy could be combined with enhanced investment in violence prevention and services for violence survivors, as well as prison education and rehabilitative programming. It would also reduce racial inequities, as disproportionality is most pronounced in long and life sentences.[86] And finally, it would also likely lead to the reduction of sentences for less serious offenses, for as legal scholar William

Stuntz emphasized, the most severe allowable penalty influences what people see as the appropriate penalty in less serious cases.[87]

In addition to reducing long and life sentences, racial inequities, and the widespread incarceration of the elderly, comprehensive sentencing reform would allow policymakers to revive rehabilitation as a penal goal. While some social scientists concluded in the 1970s that rehabilitative programming was ineffective, the research on which this conclusion was largely based was retracted in 1979.[88] More recent research shows that a number of well-executed, prison-based programs notably reduce recidivism. National Research Council researchers have concluded that some rehabilitative programs "can be effective in neutralizing or even reversing the otherwise criminogenic effects of incarceration."[89] A number of such correctional interventions are highly cost effective. These include (some) substance abuse treatment programs, education (both K–12 and postsecondary), and vocational training. Community-based prevention programs, including employment training/job assistance and outpatient drug treatment, are also excellent investments in both public safety and public health.[90] Increasing access to high-quality, early education programs also improves educational outcomes and reduces criminal justice contact.[91]

In short, a twenty-year maximum sentence is consistent with the principle of parsimony and with research showing that the vast majority of the system-involved desist from crime as they age. It would also reduce the harm caused by long-term and lifelong incarceration and the imprisonment of older adults and reduce the unfairness associated with the racially unequal imposition of these burdens. Such a policy could be accompanied by increased funding for well-executed preventative and rehabilitative programming and community-based prevention that is a better investment in public safety than long-term incarceration. However, "if the policy reforms designed to reduce long prison sentences were prospective and applied only to new convictions, then prison populations would decline only slowly."[92] For these reasons, back-end reforms that create mechanisms for prisoners currently serving long and life sentences are also important—and may be more feasible in the near term.

Back-End Reform: Toward Postconviction Review

Systems of postconviction review that allow people serving sentences longer than twenty years the opportunity to be considered for release prior to completion of their full sentence are also needed.[93] Like earned release policies, postconviction review processes reward people who take full advantage of programming and other opportunities while in prison. As a result, postconviction review processes can have a significant and positive impact on prison life and culture. In particular, consideration of prisoners' conduct during incarceration by parole boards improves morale in prisons and both encourages and rewards prisoners' involvement in rehabilitative, educational, and other programming. Research confirms that "the hope of an early parole release incentivizes inmates to invest in their own rehabilitation, and when such incentives are removed investment falls and recidivism rises."[94]

The postconviction review options currently available to people in prison are woefully inadequate. People serving long and life sentences have few opportunities to be considered for release prior to completing their confinement sentence. Sixteen states have abolished or significantly curtailed discretionary parole.[95] Prisoners in states with limited or no discretionary parole will not have the opportunity to go before the parole board to make the case that they are safe to release. In such states, the vast majority of people in prison will serve the entirety of their sentence. While other states have retained parole boards, those boards have become increasingly reluctant to release people with long or life sentences. This decline in discretionary release rates in states with parole boards is occurring despite numerous studies showing that released lifers have extraordinarily low rates of recidivism. For example, a 2011 study of released prisoners who had served life with the possibility of parole sentences found that "the incidence of commission of serious crimes by recently released lifers has been minuscule, and as compared to the larger inmate population, recidivism risk . . . is minimal."[96] A recent study by the California Department of Corrections and rehabilitation reached similar conclusions.[97]

As a result of the abolition of parole in many states, and increased caution by boards where they exist, people who were sentenced to life with the possibility of parole generally serve far longer than was the case several decades ago. For example, a recent study by Ghandnoosh shows that lifers and who were paroled in the 1980s had served an average of 11.6 years behind bars. By contrast, those paroled between 2000 and 2013 served, on average, more than 23 years in prison.[98]

In this context, many states have adopted "compassionate release" programs that, in theory, enable prisoners with serious, progressive, and terminal illnesses to petition for release. (Prior to the pandemic, roughly four thousand people died in jails and state prisons annually.)[99] However, in many states that have compassionate release programs, few patients are actually granted release.[100] In Washington State, for example, prisoners who are severely incapacitated due to age or physical disability may, in theory, be eligible for Emergency Medical Placement (EMP) outside of prison.[101] However, the number of releases generated through this program has been quite small. Between January 2012 and December 2017, only 45 of the 249 cases considered (18 percent) were approved for EMP.[102] Across the country, a variety of rules and policies limit access to EMP: restrictive medical and criminological eligibility criteria, exclusion of nonterminal but debilitating conditions, rules that allow objections by a victim advocate or prosecutor, concerns about public safety, and availability of suitable postrelease community care plans.[103]

Clemency, too, remains far too limited to serve as a meaningful method for reducing mass incarceration.[104] All states grant governors or executive boards (or both) the power to pardon or commute a criminal sentence. Historically, grants of clemency were common. But over the past four decades, clemency grants have plummeted, even as the U.S. prison population ballooned. In Texas, for example, the state executed 461 people, and Texas governors commuted the death sentences of 100 prisoners, between 1923 and 1972.[105] By contrast, Texas executed 466 people between 1976 and 2011 but granted only two capital defendants clemency during that period.[106] Insofar as clemency is designed to serve an error-correcting function and a check on the judiciary, to afford relief from undue harshness, and to help ensure that justice is tempered by mercy, the dramatic decline in clemency grants in the era of mass incarceration is nonsensical.

In short, avenues to postconviction review and "early" release have been significantly blocked even as the imposition of long and life sentences has become commonplace. This trend should be reversed, and eligibility for postconviction review should be expanded to include all prisoners who have served a certain number of years behind bars. Mechanisms for reviewing applicants should be created and expanded to facilitate this.

Like a twenty-year maximum sentence, this proposal appears radical in the context of current U.S. practices, but it is not. For example, the American Law Institute (ALI), a nongovernmental organization comprised of judges, lawyers, and legal academics, approved the first-ever revisions to the historic Model Penal Code in 2015 in which they endorsed this approach. Specifically, the revised Model Penal Code calls for state legislatures to enact a "second look" provision, that is, to create a mechanism to reexamine a person's sentence after fifteen years *no matter the crime of conviction or the length of the original sentence.* The ALI offered numerous rationales for this proposal: the proliferation of long and life sentences have fueled an unprecedented rise in incarceration rates; unnecessary incarceration is costly and harmful; the vast majority of system-involved people age out of crime; and clemency has proven to be of extremely limited utility. The ALI also noted that second-look processes can take place in a relative calm atmosphere in which the focus is on what the prisoner has accomplished during their incarceration rather than on the crime itself.[107]

A modified version of this approach would expand parole eligibility based on the age of the petitioner and the amount of time served. This approach is supported by research showing that brain development is not complete until people are in their mid- to late twenties and that recidivism declines markedly with age. An age-based review system might focus on people convicted of crimes that occurred while they were under the age of twenty-six (or twenty-eight) and people who are at least fifty (or fifty-five) and have served a minimum confinement term of fifteen (or twenty) years.

In such an approach, people sentenced for crimes committed while they were adolescents or young adults and who had served fifteen or more years in prison could be eligible for postsentence review. Similarly, people fifty or older who had served fifteen or more years would be eligible to be considered for release. Both of these back-end approaches—expansion of parole to all prisoners or on the basis of age and time served—offer several advantages. In particular, the expansion of parole eligibility could logically be paired with the reinstatement of rehabilitation as a central purpose of punishment. As noted previously, this would mean reinvesting in effective correctional programming such as higher education and vocational training, which have been shown to reduce both infractions and recidivism.[108]

However, the efficacy and impact of these back-end reforms depend entirely on the adoption of practices that assess and reward rehabilitation and provide a meaningful opportunity for discretionary release. As noted previously, people serving sentences of life *with* the possibility of parole are spending far more time behind bars than was the case several decades ago, and many die while still in prison.[109] Against this backdrop, legal experts have identified a number of "best practices" that would help to remedy these and other problems that plague many parole systems around the country.[110] These recommendations include the following:

- For extremely long and life sentences, release eligibility should occur no later than fifteen years after the conviction. This recommendation is based on the Model Penal Code produced by the ALI.[111] The implication of this recommendation is that LWOP sentences should be replaced with life *with* the possibility of parole sentences.
- There should be a meaningful presumption of release at first eligibility for review, such that the majority of prisoners are released at that time. This

recommendation is predicated on the view that prison sentences longer than fifteen years are not required to achieve "modified just deserts." As a result, prison stays that are longer than fifteen years can be justified only if necessary to incapacitate clearly dangerous people.

- The use of risk assessment tools by parole boards should be carefully considered. If used, risk assessment tools should be validated on local populations, and their connection to and implications for racial and socioeconomic inequality should be closely evaluated. The ethics of including static risk factors over which people have no control (such as whether a person lived as a child with both parents) should also be carefully considered. The ALI recommends, "As a first step, states should open their risk assessment tools to vigorous, public challenges of the tools' statistical underpinnings, as well as their application to individual offenders. We also recommend that each parole board scrutinize their risk assessment tool through the lens of race, identifying how each factor differentially affects racial minorities."[112]

- Decision-making tools should be structured, policy-driven, and transparent. Prisoners eligible for release should have the right to legal representation and must have the opportunity to access and challenge the validity of any risk assessment tools utilized.

- Perhaps most important, parole boards should focus on whether rehabilitation and maturation has occurred rather than focus on the original crime. For this reason, victim input should be limited to informed insights about the future risk potential of the inmate and comments about conditions of release.[113]

Getting from Here to There: Undermining the Myth of Monstrosity

Comprehensive sentencing reform that reduces long and life sentences and creates viable postconviction review and release mechanisms is clearly needed. What is less clear is how advocates can get such laws passed given the durability and power of the myth of monstrosity. As historian Khalil Gibran Muhammad notes, public discussions of the nature and causes of violence are very much bound up with the racial politics of blame.[114] Racist images of Black depravity, remorselessness, and violence serve not only to sustain White supremacy but also to deflect attention from structural inequalities. Similarly, the criminal legal system is built on the assumption that the causes of violent behavior can be found solely within individual defendants. For this reason, there are few avenues in the criminal legal system for challenging the assumption that criminal defendants are simply flawed individuals who were born with a predisposition to violence. Legal scholar Austin Sarat explains:

> The state will only punish responsible agents, persons whose "deviant" acts can be said to be a product of consciousness and will, persons who "could have done otherwise." As Blackstone put it, "to constitute a crime against human laws, there must be, first, a vicious will, and, secondly, an unlawful act consequent upon such vicious will." Thus the apparatus of punishment depends upon a modernist subject and conceptions of will that represses or forgets its "uncertain, divided, and opaque" character.[115]

Criminal punishment thus rests on the myth that all people possess and express a will that is absolutely and uncomplicatedly free.[116] However, in capital cases, the U.S. Supreme Court has recognized that this may not be the case and requires that sentencing decisions consider individual circumstances in order not to violate the Eighth Amendment's prohibition of cruel and unusual punishment. As a result, defense attorneys representing clients who face the death penalty do have the opportunity to introduce evidence of "mitigating circumstances" in the sentencing phase of capital trials.

Yet even where such opportunities exist, such evidence is too often dismissed. Social psychologist Craig Haney, who has collected and presented evidence of mitigating circumstances in numerous capital cases, notes, "A simple and seemingly irrefutable assertion that 'not everybody' exposed to one or another set of destructive background factors engaged in violent crime is used to trivialize what, in virtually any other context, we would all recognize as critically important to the decision at hand."[117] In particular, this "not everybody" fallacy is used to dismiss what would in other circumstances constitute clear evidence that a person's biographical experiences are related to their subsequent behavior.

While intuitively appealing to many, the "not everybody" argument ignores the reality that people's experiences of broadly similar circumstances are not identical. Evidence that some smokers do not develop lung cancer, for example, does not mean that a causal relationship between smoking and cancer does not exist, but rather suggests that the risk smoking poses is mediated by other factors. Similarly, gender, poverty, the age at which a person experienced abuse, the existence or absence of alternative sources of support, and myriad other factors mediate the long-term effects of childhood abuse, neglect, and trauma. Invocations of the "not everybody" argument sweep these nuances aside, wrongly dismiss all evidence indicating that social biography matters, and work to bolster the myth of monstrosity.[118]

In short, the disruptive impact of legal mechanisms that allow for the introduction of potentially mitigating evidence has been diminished through the routine invocation of the "not everyone" argument. This disruptive potential is limited for another reason as well: juries' willingness to treat evidence of abuse and trauma as grounds for mercy is shaped by race. Summarizing his observations of numerous capital cases involving Black defendants, Haney concludes:

> A particular kind of racially discriminatory death sentencing comes about as a result of an "empathic divide" that exists between many white jurors and African-American defendants. White jurors may have an especially difficult time understanding the mitigation that inheres in the structure of the lives that many African-American defendants have led. The empathic divide describes jurors' relative inability to perceive capital defendants as enough like themselves to readily feel any of their pains, to appreciate the true nature of the struggles they have faced, or to genuinely understand how and why their lives have taken very different courses.[119]

Findings from experimental studies confirm Haney's observation. These findings show that evidence regarding mitigating circumstances that may be perceived as exculpatory for White defendants is often ignored, or even interpreted as incriminating, when defendants are Black.[120] For example, although being raised in an abusive home is sometimes interpreted as a mitigating circumstance for White defendants, the same background often works to pathologize Black defendants, casting violence as a way of life.[121]

Some legal scholars have proposed that opportunities to present evidence of mitigating circumstances be expanded to non-capital cases.[122] Creating a new set of jurisprudential practices to enable consideration of defendants' backgrounds and circumstances might help remedy the criminal legal system's ignorance of the vast body of social scientific research showing the frequency with which abuse and trauma precipitate acts of violence. However, research showing that the meaning people make of mitigating circumstances is influenced by the race of the defendant casts doubt on the capacity of such an approach to bring about a more just and fair system.[123] Moreover, the viability of this idea in a system in which roughly 95 percent of all defendants facing felony charges plead guilty under the weight of extraordinarily harsh sentencing laws is unclear.[124] The inclusion of evidence of mitigating circumstances might make a difference in a small number of cases that go to trial, and may help chip away at the myth of monstrosity but also risks exacerbating racial inequities.

Recent research suggests some other possible avenues for addressing the failure of the public to appreciate the role of social circumstances and trauma in the generation of violence. Politicians who reiterate their commitment to harsh penalties in cases involving violence do appear to be reading the public opinion reasonably accurately. That is, many members of the public do support harsh penalties for people convicted of violent offenses, and nearly all express more support for punitive responses to violent (as opposed to property) crime.[125] Interestingly, though, research also suggests that public preferences on this issue are not rooted in past experience with violence, fear of victimization, or the risk of crime respondents face. In other words, people who have experienced violence, or live in areas that put them at higher risk of it, are not more punitive than others. Instead, the widespread preference for long sentences in response to violence is associated with traditional views about individual responsibility and accountability, as well as racial resentment and authoritarianism.[126]

These findings have mixed implications for the prospects of change in this area. On the one hand, insofar as penal attitudes are largely untethered to one's actual or perceived risk of victimization, potential increases in the crime rate may not doom efforts to shift popular beliefs and preferences about punishment (though much will hinge on the extent to which any such increases are highlighted and how they are framed, as developments in 2021 are making clear). On the other hand, the fact that support for punitive responses to violence is rooted in values rather than experience means that advocates of alternative responses to violence may have to make the case that less punitive responses to violence comport with traditional values. For example, proponents of restorative justice often emphasize the ways in which restorative justice practices respect and serve the value of accountability. Emphasizing these kinds of connections may help dislodge the widely accepted idea that the only way to hold people accountable is through long prison sentences.

While it is thus conceivable that motivated politicians could argue for alternative ways to address the problem of violence, few politicians on either side of the aisle appear inclined to attempt this. They have no political incentive to do so, at least not yet. In the meantime, many advocates are doing important cultural work by disseminating narratives that challenge the myth of monstrosity. Some groups, such as the Alliance for Safety and Justice, amplify the voices of the survivors of crime and violence—especially survivors of color whose voices are often omitted or silenced—who do *not* favor the current approach to public safety. Other advocates disseminate and amplify the stories of people who were at one point convicted of violence but are now leading lives of peace and integrity, whether behind bars or not.

These and other cultural strategies are essential to counter the myth of monstrosity, which has thus far prevented consideration of comprehensive sentencing reform. In the meantime, more minor reforms may help dislodge the image of people who have been convicted of an act of violence as monstrous others. For example, requiring that confinement institutions adopt trauma-informed practice would constitute a minor step toward acknowledging the histories of victimization that abound in jails and prisons. Similarly, improving the conditions of confinement (around medical care, visitation, and the use of solitary confinement, for example) would acknowledge the humanity of people involved in the criminal legal system. These more minor reforms may also help lay the foundation for a badly needed and more sweeping transformation of our approach to the problem of violence.

Stories from Inside

Through my work as a volunteer and teacher at the Washington State Reformatory in Monroe, I have become well-acquainted with a number of incarcerated people whose life stories exemplify the central themes of this chapter. The following accounts were developed in dialogue and partnership with those whose biographies I share and are intended, in part, to help readers understand how interpersonal violence grows out of the harmful social conditions that traumatize and destabilize young people.[127] Many people in these circumstances receive long or even life sentences at a young age without ever having had an opportunity to develop an alternative life trajectory outside of prison. Observation of these facts does not imply that people who commit violence should not be held accountable for the harm they caused, but they do suggest that responsibility is best understood as shared. They also raise questions about whether long-term confinement is the only—or most meaningful—way of promoting accountability and underscore the idea that investments in child, family, and community well-being are not only social welfare investments; they are also investments in public safety.

A second theme that emerges from these stories involves the importance of the sentencing policy shifts that have occurred across the country. As discussed previously, one effect of the enactment of tough sentencing laws has been the enhancement of the "trial penalty" (that is, the gap between the sentences imposed via guilty pleas versus at trial) and an increase in the number of people (including the factually innocent) who plead guilty out of fear of the consequences of not doing so.[128] Conversely, those who exercise their right to a trial are often penalized mightily for doing so. In one case I describe, for example, the defendant (Chris) declined to go to trial solely because the risk of doing so was too great. In another, the defendant (Anthony) rejected a plea deal that would have entailed a fifteen-year sentence—only to be sentenced to over one hundred years behind bars. The actual or implied threat of extraordinarily long sentences thus casts a long shadow over the criminal legal process. In addition, the near-abolition of parole in Washington State in 1984 (and in fifteen other states as well) means that the vast majority of prisoners, including those whose stories I summarize, will not have an opportunity to earn release from prison by demonstrating to a parole board that they are now safe to release.[129] I am thrilled to report that one of these men, Eugene Youngblood, received a unanimous recommendation from the Clemency and Pardons Board in 2019 and was released from prison in March 2021.

Finally, these stories help explain one of the most persistent and enduring research findings in criminology: people who commit unusually serious crimes and serve many years in prison but are eventually released have remarkably low rates of recidivism.[130] These extraordinarily low levels of recidivism reflect the fact that the vast majority of people sentenced to prison, including people convicted of a serious violent crime, mature and become safe to release, even when the conditions of confinement are far from ideal.

Although four of the five people who shared their experiences with me remain behind bars, their lives exemplify the maturation and growth that explains why so few released lifers return to prison despite all the hardship they endure. In all of these cases (and so many others), those who committed serious harm years ago work tirelessly to make amends and improve the lives of others, despite the fact that they will not be able to earn much or any time off their sentence by doing so.[131] Policies that deny people the opportunity to demonstrate their growth and maturation are thus in tension with the experiences of many prisoners who do in fact mature, as well as with human rights norms regarding the ways in which life sentences violate the right to dignity and evidence of exceptionally low rates of recidivism among people sentences to long and life sentences.

Christopher Blackwell

Chris was born in Oregon in 1981 and lived with both parents for a short time. However, his mother left to escape his alcoholic father's abuse when he was quite young. After regularly experiencing physical and emotional abuse at the hands of his father, Chris joined his mother in the Hilltop neighborhood of Tacoma, Washington, at the age of six, where he spent most of his childhood. Unfortunately, Chris's plight did not get easier after he moved in with his mother. In Tacoma, he was abused by his aunt, cousins, and mother's boyfriend; he was also surrounded by family members who sold drugs and regularly got drunk, high, or both. Because his mother worked two jobs to make ends meet, Chris was on his own and largely unsupervised from a very young age. By fourth grade, he was spending his time with older kids who had dropped out of school and were smoking marijuana. He changed schools regularly and attended only sporadically. He was held back in fourth grade due to poor attendance, discipline issues, and academic difficulties.

At age twelve, Chris stole a car, was involved in a high-speed chase with the police, and subsequently spent a year in juvenile detention. Upon his release, most of his criminal activity was aimed at generating money so that he could purchase drugs and alcohol. As a result of this activity, he was in and out of juvenile detention throughout his adolescence, where he was frequently assaulted and spent significant time in segregation. He also felt unsafe in his home and neighborhood and began carrying a gun at age thirteen. Eventually, he spent time in a "boot camp" program where, to his surprise, he thrived as a result of the structure, the sense of camaraderie, and the realization that he could live a different kind of life than the one he had been living in Tacoma.

The experience led Chris to attempt to join the military at age eighteen. Despite the active support of some of the sergeants who came to know him, however, he was unable to join as a result of his criminal record. Instead, upon his release he moved into a hotel and became a mid-level drug dealer. After racking up several nonviolent charges, Chris participated in several robberies. In one of these, he and his friends decided to rob a rival drug dealer whom they believed to be unprotected. Upon arriving at the intended victim's house, they discovered that a party was underway. In this context, Chris committed the crimes of Robbery I and Burglary I, during which he "shot Joshua May and caused his death."[132] Chris pled guilty to first-degree murder; had he gone to trial he may have faced a sixty-year sentence. He is now serving a sentence of 549 months, or forty-five years.

Photograph of Christopher Blackwell

Now thirty-nine years old, Chris recognizes the pain and suffering his actions caused and seeks through his daily activities to make amends. Toward this end, he is active in a number of programs, including the Concerned Lifers Organization, HEAL (Healing Education and Accountability for Liberation), Alternatives to Violence, various anger management programs, Understanding Family Violence, Smart Recovery (a substance abuse program), the Freedom Project, Bridges to Life (a restorative justice program), the Inside/Out Dad Program (a parenting class), and more. A high school dropout, Chris never thought he would pursue a college degree, but he recently earned his Associate of Arts degree through University Beyond Bars and is now working on his bachelor's degree. Chris has become a prolific writer whose work appears in such outlets as the Marshall Project and the *Washington Post*.[133] He is an accomplished artist who creates unique, Native American–inspired crafts which he often donates to nonprofit organizations and to tribal elders in Native American communities.

As a person who has been the beneficiary of other prisoners who made an investment in him, Chris has a passion for "paying it forward." He devotes much time and energy to mentoring his eighteen-year-old goddaughter, Aryanna. Chris has known Aryanna's father for years and decided to step in and help support her after her father developed a substance abuse problem and became less available to her. Although Chris's incarceration limits his ability to support her, he has focused on making sure that Aryanna knows she is loved and cared for and that no matter what she is facing, Chris will always be there to talk and lend her his emotional support. He also works hard to provide financial support, including helping her pay for a car and attend college.

Aryanna is deeply thankful for Chris's support and says about Chris, "Any time I need him he is there for me." She has found his advice and encouragement invaluable and reports that Chris is one of the only people who truly understands how she feels about virtually everything. Based on her many experiences and interactions with Chris, Aryanna says, "Chris is one of the best people I know." Appreciating what it is like not to have a supportive father, Chris finds great comfort in knowing he is helping Aryanna feel loved and navigating the challenges of life. Recently he married the woman he calls "the love of his life."[134]

Absent a change in policy, Chris is unlikely to be released from prison until 2045, despite his evident maturation, dedication to mentorship and service, and devotion to his family.

Jeff Foxx

Jeff Foxx, the youngest of four children, was born in Seattle to a single mother in 1974. His mother struggled with paranoid schizophrenia, and when Jeff was three or four years old, she moved to Yakima, alone. As a result, Jeff and his three sisters were placed in what was to become the first of a series of foster homes. Initially, Jeff and his siblings were housed together, but over time the children were separated. Sadly, Jeff experienced both physical and sexual abuse in more than one of his foster homes. He began having trouble focusing in school and had to repeat the fifth grade.

At age twelve, Jeff moved into his fifth foster home, in Seattle's Central District. Around the same time, his father was murdered. Drugs and gangs dominated the neighborhood in which Jeff now lived, and he had to be very careful navigating the area. He faced a good deal of pressure to join a gang but was able to resist. By seventh grade, however, he was unable to focus on his schoolwork despite his enrollment in advanced classes. Still, at the start of high school, Jeff worked, played sports, and dreamed of living with his sisters someday.

Eventually he did move in with his oldest sister, but the situation was not as he had hoped. Jeff then moved in with another sister, who was caring for their mother. During this time, a series of father and older brother figures whom Jeff trusted left the area, and this triggered Jeff's long-standing sense of abandonment. Around this time, he met a friend of a friend who was a drug dealer. Jeff needed money, and when offered the chance he began selling drugs. As street life consumed more of his time and energy, he quit sports and was eventually expelled from high school for poor attendance.

By the time he was seventeen, Jeff was quite anxious about how he would survive after aging out of the foster care system. He had no plan for supporting himself legally. Instead, he became highly involved in selling drugs and had no vision for his future outside of that world. Around this time, he was robbed and shot at several times, and he began to carry a gun for his protection. Shortly after Jeff turned eighteen, friends reported that some of the people who sold drugs for him were planning to rob him, and he began to fear for his life. In the context of these tensions, eighteen-year-old Jeff shot and killed four people whom he believed were plotting to harm him. He was convicted of aggravated murder in 1993 and was sentenced to life without the possibility of parole.

Now forty-seven years old, Jeff struggles daily with the consequences of his past actions, which he describes as "gruesome," and dedicates his life to attempting to make amends. He does not feel that just spending time behind bars is a meaningful way to make amends. He therefore mentors young men wherever he can. Over the years, he has also been highly involved in his church community and a variety of other prison-based programs, including the Alternatives to Violence Project, Non-Violent Communication, Men of Compassion (which serves ailing and terminally ill prisoners), HEAL, the Concerned Lifers Organization, the Black Prisoners Caucus, and many others. Jeff also serves as a trained facilitator for Roots of Success (an environmental literacy program). He earned his GED while at Walla Walla and his Associate of Arts degree through University Beyond Bars, for which he now serves on the prison advisory committee. Jeff also works as a graphic designer for Correctional Industries.

Those who know Jeff best report that he is a thoughtful, engaged, compassionate, and gentle man who consistently looks for opportunities to be of service and struggles mightily with guilt and remorse regarding his past actions. He devotes much of his time to his family, including his wife, Michelle, and his twenty-four-year-old stepdaughter, Mekiala. Michelle and Jeff have been married for over ten years. Throughout this time, Michelle says, "Jeff has always been there for Mekiala and me. He is loving, loyal, and very patient. He has such a drive to not only continue changing his life but also to becoming a better person and making sure the next young man does the same." According to Michelle, when she lost her job just after they were married, Jeff stepped in and helped her with the bills; when she is feeling down, he is always there to lift her up. Despite the challenges of having an incarcerated spouse, she feels strongly that their shared faith will get them through anything that comes their way. Mekiala similarly reports that she and Jeff have a strong bond that cannot be broken; she is able to talk to Jeff about any and all challenges and finds that he is an excellent listener and a constant source of support.

Photograph of Jeff Foxx

Jeff was barely eighteen years old—and therefore a legal adult—at the time he committed his crime. As a result, he will never have the opportunity to go before the Indeterminate Sentencing Review Board to be considered for release absent any change in policy, despite his remarkable growth, kindness, dedication to his family, and commitment to nonviolence.[135]

Ray Williams

Born in 1980, Ray lived with his mother until he was two years old, then with his grandparents until he was six. He recalls the years he spent on his grandparents' farm as the happiest time of his life; he enjoyed learning to read and helping out on the farm. His mother returned for him when he was six years old, after which time he lived with her, her boyfriend, and a new stepbrother in a trailer in Yelm, Washington. In this new environment, Ray witnessed the abuse of his mother by her boyfriend on a daily basis, including a stabbing triggered by her failure to make dinner according to her boyfriend's specifications. Ray also experienced emotional and physical abuse at the hands of both his mother and her boyfriend, and found himself in and out of school as his mother repeatedly left, and returned to, her abusive partner.

Ray ran away from home for the first time at the age of nine, but was returned to his mother shortly thereafter by Child Protective Services (CPS). Although the family was required to participate in counseling, Ray recalls no meaningful change at home and that the abuse continued. At thirteen, he ran away from home for good and began living alone on the streets of Olympia. After he returned to school, however, CPS became involved in his life once again, placing him in a series of foster homes. In one of these, Ray was abused by the biological son of his foster parents, who, among other things, forced him to inhale gasoline.

As a teenager, Ray cycled through group homes, juvenile detention, and the streets. He felt safest being homeless, so he stayed on the streets as much as possible, supporting himself by panhandling. At the age of sixteen, he broke into a house and stole a gun, which he planned to sell. He was arrested and charged with Burglary I, waived into adult court, and at the age of seventeen, sentenced to thirty-six months in an adult prison. This conviction was his first strike.

Ray was released from Clallam Bay state prison in 1997 and lived for a short time in a homeless shelter in Port Angeles. By age twenty-one, he had rebounded: he owned a window-washing and pressure-cleaning business, a house, a boat, and a truck, and he had a girlfriend and a young son, Hunter. His luck changed in 2003, however, when he discovered his girlfriend in bed with another man at a friend's house. In the heat of the moment, Ray assaulted (but did not seriously injure) the man. Because the event took place in a home that was not his own, Ray was again charged with Burglary 1. He reports that he pled guilty to this crime because he was told that if he did not, he could be charged with endangerment of a child. (His son was present at the time of the assault.) He was convicted and was sentenced to forty-eight months in prison. This was his second strike.

In prison again, Ray earned as much time as he could off his sentence in the hopes of being reunited with his son. But upon his release, he was, in his words, "a hot mess." Compelled to provide an address to which he could be released, Ray went to live with his mother, where things did not go well. In this context, his mental health deteriorated. His long-standing substance abuse issues worsened, and he turned to methamphetamine. Alarmed by his deteriorating mental state, suicidal thoughts, and anger, Ray presented himself to healthcare professionals and requested assistance. After being evaluated, the facility determined that Ray did not need to be treated or institutionalized. He was unable to secure the mental health services he felt he needed.

Soon, Ray was homeless again and living in his car. His substance abuse had become severe. He observed that an acquaintance, a middle-aged man, frequently had teenage girls in his apartment. Ray soon learned that this man was using drugs as a lure and was engaged in a variety of illegal activities involving the young women. Enraged, Ray went to the apartment with a gun and ultimately shot the man in the lower leg, injuring him. Representing himself in the case that ensued, Ray pled guilty to Assault II. This was his third strike. Ray was sentenced to life in prison without the possibility of parole in 2008. Absent the three-strikes law, the longest sentence that could have been imposed for Assault II would have been 120 months, or ten years.

The first few years of Ray's incarceration were a haze; he focused mainly on staying out of trouble, learned to play guitar, and working as a screen printer for Correctional Industries. After the shop was closed, he helped start the Sustainable Practices Lab, in which prisoners repaired bikes and furniture and made signs for state institutions and nonprofit organizations. At Walla Walla, Ray was invited to serve in a leadership role for a new program, Redemption, which he did. He was later transferred to Clallam Bay, where he initiated and served as a facilitator for Redemption.

In 2016, Ray interceded to prevent a prisoner from killing a correctional officer, which he downplays as just part of his ongoing commitment to do the right thing. Eventually, staff recognized Ray's role in ending the assault and transferred him to Washington State Reformatory, where programs are more readily available. Today, Ray works in WSR's welding shop, has produced an album, is pursuing his associate's degree through University Beyond Bars. He is a leader in the Redemption Program, an active member of the Concerned Lifers Organization, helps facilitate nonviolent communication, and is a founding member of the State-Raised Working Group, which works with state and community organizations to increase the life chances of foster youth.

Photograph of Ray Williams

Despite his maturation, dedication to defusing conflict, and insight regarding his past challenges, Ray can expect to spend the rest of his life behind bars absent a change in state sentencing policy.

Anthony Wright

Born in 1972, Anthony Wright was raised by both parents in the Los Angeles area. Although his family was a loving one, the neighborhood in which they lived was inundated with drug and gang activity. By the time Anthony was ten, neighborhood gang members routinely asked him where he was from so that they could identify the gang to which he belonged. For protection, Anthony began to affiliate with his neighborhood gang and soon became preoccupied with rivalries with other gangs. When he was fifteen, he was sent to juvenile detention for committing "malicious mischief." Undaunted, he grew up admiring successful drug dealers and sought to be one himself. He assumed, based on his surroundings and observations, that he was unlikely to survive into adulthood.

Anthony spent his adolescence in and out of juvenile detention, which he now describes as a "school for criminals." His early adult years looked much the same until, in 1992, he discovered that he could make more money selling drugs in Spokane, Washington, than in Los Angeles. He continued selling drugs in both locales; he was also a father to several children and had started a number of legitimate businesses. Eventually, Anthony was set up for a robbery by an acquaintance who also sold drugs. Afterward, Anthony and two friends went to confront the robbers in their house in Spokane. Waiting outside, Anthony saw the man who had robbed him through a window and attempted to shoot him. His co-defendants also shot into the house, and one of the bullets tragically killed a three-year-old child Anthony and his co-conspirators did not know was inside.

Anthony was devastated when he learned of the child's death, after which, he reports, he "went into denial" and stayed that way through the trial and into the early years of his incarceration. Upon his arrest, he was offered a sentence of 180 months (fifteen years) if he pled guilty to being an accomplice to Murder 1 or 2, conditional on his willingness to testify against his co-defendants.[136] He declined to do so. At trial, he was convicted of one count of first-degree murder, one count of attempted first-degree murder, and six counts of first-degree assault. He received a sentence of 1,660 months, or

138 years, and now confronts on a daily basis the fact that he will likely die behind bars.

Anthony also struggles with the guilt he feels for helping to create a situation in which a three-year old lost her life. Although it appears that Anthony was not directly responsible for her death, he takes responsibility for organizing the retaliatory effort that resulted in her death. As he puts it, "I ruined many lives. Because of my actions, Pasheen's brother and sister have grown up without her. She never got the chance to attend school, drive her first car, make life decisions, just be who she wanted to be. I think of that every day, and every time I think of my kids."

Although Anthony knows there is no way to compensate for the loss of the life of a child, he seeks to make amends in any way he can. Following his mother's advice to "bloom where you are planted," he works every day to help other incarcerated people discover and develop their potential. Anthony works closely with prisoners seeking to leave the gang life, helping them navigate that complex and often dangerous process. He is involved in a variety of programs, including Alternatives to Violence, HEAL, and Men of Compassion, in an effort to reduce violence both inside and outside the prison and serve those in need. He also serves as a facilitator for Alternatives to Violence.

Anthony was one of University Beyond Bars' first four students and is a founding member of its Prisoner Advisory Committee. He earned his Associate of Arts degree in December 2011 and is now working on his bachelor's degree. On behalf of UBB, he facilitates the College Prep Math courses and tutors students in all levels of math, from pre-algebra to calculus. He also serves on UBB's Prison Advisory Board and reports that UBB has helped him realize how important a role he can play in helping others realize their worth.

One young man whom Anthony mentored during the formative years of eighteen to twenty-six says, "Anthony was patient and challenged me in ways that promoted growth and development despite the sometimes arrogant, sometimes impulsive young man I was. . . . Anthony Wright taught me that being a mentor is more than just directing younger men in the way they should go. It is putting rubber to the road and hitting the pavement right alongside with them, because their triumph is your triumph. I'm almost thirty now, nearly done with my sentence, but Anthony Wright has been right by my side, if not physically then certainly in spirit, every step of the way."

Photograph of Anthony Wright

Despite his remarkable maturation, kindness, and advanced education and skills, Anthony will not have the opportunity to be considered for release absent any change in policy.

Eugene Youngblood

Eugene Youngblood was born in 1973 to a young single woman who had recently moved to Los Angeles in the hopes of becoming a movie star. Instead, she was arrested and incarcerated when Eugene was an infant. Although his father lived nearby, Eugene's paternal grandmother became his caretaker and he rarely saw his father. His grandmother worked hard to ensure that Eugene was busy with activities after school and did not interact with the gang members who dominated the neighborhood. However, his grandmother died when he was just ten years old, and he subsequently moved in with an aunt who struggled with substance abuse issues and did not pay close attention to his well-being or whereabouts.

By the age of eleven, Eugene was spending more and more time with the local gang, members of which sometimes looked after and fed him. By thirteen, he was actively involved with the gang to which he now felt indebted. By the age of fourteen, he had dropped out of school and was delivering cocaine for the gang. His drug-dealing activities took him back and forth between California and Washington over a period of years. At eighteen, Eugene was living in Tacoma when he was asked by friends to confront some rivals with whom they had a conflict. He agreed to do so, although he has long maintained that he was not present when the confrontation actually took place. During this confrontation, two young men, eighteen-year-old Tyrone Darcheville and sixteen-year-old Arthur Lewis Randall Jr., were shot and killed.

Eugene was charged with two counts of murder in the first degree, to which he pled not guilty. During his first trial, his co-defendant was found guilty, but the jury could not reach a verdict regarding Eugene. In a second trial, Eugene and another co-defendant were both found guilty, although a juror noted at the time that it was much more difficult for the jury to reach this conclusion regarding Eugene.[137] Eugene was convicted of two counts of first-degree murder as well as conspiracy to commit murder and received a 780-month (sixty-five-year) sentence.

During the early years of his incarceration, Eugene remained loyal to the gang and, accordingly, racked up an estimated seventy infractions before his twenty-fifth birthday. Today he recognizes that he caused much harm during this time, and although he has always maintained that he was not present when the two victims were killed, he acknowledges that he had previously engaged in violence. During the latter part of his incarceration, Eugene actively rejected the "gang code" that he accepted in his youth and spent much of his time and energy engaging young gang members and supporting those who were attempting to exit gang life. He also worked hard to change prison culture such that redemption, responsibility, and participation in positive programs—not toughness or the willingness to commit violence—are the basis of respect. He became a leader in the Black Prisoners Caucus, which works to break the cycle of poverty, violence, and incarceration, and the Concerned Lifers Organization, and participated in the Redemption Program, HEAL, and more. He also became a master trainer for the Roots of Success program, an environmental literacy program that emphasizes job readiness and reentry skills.

In keeping with his goals and priorities, Eugene befriended a young man, Travis Turner, who at the time identified as a White supremacist. Despite their obvious differences, Eugene recognized that he and Travis had something important in common: they had both been taught to hate another group of people and accepted this ideology without question. Eugene nonetheless reached out to Travis and eventually became a role model and mentor for him. Eugene helped facilitate Travis's exit from the gang he was affiliated with and his efforts to address his substance abuse. Inspired by Eugene's example, Travis has become involved in the Concerned Lifers Organization, Toastmasters, Non-Violent Communication, University Beyond Bars, debate

Photograph of Eugene Youngblood

team, and more. On Eugene's advice, Travis also enrolled in HEAL, which, he reports, "has allowed me to open up about my past and allow healing to take place, stop running, stop burying my past. . . . I feel so much better."

For years, Eugene and Travis provided important leadership and support for other men attempting to change prison culture, and recently they co-facilitated a group of men working through the Redemption curriculum. About Eugene, Travis recently wrote, "I was changed by a Black man, a man who the state says will spend the rest of his life in prison. A man who truly cares what I am doing, how I am doing, feeling, what I am working on, what I am reading, what events to go to get some knowledge, some information to be more successful. . . . He truly cares for my wellbeing. I don't believe I ever had that before."

On June 14, 2019, the Clemency and Pardon Board unanimously recommended that Eugene Youngblood's virtual life sentence be commuted. Governor Jay Inslee eventually signed off, and Eugene was released in March 2021. He is thrilled with his newfound freedom, overjoyed to be reunited with his daughter and other family members, and delighted to be working for the Freedom Project, a local nonprofit that seeks to dismantle mass incarceration and address the harm that it has caused in communities of color.

Summary

About the death penalty, Haney writes:

> Our system of death sentencing . . . leads us to view capital defendants as genetic misfits, as unfeeling psychopaths who kill for the sheer pleasure of it, or as dark, anonymous figures who are something less than human. The public is given access—in some cases, an amazing amount of access—to only superficial and schematic details of the lives of capital defendants, typically only those "facts" that underscore their deviance and that facilitate their dehumanization. Since we can tolerate eliminating from the human social order only those who by their very nature stand outside its boundaries, the long-term viability of the system of death sentencing requires that capital defendants be depicted in this fashion.[138]

The elimination of criminal defendants from the social order is uniquely complete in the capital cases on which Haney focuses. But incarceration, and especially long and life sentences, are also forms of exclusion and elimination. In this chapter, I have argued that the belief that this long-term exclusion and expulsion are necessary and appropriate rests on the depiction of people who have been convicted of a violent crime as monstrous others who bear sole responsibility for the violence that occurred.

The reality is much more complicated. Violence has many antecedents, including personal trauma and state violence. Moreover, mass incarceration is itself a form of structural violence. Long and life sentences fuel mass incarceration and fail to make us safe because they do not deter more than short sentences, because the risk that someone will reoffend declines dramatically with age, and because imprisoning older people is both inefficient and costly.[139] The routine imposition of long and life sentences is also unethical and inhumane: the denial of hope, the mass incarceration of elderly and often frail prisoners, and the racially unequal imposition of these and other harms should be of great concern. To make matters worse, the current policy regime does little to meet the needs of most crime survivors, the vast majority of whom do not receive the services and compensation they need and deserve.[140] Comprehensive sentencing reform, including the adoption of a statutory maximum of twenty years, as well as social investments in disadvantaged communities are clearly needed if we are to reduce both interpersonal and state violence.

6
Violence and Restorative Justice

Although U.S. crime rates have been falling for decades, and remains low by historical standards even in 2021, the risk of violence remains unacceptably high in some disadvantaged communities. People of color, people living in poverty, and the disabled experience violence far more frequently than others.[1] In some neighborhoods, the homicide rate is more than one thousand times higher than in others located just a mile away in the same city.[2] The neighborhoods with the highest rates of violence are also those from which people who are entangled with the criminal legal system are overwhelmingly drawn.

Violent victimization is highly correlated with negative mental health and social outcomes such as PTSD, socioemotional distress, and reduced quality of life (presumably as a result of the trauma associated with violent assault).[3] Violence survivors tend not to experience a conventional grief process; instead, the trauma is prolonged and often remains unresolved well after victims' cases are processed (if arrest and prosecution occur).[4] Studies show that individuals who are exposed to trauma (including violent victimization) are at increased risk for physical illnesses, and that poor physical and mental health impacts survivors' ability to engage in education and the labor market.[5] As a result, the experience of violence by young people may have a significant impact on their transition to adulthood and life course trajectory.[6] To the extent that this is the case, violent victimization may also contribute to both socioeconomic and health inequality over the life course.

Current criminal justice and sentencing policies do not serve violence survivors well, especially those who are from disadvantaged communities. Most victims never enjoy their "day in court," either because they do not file a police report or because arrest and prosecution do not occur.[7] As Danielle Sered points out, the fact that roughly half of all people who experience violence do not report the crime to the police means they prefer *nothing* to what the state has to offer.[8] Even among people who do report their victimization to authorities, most do not receive the services they need.[9] People who are poor and/or of color are especially unlikely to receive needed services.[10] Moreover, many survivors who have contact with the criminal legal system are dissatisfied with the process, and too many experience revictimization that amplifies their psychological distress.[11] In fact, some studies find that newly created opportunities for victim participation in the conventional criminal justice process exacerbate rather than alleviate survivors' trauma.[12]

Although policies that allow for the imposition of long and life sentences are often said to reflect survivors' preferences, this is misleading. Long prison sentences do little to mitigate the negative effects of violence, are not favored by many people who have been harmed, and often end up punishing people who are themselves victims of abuse, crime, and violence. A recent national survey found that 61 percent of those who have experienced interpersonal violence favor shorter prison terms and enhanced spending on prevention and rehabilitation; only 25 percent preferred sentences that keep people in prison as long as possible.[13] Similarly, significant majorities of survivors of all political orientations favor investing public safety dollars in education rather than in prisons and jails.[14] In California, crime victims are a leading force in the movement for criminal justice reform.[15]

As Sered vividly illustrates in *Until We Reckon*, survivors' emotional responses to their victimization and their thoughts about crime policy are complex, ambivalent, and varied. The assumption that all victims feel the same way and want the same thing is an artifact of the amplification of some survivors' voices and the neglect of others. Too often, survivors who have complex thoughts and feelings about what should be done about the problem of violence are shut out of the media and the policymaking process. Increasingly, however, people who have been harmed and are from disadvantaged communities are mobilizing to ensure that their concerns about the lack of social services for crime victims—as well as about police brutality and mass incarceration—are heard.[16]

In addition to homogenizing and oversimplifying the views of people who have been harmed, policymakers tend to imagine people who have experienced violence and those who are justice-involved as two distinct and unrelated groups of people. But, as has been discussed throughout this book, people who have experienced violence are notably overrepresented among arrestees, prisoners, and ex-prisoners.[17] Put another way, most system-involved people are also survivors of violence and abuse. And, as noted previously, there is evidence that the experience of violence increases the risk of subsequent justice involvement. One study, for example, found that Black Americans who have experienced four or more traumatic, violent events are more than four times more likely to be arrested, jailed, or imprisoned than those who have not experienced violent trauma, even after controlling for factors such as poverty that increase the risk of victimization.[18]

Long prison sentences consume significant public dollars that could be reallocated to improve victim services and enhance crime prevention efforts. For example, increasing access to high-quality, early education programs improves educational outcomes and reduces subsequent criminal legal system involvement.[19] Nevertheless, the U.S. Department of Education has acknowledged that "children in countries as diverse as Mexico, France and Singapore have a better chance of receiving preschool education than do children in the United States."[20] Numerous other public safety interventions that do not involve incarceration have also been found to be highly cost-effective. These include employment training/job assistance in the community and out-patient drug treatment.[21] Community organizations that focus on violence prevention and strengthening communities have also been found to notably reduce violent crime.[22] Within prison settings, substance abuse treatment, education (both K–12 and postsecondary), and vocational training are also cost-effective means of reducing recidivism and improving public safety.

These facts and figures provide compelling grounds for ending the imposition of excessive sentences and for reallocating resources toward violence prevention and accessible victim services. Yet such facts and figures are rarely mentioned in policy discussions of violence or in the response to individual cases in which violence occurred. Instead, the assumptions and images associated with the myth of monstrosity tend to dominate the tenor and content of these discussions. It is clear that our ability to consider and enact reasonable and effective antiviolence policies will remain stymied as long as the myth of monstrosity prevails. In this chapter, I argue that increased investment in restorative justice (RJ) alternatives and recognition of the important principles and lessons that RJ offers, will help dislodge the cultural centrality of the myth of monstrosity and provide a more effective and humane way of responding to the problem of violence.

Understanding Restorative Justice

Interventions based on RJ principles generally "involve, to the extent possible, those who have a stake in a specific offense to collectively identify and address harms, needs and obligations, in order to heal and put things as right as possible."[23] From an RJ perspective, crime and other forms of harm are a violation of people and relationships—the relationships between the responsible party and their family, friends, the people they have harmed, and the community—as opposed to a crime against the state. The RJ framework rests on three additional underlying principles: (1) the focus should be on the harm done; (2) wrongs or harms result in obligations; and (3) engagement and participation by all parties is ideal.[24] RJ entails repairing the harm caused by the wrongdoing (restoration); encouraging appropriate responsibility for addressing needs and repairing the harm (accountability); and involving the impacted, including the community, in the resolution (engagement) wherever possible.[25] In the process of coming together to restore relationships, the affected parties are provided with an opportunity to heal through the reintegration of those harmed and those who caused the harm.[26] Since harm is the central problem in a restorative framework, RJ requires a response that avoids committing further harm.

RJ is thus best understood as a philosophy and set of principles that guide alternative responses to harm and violence rather than as a fixed set of practices that are uniformly applied. Still, direct interaction between the person who experienced harm and the person who caused it is at the heart of most (but not all) RJ initiatives.[27] These processes provide people who were harmed the opportunity to meet the person(s) who harmed them in a safe and structured setting; to tell the person who caused the harm about its physical, emotional, and financial impact; to receive answers to lingering questions about the harm and the factors that led to its commitment; and to be directly involved in developing a restitution or agreement plan going forward.

RJ has roots in some indigenous communities and emerged in Western criminal legal systems in the 1970s, with "victim-offender reconciliation programs" and "victim offender mediations" in Canada and the midwestern United States.[28] These approaches focus primarily on restoring "the right relationships" that should exist between two parties.[29] The core practices that emerged under this philosophy include "victim-offender mediation," "victim-offender dialogues," group conferences, and RJ circles. (Note that the term "offender" is no longer considered appropriate or helpful.) The initial impetus for "victim-offender mediations" grew out of a desire to create a more effective approach to dealing with juveniles. Ideally, these mediations result in a consensus agreement about activities the responsible party will undertake to meet the needs or expectations of the person who was harmed.[30] "Victim-offender dialogues" involving serious violence grew out of these processes and have been primarily driven by people who have experienced harm.[31] That is, many dialogues involving the harmed party and the person(s) who caused the harm are not stipulated by the court, but rather are initiated by the person who experienced harm and often occur while the person who caused harm is incarcerated.

Another RJ practice called family group conferencing was introduced in the United States in the mid-1990s. Conferencing is an adaptation of a traditional

Maori process for resolving community problems and involves a dialogue between the harmed party, the responsible party, their supporters, and a facilitator. Family group conferencing differs from "victim-offender reconciliation" programs or "victim-offender mediations" in its inclusion of a broader array of community members in the dialogue about the harm.[32] The dialogue is meant to explore what happened, the impact of the harm, and what needs to happen to make things as right as possible. Every participant has an opportunity to speak to the issues and to collectively develop an agreement about obligations going forward.

Similarly, circle processes, based on Native American talking circles, involve the person who experienced harm and the responsible person as well as interested and affected community members in a facilitated dialogue. The process often involves preconferencing or separate circles for the various parties before they are brought together to determine an action plan. Sentencing circles are a consensus process aimed at addressing harm, accountability, and healing.[33] They involve "a broad holistic framework [that includes] crime victims and their families, an offender's family members and kin, and community residents in the response to the behavior and the formulation of a sanction which will address the needs of all parties."[34] Non-Aboriginal groups in Canada and the United States have been experimenting with sentencing circles for some time.[35]

Although systematic information about the prevalence of RJ in the United States does not exist, it appears that initiatives based on this philosophy have expanded in recent decades. As of 2015, thirty-three states had enacted laws that mention or require some form of RJ.[36] At least in the United States, however, it appears that most RJ programs involve juveniles rather than adults, and most exclude cases involving serious violence.[37]

Existing RJ programs differ across at least two important dimensions. First, RJ interventions vary in terms of whether they entail diversion from jail and/or prison. Some RJ diversion frameworks provide an alternative dispute resolution process that largely replaces the role of the juvenile or criminal courts. Other diversionary initiatives, such as the Common Justice program in Brooklyn, New York (described by Sered in *Until We Reckon*), partner with the courts to divert cases and, pending a resolution that is satisfactory to all, lead to a reduction or dismissal of charges. In such cases, the result may be that a confinement sentence, and possibly a criminal conviction, are avoided altogether. By contrast, some RJ-inspired interventions are based primarily in jails or prisons and have no impact on sentencing, although they could conceivably impact postconviction review process such as parole and clemency. These interventions seek to facilitate dialogue between people who are incarcerated and the person(s) they harmed and, in the process, stimulate a healing process for victims and responsible parties alike. Proponents of this approach also seek to reduce recidivism among participants who are released from jail or prison.

Research on the Efficacy of Restorative Justice Programs

A growing number of studies evaluate RJ programs. Variation along the dimensions described earlier as well as the types of harms included, the age of the persons involved, and the difficulty of random assignment makes conducting these evaluations and summarizing their findings tricky. Still, there is a growing body of evidence that programs informed by RJ principles hold a great deal of promise in terms of improving survivor well-being, reducing recidivism, and, in some cases, decreasing reliance on prisons and jails.

Victim Satisfaction

When given the option, many people who have experienced violence and other harms choose to participate in RJ alternatives.[38] A recent multistate study found that victims who choose to participate in an RJ-mediated dialogue do so for a variety of reasons: to help (and pressure) the responsible party to address the underlying issues; to learn why the responsible party committed the crime; to communicate to the responsible party the impact of the crime; and to increase the chances that the responsible party will not harm others in the future.[39]

Studies of RJ programs generally indicate that all involved parties report high levels of satisfaction.[40] In fact, expression of satisfaction is consistent for both victims and responsible parties across sites, cultures, and offense seriousness. Typically, 80 to 90 percent of participants report being satisfied with mediated dialogue processes.[41] For any given mediation, the victim and the responsible party tend to report similar levels of satisfaction, regardless of the type of offense or the restitution agreed upon. In addition, research tracing the impact of RJ conferencing on posttraumatic stress symptoms associated with robbery and burglary found that RJ practices notably reduce the traumatic impact of crime. Specifically, participants in RJ conferences reported a more than 40 percent reduction in posttraumatic stress symptoms immediately and six months after participation.[42] The authors of one recent meta-analysis of RJ alternatives to the traditional juvenile justice system state, "Victims reported improved perceptions of fairness, greater satisfaction, improved attitudes toward the juvenile, are more willing to forgive the offender, and are more likely to feel that the outcome was just."[43] Research suggests that victims' satisfaction is likely to correlate directly with their perception of the process rather than with the outcome.[44] That is, harmed parties who feel that the process was conducted in a fair and thoughtful manner are likely to report high levels of satisfaction, regardless of the nature of the restitution or outcome.

Victim satisfaction also reflects increased feelings of safety. For example, one study found that victims who participated in mediation in lieu of the criminal legal process reported feeling safer than they had not only before the mediation but also before the harm occurred. By contrast, victims who went through traditional court processes reported that the experience had substantially *lessened* their sense of safety.[45] Survivor satisfaction also appears to reflect the positive impact of RJ processes on perceptions of fairness. A study of people who experienced burglary in Minneapolis, for example, found that 80 percent of those who went through mediation experienced the process as fair, compared with only 38 percent of those who had participated in standard court processes.[46]

Recidivism

Although RJ as a framework tends to focus on repairing harm in the present situation, the efficacy of any form of criminal legal intervention is often measured in terms of its capacity to reduce recidivism. And many survivors elect to participate in RJ processes precisely because they hope doing so will ensure that the person who harmed them will not harm others in the future.[47] For these reasons, many studies assess whether RJ processes impact the likelihood of future harm. Although there are significant methodological challenges associated with these evaluations, many studies do find that RJ programs reduce future violations.[48]

One recent and exhaustive meta-analysis, for example, found that RJ conferences cause a "modest but highly cost-effective reduction in the frequency of repeat offending by the consenting incarcerated/formerly incarcerated individuals randomly assigned to participate in such a conference."[49] Another meta-analysis of a sample of 11,950 juveniles found that RJ programs generated a 34 percent reduction in recidivism.[50] In addition, some studies find that when former participants did reoffend, their crimes were less serious than those committed by people who had not gone through RJ processes.[51] However, a recent large meta-analysis that found only modest reductions in recidivism among juvenile participants notes that these effects were found to be smaller where researchers were able to randomly assign people to RJ and traditional processes.[52] This finding raises the concern that some of the reported impact on RJ processes on recidivism may reflect the fact that people who choose to participate in RJ are different from those who do not. Additional research is needed to assess this possibility.

Most of these studies pertain to RJ processes that occur after conviction. Less is known about diversion programs that keep people out of the criminal legal system and are based on RJ principles. However, evaluation of an RJ program that was designed to divert defendants from incarceration found that recidivism rates were significantly lower for program participants than for members of the comparison group.[53] The aforementioned meta-analysis of RJ programs for juveniles similarly found that diversion programs were associated with greater reductions in recidivism than non-diversion models.[54]

Overall, then, there is reasonably strong evidence that RJ practices, particularly those that keep people out of the criminal legal system, reduce recidivism relative to conventional alternatives, though important questions remain about how selection bias, age, and other factors may affect this process. Importantly, most of these studies evaluate programs that mainly involve facilitation of dialogue between harmed and responsible parties; the trauma of those who have caused harm is addressed in some, but not all, of these programs. It seems likely that doing so in a more consistent manner would generate further reductions in recidivism.

Unfortunately, most RJ programs do not include cases that involve violence. Yet RJ mediation and other alternatives may be most effective in such cases. For example, one Canadian study found no significant impact on future violations for individuals convicted of low-level offenses, but did report a 38 percent reduction in recidivism for people who committed violent crimes.[55] Another study found a direct and positive correlation between the long-term success of the program (measured mainly in terms of recidivism) and the seriousness of the offense.[56] The implication of these findings is that RJ programs may have the most potential to improve victim healing and reduce recidivism if they include cases that involve interpersonal violence.[57] While these findings may seem counterintuitive, they are consistent with evidence that survivors of violence experience the greatest level of trauma, and thus that a healing-centered approach will provide the most benefit to them.

Limitations of (Many) Restorative Justice Programs—And How to Address Them

Existing RJ programs have a number of limitations, although many of these are remediable. The first has to do with the limited access to RJ that results when programs only facilitate dialogue between people who experienced harm and *the specific person* who harmed them. If the person who caused the initial harm is never arrested and convicted, and is not identified through some other process, then harmed parties are unable to benefit from many existing RJ programs. This is an important limitation. One possible solution is to expand the options for the involvement of "surrogate" victims: harmed parties who wish to share their experiences with people who have caused similar kinds of harm. For example, the Insight Prison Project in California and the HEAL program in Washington State arrange for people who have experienced certain kinds of harm (such as robbery or assault) to dialogue with people in prison who were convicted of those same offenses. Many of the survivors who participate in these processes report that doing so is extremely valuable to their own healing.[58] It is unclear whether this approach will yield reductions in recidivism, though many former prisoners report that participation in these programs expedited their own transformation and recovery.[59]

Second, the success of an RJ-based intervention also depends on responsible parties' willingness and ability to engage in a dialogue without further harming the person who experienced trauma. Survivors who wish to participate in an RJ process are unable to do so when these conditions do not exist (although here, too, the use of surrogates may be helpful). Increased investment in the process of preparing people who have caused harm to participate in RJ processes that do not exacerbate harm may help to address this constraint.

Third, although participation in some RJ programs may serve as a substitute for, or part of, a defendant's court sentence, most are not designed as an alternative to criminal sentences and, consequently, are not designed to reduce the number of defendants sentenced to jail or prison.[60] To the extent that this is the case, the potential of RJ to help ameliorate the harm associated with mass incarceration is limited. An obvious response to this limitation is to expand the number of RJ interventions that serve as a substitute for incarceration and, ideally, criminal conviction.

Fourth, many RJ programs, especially those offering an alternative to traditional court processes and incarceration, are available only to juveniles and/ or to adults charged with low-level offenses.[61] The use of RJ frameworks that include adults charged with or convicted of more serious criminal offenses, especially violent crimes, has been more controversial, although support for this appears to be growing. Although some argue that RJ alternatives cannot reduce the use of incarceration, this argument rests on the erroneous assumption that RJ interventions that involve diversion *cannot* include cases involving violence.[62] In fact, as noted previously, the evidence suggests that the positive impact of RJ may be greatest when the harm caused is comparatively serious.[63] Moreover, the potential to reduce incarceration is also greatest when cases involving more serious harms are included. The Common Justice program in Brooklyn described by Sered works only with people who experienced violent crime, and it has achieved remarkable results.[64] For these reasons, expansion of RJ-based diversion approaches that include, and perhaps even prioritize, cases involving violence is warranted.

Fifth, cultural differences, bias, and racism cast a shadow over attempts to build RJ programs that benefit everyone. For example, a recent study found that schools with more Black students were less likely to employ RJ techniques than schools with fewer Black students.[65] The risk of maintaining or exacerbating preexisting racial disparities in the criminal justice system is heightened when RJ programs are not intentionally race-conscious. Practitioners should be aware of the role of racial and other biases and take active steps to ensure racial equity in the availability and process of RJ.

Finally, the issue of scalability remains challenging. It is, at this juncture, unclear whether and how diversion frameworks based on RJ principles can be "scaled up" in a way that leads to meaningful improvements in victim well-being and public safety even as they reduce mass incarceration. Yet the answers to these difficult questions will never be ascertained in the abstract. Rather, increased investment, effort, and experimentation with RJ alternatives is needed to inform assessments of the scalability of these approaches.

Summary

The twin problems of mass violence and mass incarceration have devastating effects on poor communities across the country, and communities of color have been especially impacted. Current criminal justice practices and policies do not meaningfully improve public safety[66] or address survivors' needs.[67] In this context, interest in RJ frameworks is growing. With its emphasis on ameliorating harm, RJ is a promising alternative to conventional criminal justice practices, especially when paired with diversion, focusing on situations involving comparatively serious harm, and addressing the trauma and deprivation that people who cause harm have also experienced.

As currently practiced, RJ has limited reach, mainly because most initiatives limit participation to cases in which all directly involved persons are available and willing to participate. In addition, the exclusion of cases involving adults and/or violence severely limits the potential impact of many existing RJ programs. But as discussed in this chapter, studies suggest that RJ is most effective in cases involving violence. The exclusion of cases involving more serious harm denies people who have experienced the gravest injuries the opportunity to reap the benefits associated with RJ. It also reduces the capacity of RJ interventions to meaningfully reduce mass incarceration.

The expansion of RJ programs, practices, and principles is overdue. Ideally, these programs would include adults as well as juveniles, and cases involving violence. While important questions about scalability remain unresolved, developing the institutional capacity to operate RJ-inspired interventions that target violence and survivors of color is an important step toward ameliorating the harm associated with both violence and mass incarceration.

Embracing and expanding RJ responses in the aftermath of violence (and in lieu of incarceration) would have a number of other benefits as well. For example, the expansion of RJ processes would be built on recognition of the fact that people who cause harm at one point in their lives are human beings who have likely experienced a great deal of trauma and can and should remain connected to others rather than be cast aside and presumed to be incapable of growth and maturation. More generally, RJ's emphasis on the importance of relationships is a healing antidote to the isolation, shame, and stigma associated with more conventional approaches to punishment. RJ alternatives serve as an important reminder that holding people responsible and accountable for the harm they cause does not necessarily entail incarceration. And after decades of mass incarceration, recognition of the fact that all human beings are fallible, and most are capable of accountability and making amends, is an essential component of the healing journey upon which we must embark.

7

Rethinking Drug Policy

The drug war has been vigorously fought and has produced many casualties. The number of drug arrests taking place each year nearly quadrupled in recent decades, from just over a half a million in 1981 to a peak of nearly 1.9 million in 2006. Because many people arrested on drug charges are also convicted, fined, incarcerated, and even deported, the human and fiscal costs associated with the antidrug campaign have been massive. Roughly 400,000 U.S. residents are behind bars as a result of a drug conviction.[1] Upward of a million more are on probation or parole as a result of a drug conviction.[2] These misguided interventions have unfolded in a wildly disproportionate manner.[3] As noted in chapter 4, preexisting racial inequities were magnified between 1980 and 2006, as the (comparatively low) White drug arrest rate doubled while the Black drug arrest rate more than tripled.[4] The harm that results from drug law enforcement has thus been quite unevenly distributed, with Black and brown people bearing the brunt of it.

The war on drugs represents one of the least effective ways of responding to substance use that humans have ever devised. Punishing people who use drugs does not improve their health and well-being, or address the circumstances that fueled their drug use in the first place.[5] In fact, punishment merely adds to the trauma with which many people with substance use disorder contend, while incarceration puts them at grave risk of overdose upon their release from jail or prison.[6] Moreover, the drug war has failed to achieve its stated objectives, namely, reducing the supply and increasing the price of drugs in order to deter their consumption. Despite spending billions of dollars to achieve these goals, illicit drugs remain more ubiquitous and affordable than ever.[7] Similarly, efforts to disrupt local drug markets through law enforcement do not reduce crime[8] and have not reduced the supply of drugs, but do often trigger competition and violence.[9]

While the U.S. government has spent billions of dollars in a futile attempt to control the supply and raise the price of illicit substances, affordable housing has grown ever scarcer, behavioral health treatment is difficult to access for many, and drug treatment remains underfunded. Over 7 million Americans struggle with a substance use disorder involving one or more illicit drugs;

only about one in five receive the treatment they need.[10] The approach to chemical dependency that is most efficacious for many people—medication-assisted treatment—remains especially difficult to access.[11] In this context, the U.S. overdose death rate has reached record levels, and is 3.5 times higher than the average rates found in seventeen other high-income countries.[12]

It is clear that the drug war has failed and must end. The question is: How—and what should replace it? As advocates of decriminalization and legalization point out, arrest, conviction, incarceration, and criminal legal system supervision compound drug-related harm and do not meaningfully reduce harmful forms of drug use, crime, or violence. Ending the destructive involvement of the criminal legal system in the lives of people who use drugs is therefore an important objective. In and of itself, though, this is not be enough; addiction often stems from trauma and causes its own, often devastating kind of suffering that is not addressed by decriminalization or legalization alone. Moreover, decriminalizing drug possession in isolation ignores the fact that unregulated drug markets also cause significant damage. For example, the content and potency of illicit substances are wildly variant; this uncertainty increases the risk of overdose. In recent years, the spread of fentanyl and other potent, synthetic opioids led to a surge in overdose deaths.[13] Illicit drug markets are also characterized by high price markups and profit margins, as well as unregulated competition among traffickers and dealers, all of which contributes to systemic, drug-related violence.[14]

Untreated addiction and unregulated drug markets cause significant harm even to people who do not use or sell drugs. For example, some people with substance use disorders commit property crimes and engage in other criminal activities such as drug sales in order to generate revenues that can be used to obtain drugs.[15] These ancillary crimes disproportionately impact poor people and people of color, and drive significant criminal legal system involvement. In fact, more than one in five people (21 percent) sentenced to state prison or jail are behind bars for committing crimes aimed at obtaining drugs or money for drugs.[16] This figure includes nearly 40 percent of those who are incarcerated as a result of a property crime conviction as well as 14 percent of those who are serving time for a violent crime. Thus, in addition to the roughly 400,000 people who are incarcerated as a result of a drug law violation, nearly a half a million more are behind bars for engaging in illegal conduct that was intended to enable the acquisition of illicit drugs.

In short, while drug policy reform advocates are right to emphasize the harm that criminal legal system involvement causes to people who use drugs, unmanaged chemical dependency and unregulated illicit drug markets also generate significant suffering. Ideally, an improved drug policy response would reduce the harm caused by criminal legal system involvement *and* the suffering that stems from unmanaged addiction *and* the harm that flows from illicit and unregulated drug markets. The kinds of reforms that most states have enacted in recent years, such as measures that reduce the penalties imposed on people convicted of drug possession, do next to nothing to address these latter harms. In fact, drug courts actually appear to *increase* drug arrests and incarceration in the aggregate, as was discussed in chapter 4.

Drug legalization and regulation, accompanied by a massive increase in investments in affordable housing and all forms of drug treatment (as well as behavioral health treatment) are likely the most efficacious way to reduce drug-related harm. Unlike drug courts and even decriminalization, legalization would enable regulation of the drug market and, therefore, greater control over the potency and contents of consumed drugs. Contrary to popular mythology, legalization need not result in the commercial sales of drugs such as heroin and methamphetamine at the neighborhood store. Rather, under some versions of a legalization scheme, distribution would be managed by health professionals who prescribe and supply pharmaceutical versions of, or substitutes for, popular street drugs to people for whom other forms of treatment have been unsuccessful. This approach would notably reduce crime; it would also address the problem of unregulated drugs and shrink the illegal market for drugs.[17]

While this approach to legalization—paired with significant social investments—has significant promise, political realities mean that this option is unlikely to occur across the United States in the near future.[18] In theory, statutory decriminalization, which entails the legislative reduction or removal of criminal sanctions for possession of small amounts of illicit drugs, could be a way of moving toward legalization while also reducing the harm caused by the criminal legal system. Examples from the European context are encouraging. In Portugal, for example, the decriminalization of recreational drug use has been accompanied by reductions in substance abuse, in drug-related health problems, and in the arrest and incarceration of drug users.[19] Portugal has been able to achieve some of these outcomes because it also made significant efforts to address the underlying social and economic conditions that fuel harmful forms of substance use and to employ harm reduction techniques in a variety of settings.[20]

By contrast, in the United States, most decriminalization measures merely reduce drug possession from a felony to a misdemeanor or substitute civil penalties for criminal ones. For example, Oklahoma's House Bill 1269, enacted in 2019, made user-amount possession of any drug a misdemeanor (rather than a felony).[21] While reclassifying drug possession as a misdemeanor does alleviate the particular burden caused by *felony* conviction, misdemeanor convictions and associated short-term jail stays also cause significant harm.[22] Other decriminalization bills have replaced criminal penalties with fines, a civil sanction. Such measures are also of limited utility, mainly because the imposition of fines—which are not typically assessed in a way that reflects people's ability to pay—often leads to the accumulation of legal debt owed by poor people.[23] This debt, in turn, has a host of negative consequences and fuels subsequent criminal legal system involvement.[24]

In short, in recent instances of decriminalization in the United States, drug possession remains subject to either criminal penalties or civil sanctions that often lead to some form of criminal legal system involvement. Policies that treat drug possession as a misdemeanor crime or civil violation also continue to treat drug use as "policeable" behavior. Sociologists Daniel Gascón and Aaron Roussell coined the term "policeability" to refer to the organizational, interactional, and historical processes by which certain people, behavior, and issues come to be understood as appropriately and effectively resolved by police involvement.[25] Treating drug possession as a misdemeanor crime or civil violation subject to a fine does not disrupt the policeability of drug use. Currently, drug possession is the most frequently arrested offense in the United States, occurring once every twenty-five seconds.[26] The police continue to be tasked with drug law enforcement even if violations constitute misdemeanors or civil violations. Moreover, the negative outcomes that often accompany police encounters are particularly acute for individuals wrestling with behavioral health issues.[27]

In November, Oregon voters passed a decriminalization bill that appears, at first glance, to avoid generating legal financial obligations that, if unpaid, could trigger police stops and short-term jail stays. This new law specifies that people who are found to be in possession of small amounts of a controlled substance are required to either pay a $100 fine *or* to complete a health assessment.[28] The latter option is intended to enable arrested parties to avoid the debt-jail cycle and future police stops, and is a step in the right direction. However, there is reason to believe that vulnerable and marginalized people who use drugs (especially those who lack access to housing and transportation) may not have the wherewithal to complete the health assessment. Because it is likely that people experiencing homelessness and behavioral health challenges comprise a significant share of those arrested for drug possession, it seems that even the Oregon decriminalization measure may not reduce the extent to which the most vulnerable drug users are arrested and fined and therefore cycle in and out of jail.

Statutory decriminalization alone also leaves drug markets unregulated, and fails to address the fact that some people who are contending with unmanaged addiction will resort to committing property and other crimes to generate monies that can be used to purchase drugs. It may also worsen racial inequities by shifting the enforcement focus to drug delivery arrests, which are characterized by even higher levels of racial disparity and are far more likely than drug possession to trigger a prison sentence.

Ironically, responses to substance abuse that entail *de facto* decriminalization (as opposed to formal, statutory decriminalization) and remove *all* sanctions for drug possession may offer some advantages over formal legal changes that reduce (but do not eliminate) penalties for drug possession, particularly when combined with housing, behavioral health treatment, and improved access to medication-assisted treatment (MAT). This chapter identifies several programmatic and policy shifts that could facilitate the *complete* removal of sanctions for the most vulnerable drug users and can be combined with housing and other forms of support. In particular, I argue that a significant expansion of harm-reduction-oriented response models would entail de facto legalization for the most vulnerable. The benefits of this approach could be greatly enhanced if we also dramatically expand access to MAT and affordable housing, including Housing First facilities.

If brought to scale, these programmatic and policy changes would greatly reduce drug-related suffering, the harm associated with the illicit drug market, and the misery caused by the involvement of the criminal legal system in the lives of people who use illicit substances. They may also help pave the way for legalization and regulation of the drug market in the longer term. However, in making the case for these alternative approaches, I argue that they can, and should, be adopted in the near term. I also consider critiques of these approaches from both the left and the right, and explain why I continue to believe that these measures can bring about transformative change and meaningfully reduce human suffering.

Toward—and beyond—Harm Reduction Drug Policing

People who contend with behavioral health issues—including mental illness and/or substance abuse—frequently cycle in and out of the criminal legal system, especially courts, jails, and probation offices, as a result of drug law violations and other comparatively minor charges. This is especially true for people who live unsheltered. This pattern stems, in part, from the fact that behavioral manifestations of extreme poverty, unmanaged mental illness, and drug use trigger many calls for police assistance, particularly when those behaviors occur outdoors. A recent study in Portland, Oregon, for example, found that half of all 911 callers requested police assistance in addressing situations involving people who are perceived to be homeless and disorderly.[29] (Sociologist Chris Herring's research in San Francisco suggests that recent upticks in many cities for such calls for service are linked to gentrification.)[30] Given that there are an estimated 240 million calls to 911 for emergency assistance in the United States each year,[31] these findings suggest that civilian requests for assistance play an important role in fueling the arrest and incarceration of many people who live unsheltered and struggle with behavioral health challenges, including substance use disorders.

As a result of these dynamics, people who live in extreme poverty and have unmet behavioral health needs comprise a large share of those who cycle in and out of jails. A recent study in King County, Washington, found that 58.6 percent of the "familiar faces" who were booked into jail four or more times in the previous year were living unsheltered; 94 percent had been diagnosed with either a chemical dependency issue or a mental health issue (often both).[32] Nationally, more than 60 percent of people in jail have histories of mental illness and/or substance use.[33] Of course, jail often makes matters worse by disrupting benefits, medication, employment, and housing, families, and by creating the mark of a criminal conviction and exposing people to additional trauma. Even short jail stays decrease employment and tax-related government benefits,[34] increase homelessness,[35] and exacerbate racial inequities.[36] The effects of jail are even more detrimental for people with mental illness and/or substance abuse issues, who, if jailed, are often taken off Medicaid, receive inadequate care, and are more likely to be sanctioned for rule infractions, among other harms.[37]

If the damage associated with arrest and jail is to be avoided, advocates must figure out how to address the public demand for a response to people who live outdoors and contend with behavioral health issues in a way that ameliorates rather than compounds harm. In what follows, I argue that community-based, long-term, harm-reduction-oriented responses to people contending with extreme poverty and unmet behavioral health issues can serve as alternatives to law enforcement and/or displacement (sweeps), and represent a viable and transformative way to do so. Such initiatives can notably reduce system involvement and other harms even in the absence of formal, statutory decriminalization or legalization, in part because they create spaces in which drug possession is no longer treated as a crime. If accompanied by other progressive policy shifts and prosocial investments, the positive impact of these harm reduction initiatives would be greater still.

To support and illustrate this argument, I trace the history and evolution of this kind of approach as practiced in Seattle, Washington. LEAD, which originally stood for Law Enforcement Assisted Diversion, was one of the nation's first prebooking diversion initiatives and was launched in 2011. From its inception, LEAD sought to reduce individual and community-level harms associated with unmanaged drug use and sales and sex markets—and conventional criminal legal responses to these issues—by diverting people who would otherwise be arrested on low-level drug (or other) charges into intensive, community-based, case management guided by harm reduction principles. LEAD as Law Enforcement Assisted Diversion, sometimes called LEAD 1.0, is now in place or in development in roughly one hundred jurisdictions around the country.[38]

In recent years, however, LEAD in Seattle has evolved considerably. Police no longer serve as gatekeepers to services, and LEAD 2.0, which stands for Let Everyone Advance with Dignity, is now part of a collaborative initiative called JustCARE that uses hotels and motels to provide interim supportive housing and support to people who live unsheltered during the pandemic. In what follows, I describe LEAD's evolution and its current involvement in JustCARE. To do so, I draw on the research I conducted as part of a process evaluation of LEAD 1.0 in 2013–15[39] as well as more recent research on LEAD 2.0 and JustCARE.[40]

LEAD 1.0: Law Enforcement–Assisted Diversion

The adoption of LEAD in 2011 marked a dramatic shift in Seattle's approach to drug markets and associated problems. Like many urban police departments, the Seattle Police Department (SPD) was actively engaged in the drug war through the late 2000s. In fact, the city's drug arrest rate was comparatively high,[41] and levels of racial disproportionality in drug law enforcement outcomes were extraordinarily pronounced, even by U.S. standards. In 2006, for example, the drug possession arrest rate for Black people in Seattle was 13.6 times higher than for White people; for drug delivery arrests, it was 21 times higher.[42] (Full disclosure: I was part of a research team that documented and sought to explain these remarkably high levels of racial disparity.)[43]

In response to the severity and persistence of racial disparity in Seattle's drug arrests, attorneys with the Racial Disparity Project mounted a selective enforcement challenge on behalf of a consolidated group of nineteen criminal defendants in 2003. All of the defendants involved in this "criminal class action" case were Black and/or Latino, and all had been arrested for delivering drugs in the downtown area. As a group, the defendants were alleged to have delivered an amount of crack cocaine weighing the equivalent of six plain M&Ms. Collectively, they faced the prospect of well over one hundred years in prison.

Perhaps unsurprisingly, the litigation that ensued proved to be lengthy, complex, and time-consuming. At the same time, the persistence of visible drug activity continued to generate significant community pressure on authorities to "do something" about drugs. By the late 2000s, all of the main actors were dissatisfied with the status quo, including the SPD itself. Eventually, litigation fatigue and the persistence of significant public concern about Seattle's still-active drug markets inspired the SPD, the King County Prosecutor, the ACLU, the Racial Disparity Project, and other organizations to work together to identify an alternative approach that avoided reliance upon jail and prison— but also took seriously the harm associated with untreated addiction and drug market activity.

The result, eventually, was the development of LEAD. The original version of LEAD was often described as a prebooking diversion framework in which police officers could refer people with extensive criminal legal involvement to long-term care and services. The harm reduction philosophy was (and remains) central to LEAD, and holds that some people will always engage in behaviors, such as drug use, that may cause harm to individuals and those around them.[44] From a harm reduction point of view, the active intervention of the criminal legal system is often counterproductive and harmful. Harm reduction practitioners also emphasize that the path toward abstinence is often long, and sometimes is nonexistent, even when people strive to achieve sobriety. Nonetheless, meaningful reductions in human suffering can be achieved, even in the absence of abstinence. For this reason, the LEAD model does not require abstinence as either a precondition or a goal.

Early in the process, Seattle LEAD stakeholders expanded the potential participant pool from people who had been arrested (or were arrestable) on low-level drug charges to include people who engaged in sex work in order to ensure significant participation by women who suffer from addiction and/ or extreme poverty. Stakeholders subsequently expanded the list of divertible offenses to include misdemeanor theft, misdemeanor property destruction, criminal trespass, unlawful bus conduct, and obstruction of a police officer.[45] Other jurisdictions have identified yet more "LEAD-eligible" offenses.[46]

Initially, people were referred to LEAD through "arrest referrals" in which LEAD-trained police officers and sergeants divert people against whom the officer has probable cause for arrest on a LEAD-eligible charge. In such cases, officers offer diversion as an alternative to a jail booking (hence the description of LEAD 1.0 as a "prebooking diversion" framework). If the individual accepts the offer, the officer contacts a LEAD case manager to whom the officer relinquishes physical custody, and the case manager begins to work with the referred individual.

Over time, many LEAD sites created a "social contract" referral process that makes it possible for officers or others to refer to LEAD a person who is struggling with unmanaged addiction and/or extreme poverty, without requiring a precipitating arrest or probable cause for arrest. When a social contact referral occurs in LEAD 1.0, police run a background check to confirm that the referred person *has* been system-involved. The rationale for this is surprising: whereas drug courts and other postbooking diversion programs often deem people with extensive criminal histories or unmanaged drug use to be *ineligible* for diversion, LEAD 1.0 treats both drug use and ongoing criminal legal involvement as indications that LEAD referral *is* warranted. (There are no per se criminal background exclusions for people referred through the social contact referral process.)

Upon referral to LEAD, case managers conduct an intake assessment and work with the participant to identify the participant's most pressing needs and priorities. In the following days and weeks, case managers work closely with participants to create a plan for addressing their needs. Case managers use motivational interviewing to assist participants in identifying their own goals and support them as they work to meet those goals. These plans may include assistance in obtaining housing, public benefits, health insurance and healthcare, behavioral health treatment, education, job training, job placement, licensing assistance, transportation, small business counseling, child care, or other services.

Several core operating principles guide LEAD's provision of social services. First, consistent with the harm reduction philosophy, LEAD case managers focus on individual and community wellness; that is, they seek to reduce harm related to unmanaged behavioral illness—harms that participants cause to themselves and to others—as well as the harms that are caused by the war on drugs and the marginalization and criminalization of drug use, mental illness, and poverty. Recognizing that not all LEAD participants will pursue sobriety, and that setbacks are common even for those who do, harm reduction case managers emphasize that meaningful improvements can be fostered and achieved in the absence of abstinence.[47] The theory is that by engaging and developing meaningful relationships with people participating in LEAD, helping them to identify and articulate their own goals, and providing emotional, practical, and financial support as they work toward those goals, harm reduction case management increases LEAD participants' ability to stabilize their lives, address their physical and mental health issues, reduce the harmful use of drugs, and cause less harm to themselves and to others than they would absent LEAD's intervention.

Case managers hired by LEAD are accustomed to working in an intensive and hands-on manner with participants. In this street-based approach, case managers do not supply their clients with a to-do list, but rather spend most of their time outside of the office, actively seeking out and meeting with participants in the field—under bridges, in homeless encampments, in parks—continuing their intensive case management when people are housed, helping people complete paperwork, accompanying (and often transporting) them to appointments, helping them to apply for services and housing, and engaging in myriad other forms of support aimed at helping their clients achieve their stated goals.[48] In one recent (pre-pandemic) case, for example, a LEAD caseworker accompanied a participant to medical appointments, located and paid for a motel room, delivered snacks and toiletries, and drove the participant to visit her grandmother on the other side of the state—long before the woman expressed any interest in getting clean.[49]

LEAD participants' eligibility for services and benefits are not time-delimited, and the LEAD protocol does not authorize any sanctions for "noncompliance."[50] In other words, once enrolled in LEAD, participants remain enrolled for as long as they choose. Further, they cannot be prosecuted for the "referral arrest" (if there was one). Although prosecutors retain authority to file charges for prior or subsequent alleged crimes, the LEAD model requires that they work in cooperation with LEAD, which means *not* bringing charges against LEAD participants for subsequent arrests if, in their professional judgment, prosecution would undermine the participants' progress.

Early on, some stakeholders expressed concern that police officers might be more inclined to refer White people than people of color to LEAD, an entirely understandable concern given the history of racial inequities in drug law enforcement in Seattle and elsewhere. For this reason, LEAD sites are encouraged to monitor LEAD referrals to ensure that people of color and other groups that often experience bias (such as people living unsheltered) are afforded the opportunity to participate in LEAD and to identify any obstacles that may prevent this from occurring. Data regarding the racial and ethnic composition and housing status of LEAD participants in Seattle and elsewhere have been periodically collected and monitored. The most recent data show that although 64 percent of the Seattle city population is White, the majority (56.1 percent) of LEAD participants are people of color. Similarly, in San Francisco and Los Angeles, 50 to 75 percent of those participating in LEAD are people of color.[51] In all three sites, roughly 80 percent of participants are homeless. However, in some locales, the police do appear to have been more likely to refer White people to LEAD, suggesting the need to either create mechanisms that counteract this pattern or terminate the role of the police as gatekeepers to the program. As will be discussed shortly, LEAD Seattle has elected to do the latter.

The Benefits of LEAD 1.0

Outcome evaluations suggest that LEAD 1.0 was quite effective in reducing the harm associated with substance abuse and associated criminal legal system involvement. Researchers compared the system utilization of approximately 200 LEAD clients with 115 others with similar criminal records who, by virtue of the time or place of their arrest, did not participate in LEAD. The results reveal statistically significant reductions for the LEAD group in average yearly criminal legal system utilization costs compared to the control group.[52] For example, LEAD participants spent thirty-nine fewer days in jail than similarly situated people who did not enter LEAD. Similarly, the odds that a LEAD participant was sentenced to prison in the first year after enrollment in LEAD were 87 percent lower than for people who were not referred to LEAD. As a result of these reductions in criminal legal system contact and incarceration, system costs associated with LEAD participants decreased by roughly 30 percent relative to the year prior to enrollment in LEAD, while those costs for non-LEAD participants more than doubled. In San Francisco, felony and misdemeanor arrests were two and a half and six times higher, respectively, among the non-LEAD comparison group than among LEAD participants after twelve months. This difference translates to cost savings of $3,651 per person in LEAD.[53]

Researchers report that LEAD 1.0 has had a number of other positive effects as well. In particular, LEAD participants report dramatic improvements in their health and well-being.[54] For example, participants were twice as likely to be sheltered and were 89 percent more likely to have obtained permanent housing, after their referral to LEAD. Participants were also 33 percent more likely to receive legal income and/or benefits subsequent to their LEAD involvement.

Challenges Associated with LEAD 1.0

Although LEAD 1.0 produced many benefits, the paucity of needed services and resources for LEAD participants poses a significant challenge to the viability of the model. In particular, case managers often struggle to find housing for LEAD participants, mainly because affordable housing is quite limited, especially for unemployed people who use drugs and/or have extensive criminal records. Access to other needed services, including mental health and chemical dependency treatment, is also constrained. These limitations do not exist only in Seattle, of course. And they not only impair case managers' capacity to assist LEAD participants but also create certain practical and moral quandaries with which LEAD stakeholders continue to wrestle. LEAD participants do rely on and consume public services, and LEAD stakeholders in Seattle have thus far been unable to notably expand the pool of those services.

Another constraint stems from the reliance of LEAD 1.0 on the police to refer people to LEAD and "clear" those who were referred by others. In Seattle, both of these eventually became problems. Early on, the SPD notably reduced the number of people it referred to LEAD via the arrest referral process. As a result, an increasing share of participants were referred to LEAD through the social contact referral process, as is shown in Figure 7.1.

In 2020, the SPD began to slow the speed with which it "cleared" people referred to LEAD via the social contact referral process. This development underscored the risk associated with relying on police to serve as gatekeepers to services. In the context of the pandemic, and the widespread need it created, frustration regarding the SPD's failure to clear many people referred to LEAD through the social contact process grew. At the same time, stakeholders were increasingly aware of the need to reduce

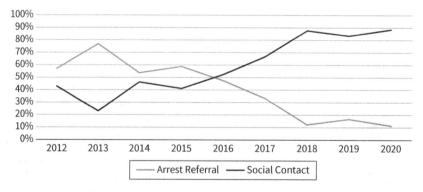

Figure 7.1 Seattle LEAD enrollments by referral type, 2012–2020
Source: Data provided by the Public Defender Association.

police contact with members of the public, especially people of color and people contending with behavioral health challenges. In this context, LEAD stakeholders removed the requirement that people who are referred to LEAD be "cleared" by the police.[55] In other words, the police no longer serve as gatekeepers to LEAD in Seattle.

Developments in the spring and summer of 2020 also fueled the birth of a new, collaborative, harm reduction framework for providing interim housing for people contending with substance abuse, homelessness, and behavioral health issues. In what follows, I describe this new framework, in which LEAD plays a crucial role.

Beyond Harm Reduction Policing: LEAD 2.0 and JustCARE

The rapid spread of COVID-19 in the spring of 2020 posed unprecedented challenges for LEAD, for a number of reasons. First, the pandemic profoundly affected the criminal legal system. In Seattle and elsewhere, police had less contact with members of the public, and arrest referrals (which had been dropping for some time) essentially ceased. Meanwhile, courts nearly closed for an extended period of time and many local jails implemented booking guidelines that excluded people arrested on drug and other low-level charges. The effort to release people from jail was stymied, though, as prosecutors and courts cited the lack of viable stabilization plans for people with complex behavioral health challenges.

Stakeholders adapted the LEAD model rapidly to respond to COVID-19's emergency conditions. The initial adaptation, called Co-LEAD (for COVID, Community, and Co-Responder), began operations in the spring of 2020 and differs from LEAD 1.0 in several important ways. First, some participants entered Co-LEAD directly from jail, as authorities sought to depopulate those facilities to reduce the spread of COVID-19 during the height of the pandemic. Second, Co-LEAD secured interim housing in hotels and motels, and uses an around-the-clock staffing model to ensure that support staff are always available to Co-LEAD participants. Third, Co-LEAD staff include naturopathic and medical doctors who work alongside case managers to assess participants' healthcare needs, test for COVID-19, and provide medical care, including prescription and pharmacy coordination. In this context, access to Suboxone and other forms of MAT was notably enhanced. And finally, Co-LEAD and other hotel providers now utilize the services of a community-based safety team whose members use de-escalation and other strategies to maintain public safety in and around the hotels and to decrease the number of 911 calls for service that occur from those locales.

While Co-LEAD was designed as an emergency response to the pandemic, its success has underscored the importance of housing to any successful effort to reduce the harm associated with substance abuse. It has also suggested the viability of a revised version of the LEAD model that does not depend on police to serve as gatekeepers, the value of a 24/7 staffing model and of interim supportive housing, and the benefits of directly employing medical staff to ensure greater access to healthcare MAT. Its reliance on community-based public safety teams also signals its commitment to minimizing police interactions with participants wherever possible.

As the pandemic continued to unfold, LEAD and Co-LEAD joined forces with a number of other community partners (including other service providers such as the Chief Seattle Club and the Asian Counseling and Referral Services) to provide an even more robust and comprehensive care response called JustCARE. This collective impact model is a community-based response to unauthorized encampments that generate many repeated calls for service. JustCARE is also an alternative to sweeps or traditional enforcement practices. Each participating organization brings a specific skill set and area of expertise to the effort: LEAD personnel conducted preliminary needs assessments in encampments and continue to provide street-based outreach for people who live unsheltered; Co-LEAD shares training and expertise regarding delivery of harm reduction case management in hotel settings; Asian Counseling and Referral Services has particular expertise regarding the provision of care for people with high-acuity mental health needs; and Chief Seattle Club provides culturally appropriate care for indigenous participants.[56]

These and other stakeholders conceive of JustCARE as an opportunity to demonstrate that a care-based, Housing First response to people struggling with poverty and behavioral health issues, and who have a large impact on neighborhoods, can succeed where sweeps and enforcement did not. JustCARE thus is characterized by (1) the end of the police gatekeeping role and a reliance instead on community referrals; (2) intensified and expanded service provision; and (3) wherever possible, the implementation of a Housing First approach. LEAD continues to play a vital role in this collaboration.

LEAD and Its Critics

While the outcome evaluations of LEAD are quite positive, the model (and the harm reduction approach to care that it embodies) nonetheless remains controversial in some circles. From the perspective of drug court advocates, harm reduction initiatives like LEAD seem far too radical. Drug courts rest on the premise that both carrots and sticks are required to compel people with chemical dependency issues to avail themselves of treatment and to succeed in it. As one state supreme court justice recently argued, "Drug courts are effective only when they combine the 'carrot' of treatment and support with the 'stick' of judicial accountability, including incarceration when needed. It is this carrot-and-stick approach that enables judges and drug court teams to use a variety of tools to help people overcome addiction."[57] From this perspective, the capacity of judges and treatment providers to threaten and inflict pain (through the use of "sticks" such as jail time) is necessary to incentivize people to pursue the correct course of action, which, it is assumed, is (abstinence-oriented) treatment.[58] At the same time, the medical model treats addiction (mainly) as a brain disorder that can be "cured" through treatment. Implicit in this approach is the idea that system involvement can end only when people are "cured" of their chemical dependency issues and achieve sobriety.[59] These ideas merge in the theory and practice of drug courts.

By contrast, LEAD and JustCARE operate on the theory that chemical dependency has many complex causes and is often rooted in trauma as well as extreme poverty. Healing occurs when traumatized and marginalized people form trusting, dependable, long-term relationships with people who help them clarify their own goals and support them in their efforts to pursue them. From this perspective, "sticks," threats, and sanctions reinforce the isolation, stigma, and hardship with which many drug users already contend and are therefore unhelpful. In fact, it is only by helping people to feel less alone and more supported that meaningful, long-term change is likely to occur. Moreover, from the harm reduction perspective, sobriety is not the only valid goal, and problematic behavior and involvement in the criminal legal system can be reduced without mandating sobriety.

As Table 7.1 shows, harm reduction initiatives and drug courts differ in a number of other important ways as well. While LEAD 1.0 sometimes involves arrest as the portal to diversion, participants referred in that manner were not booked into jail, unlike drug court participants. Moreover, participation in any version of LEAD or in JustCARE does not hinge on being charged or a guilty plea; in fact, charges stemming from the referral arrest are not filed.[60] Further, LEAD and JustCARE intentionally seek to include the most marginalized people: those with the longest rap sheets, the unhoused, and the extremely poor. By contrast, studies suggest that many drug courts "cherry-pick"

Table 7.1 Comparison of Prebooking Diversion (LEAD) and Drug Court

	LEAD 1.0	LEAD 2.0/ Co-LEAD/ JustCARE	Drug Courts
Participation depends on arrest	Sometimes	No	Yes
Participants are booked into jail on drug charge	No	No	Yes
Participation depends on pleading guilty	No	No	Yes
Incarceration as sanction for noncompliance/drug use	No	No	Yes
Evidence of reduced system involvement among participants	Yes	Not yet assessed	No
Systematic effort to include the most marginalized	Yes	Yes	No
Likely exacerbates racial inequity in drug case outcomes	No	No	Yes

less disadvantaged participants in order to achieve evidence of "success," as was discussed in chapter 4.[61]

In short, while drug court advocates maintain that the use of "sticks" by therapeutic courts is essential, the available evidence suggests that harm reduction frameworks such as LEAD notably reduce criminal legal system involvement and drug-related harm among the most marginalized groups *without* the threat of incarceration or any other sanction for noncompliance or nonabstinence. Elsewhere, sociologists Monica Bell and Forrest Stuart and I argue that harm reduction frameworks such as LEAD and JustCARE offer another important advantage as well: whereas drug courts violate important dignitarian principles, harm reduction practitioners' emphasis on accepting people "where they are at" results in more dignity and agency-enhancing interactions.

For example, as was discussed in chapter 4, drug courts assume that the root of all participants' trouble is addiction; they also assume that the answer to this problem is abstinence-oriented treatment. By contrast, LEAD and JustCARE enable participants to identify their own needs and priorities, and avoid creating any sense that drug use is either abnormal or inherently problematic. For example, the use of motivational interviewing during the intake process is intended to destigmatize drug use and allow participants to identify their own goals. Through this process, participants are also invited to consider what is and is not working in their lives and to make a plan for moving forward in a way that respects their assessment of their goals. One supervisor and former case manager explained:

> LEAD uses motivational interviewing because it's one of the best methods to really be able to tap into someone's intrinsic values and goals. And it allows them, the participants, to really define their own pathway for where they want to go and how they want to get there. So it's one of the best interventions for really tapping into . . . "What do I really want? And how do I want to achieve this?" . . . The way that motivational interviewing really aligns with drug use is it allows people to ask themselves the question . . . "What are the positives to my drug use? What are the negatives to my drug use?" And [it] really allows people to sit with the ambivalence and the reality that people use drugs for almost contrary reasons. And so there's two realities and two truths that a lot of our LEAD clients are grappling with: it's that drugs can have a negative impact on their life and their drug use is also having a positive impact, you know, it's bringing something, it's filling a need that they are trying to fulfill. And allowing people to kind of sit with both of those truths helps, almost like shin[ing] a light on to "Okay, well then . . . what are my options here? How, what are my needs? And how, what are some other alternatives if I want any to be able to fulfill those needs?"

In practice, this means that LEAD and JustCARE participants are under no pressure to participate in drug treatment. Another former case manager–turned-supervisor explained:

> When an individual gets referred into LEAD, you don't have to do treatment. All you have to do is complete a biopsychosocial intake. That's it. . . . Most folks, after they completed the biopsychosocial intake, they still engage with their case manager, and when you engage with your case manager, and you create a service plan, it is self-identified. I would tell people, "You're the driver, what do you want to do?"

Thus, whereas drug courts routinely deny participants the right to narrative autonomy, common LEAD practices afford participants the capacity to identify their own needs and priorities.

Drug courts also rely extensively on drug testing and discuss the results of these tests—and their purported meaning—in open court. By contrast, LEAD and JustCARE do not conduct drug testing, and participants choose for themselves whether, when, and how much to share about their drug use with their case manager or outreach responder. Moreover, conversations between case managers and participants take place in private spaces.[62] In these ways, LEAD and JustCARE case managers take care not to violate the bodily and psychic integrity of the people they serve.

Finally, drug court participants are frequently reminded that the courts have the authority to incarcerate them for their "failure" to comply with the requirements associated with court-mandated treatment. By contrast, LEAD operates on the theory that harmful drug use has many causes and is often rooted in trauma and other social determinants of health, such as extreme poverty, homelessness, discrimination, isolation, and shame. From this perspective, "sticks," threats, and sanctions—especially incarceration—reinforce the isolation, stigma, and hardship with which addicts already contend and are therefore entirely unhelpful. One supervisor and former case manager put it this way:

> Punishment is a, can be for some people, and at certain points in time, a short-term, you know, can cause short-term behavior change. But it does not instill long-term behavior change. It doesn't change someone's values, it doesn't change their goals. And then a lot of times it just creates more stigma and really impedes someone's ability to stabilize within their life. So what I am really committed to and what is, I think, really alluring about LEAD is the ability to, you know, find an intervention that is committed to behavior change in a way where you're taking their full human scope into account.

In short, while drug court advocates maintain that the threat of sanctions, including incarceration, are absolutely necessary, LEAD, JustCARE, and other harm reduction initiatives illustrate that this is not the case. Many positive outcomes can be achieved without the use of sanctions—and the degradation and humiliation that tend to accompany them.

LEAD is also controversial among some people on the political left, particularly police and prison abolitionists. Here, the main concern is that LEAD (as originally designed) requires cooperation with police and thus remains "firmly within the contours of the contemporary carceral state."[63] It is true that LEAD 1.0 necessitates cooperation with the police and criminal legal system officials, and that it seeks to transform rather than abolish policing altogether.[64] It is also true that referral to LEAD 1.0 (but not LEAD 2.0) is sometimes precipitated by arrest and that the police serve as gatekeepers to services in some LEAD initiatives. LEAD 1.0's reliance on arrest referral was intended to give police an alternative way to respond to people involved in unlawful behavior, one that reduces rather than compounds harm. That is, LEAD 1.0 uses the moment of (potential) arrest—which sometimes occurs as a result of civilian calls for service—to funnel people who would otherwise be booked into jail *away* from the criminal legal system. As was discussed earlier, this approach has been shown to reduce jail stays and prison admissions, thus reducing the size and scope of the carceral state.[65] On the other hand, as critics point out, LEAD 1.0 does involve the police, and the reliance on arrest referral did not reduce "policeability." As noted earlier, the newer version of LEAD in Seattle—sometimes referred to as LEAD 2.0—does not rely on arrest referral or employ police as gatekeepers.

The concern that LEAD does not sufficiently challenge the power and reach of the carceral state appears to underlie a number of associated claims, but many of these rest on a misunderstanding of the LEAD model. For example, the assertion that LEAD functions to expand police surveillance[66] appears to be unsubstantiated, as police officers (if they are involved at all) relinquish custody and control upon a participant's referral to LEAD 1.0. Moreover, police do not play an active role in LEAD 2.0. And while it is true that prosecutors retain the legal authority to file charges related to the arrest that precipitates referral, prosecutors working with LEAD are subject to a Memorandum of Understanding in which they explicitly agree not do so. In this way, LEAD reduces criminal prosecutions. Finally, concern about the fact that people in LEAD lack due process protections[67] makes little sense given that LEAD participants have not been booked into jail or charged with a crime, that LEAD imposes no sanctions for noncompliance or failure to achieve sobriety, and that participation in LEAD is not conducted under court supervision.

Evidence regarding the claim that LEAD reentrenches race and class inequality[68] is also thin. The available data indicate that the majority of LEAD participants in Seattle, San Francisco, and elsewhere are people of color living unsheltered who have cycled in and out of jail (and sometimes prison) and struggled with poverty and a host of behavioral health issues, often for much of their lives.[69] Still, it is true that police have a great deal of discretion in deciding who will be referred to LEAD 1.0, and this discretion can be exercised in ways that privilege White, housed, and middle-class people. The shift toward community referral in LEAD 2.0 and in JustCARE is intended to reduce police contact with vulnerable members of the public and ensure racial equity. For example, JustCARE has focused on neighborhoods in which people of color predominate among those living unsheltered. During JustCARE's first wave of operations, nearly three-fourths—73.5 percent—of the people offered housing and support from a JustCARE provider were people of color.

Lessons Learned

Inspired by Seattle's example, roughly one hundred jurisdictions have since established or are in the process of establishing LEAD 1.0, LEAD 2.0, or something in between.[70] The first years of LEAD's operations provide compelling evidence that collective impact and harm-reduction-oriented diversion initiatives that provide a long-term care response, do not rely on sanctions, and steer system-involved people away from the criminal legal system are, in fact, achievable and valuable. The advent of JustCARE and the move away from arrest referral and toward community referral in LEAD 2.0 suggest that these and related harm reduction initiatives may be able to avoid the problems associated with relying on police as gatekeepers in the future. As research on the human costs of extreme poverty and mass incarceration makes abundantly clear, cities, towns, and tribal communities across the United States desperately need such alternatives. Through the development and implementation of frameworks that use harm reduction principles to guide the delivery of care and services—and, in the process, achieve de facto legalization for the most vulnerable and system-impacted—municipalities may be able to transform the response to low-level crime and disorder that engenders many calls to 911 to one that notably reduces both individual and community suffering.

At the same time, it is clear that harm reduction frameworks such as LEAD and JustCARE alone cannot solve all problems. These kinds of interventions offer a way to reduce criminal legal system involvement and to connect people to long-term care and social services and housing, where they exist. But they do not transform the kinds of treatment options that are available, create housing options where they do not otherwise exist, or reduce the dangers associated with unregulated drug markets. Additional policy changes are needed to address these issues. In fact, the transformative impact of harm reduction initiatives like JustCARE would be enhanced if they were situated in a context in which other antipoverty and public and behavioral health investments, including affordable housing, were also in place. In the next section, I identify some of the most important initiatives needed to radically reduce the harm associated with unmanaged addiction and other behavioral health issues, homelessness, and extreme poverty.

Expand Access to Medication-Assisted Treatment

As noted previously, over 7 million Americans struggle with a substance use disorder involving one or more illicit drugs; only about one in five of these people receives any form of treatment in a given year.[71] The first and most obvious way to address the problem of chemical dependency is to radically expand treatment options and accessibility in the community and to ensure access to culturally appropriate treatment. This would benefit not only those who struggle with addiction but society as a whole: every dollar spent on treatment saves three dollars in crime reduction.[72]

Although some people do not receive treatment in the community because they do not want or are not ready for it, about one-third do not receive it because they lack health insurance and/or cannot afford it.[73] Compared to higher-income people, people whose incomes fall under 200 percent of the poverty line are 47 percent more likely to experience substance abuse disorder and about 33 percent more likely to lack insurance coverage.[74] Poverty thus increases the risk of both addiction and lack of access to treatment. These barriers disproportionately impact people of color. While the Affordable Care Act expanded access to health insurance and therefore to substance abuse treatment, many people remain underinsured. In fact, the Affordable Care Act is estimated to have raised the treatment rate among low-income people who would benefit from it from 8.8 to just 9.7 percent.[75] The roughly 2.1 million people who are currently living in prison or jail also have startlingly limited access to treatment, despite unusually high levels of substance dependence among prison and jail populations.[76] Clearly, economic, geographic, and other barriers to treatment must be addressed.

It is also important to recognize that some kinds of treatment are more effective than others. While most experts believe that offering various types of treatment is optimal, it is clear that MAT is the most efficacious approach for people with long-term substance use disorder who have not benefited from other approaches.[77] Yet access to MAT remains highly constrained; even people with health insurance often struggle to obtain it. For example, Medicare covers MAT using either methadone or buprenorphine (Naloxone) when medically necessary and pending pre-authorization. However, according to the American Medical Association, the requirement that patients receive pre-authorization represents a significant barrier to treatment.[78] Recent research further indicates that fewer than 1 percent of imprisoned people who meet the diagnostic criteria for a substance abuse disorder receive MAT in custody.[79]

Experts thus agree that access to MAT should be expanded.[80] Methadone and buprenorphine are effective first-line treatments for some people who use opiates, but a variety of other medications show greater promise, particularly for those for whom other forms of treatment are ineffective. These "second-line" medications include Dilaudid (hydromorphone) and heroin (diamorphine) itself. While heroin-assisted treatment may seem radical, there is compelling evidence that it is a highly effective form of treatment when combined with counseling and other services for people with long-term heroin dependency issues. For example, a recent meta-analysis of research on heroin-assisted treatment (HAT) reports, "Evidence from randomized controlled trials of HAT in Canada and Europe indicates that supervised injectable HAT—with optional oral methadone—can offer benefits over oral methadone alone for treating [opiate use disorder] among individuals who have tried traditional treatment modalities, including methadone, multiple times but are still injecting heroin."[81] Legal access to these medications enables people with long-term dependency issues to avoid overdose and withdrawal. Studies also find that many people who receive these medications generally stabilize and eventually reduce their doses.[82]

The U.S. Substance Abuse and Mental Health Services Administration has concluded that MAT programs provide a safe and controlled level of medication to overcome the use of an abused opioid and do not adversely affect people's cognitive capacities or physical functioning.[83] Moreover, studies show that crime rates fall precipitously when access to MAT increases. This is because patients are no longer compelled to engage in criminal behavior in order to obtain the money needed to buy illicit drugs.[84] Similarly, researchers have found that the recruitment of new users declines as people receiving MAT no longer feel compelled to encourage others to buy illicit drugs in order to enhance their own resources.[85] As a result, overall consumption of illegal drugs, dealing, and associated crime and violence decline when MAT is expanded.[86] Perhaps most important, the quality of life, health, and well-being of those who have suffered from unmanaged addiction for years, and sometimes decades, improves dramatically.[87] In this context, many people who have used drugs in harmful ways for decades are often able to find housing and employment and to reconnect with family members and friends. It is for all of these reasons that JustCARE employs the services of healthcare providers who are able to increase participants' access to MAT.

Unfortunately, a number of barriers currently limit access to the most efficacious medicines. For example, hydromorphone has been found to be effective for treatment of opioid use disorder in a number of studies, but is currently a Schedule II drug in the United States and is therefore not available for distribution as a treatment for addiction. Similarly, heroin is classified as a Schedule I drug in the United States and therefore cannot be prescribed.[88] Another major limitation in the use of MAT is that medications have been approved only for treatment of opiate use disorder. Similar treatment options do not currently exist for those who are dependent on stimulant drugs such as cocaine and methamphetamine, although there is some evidence that long-acting stimulants may be effective in such cases.[89] Rescheduling drugs in ways that facilitate the identification of medicines that are effective in the treatment of addiction, and investing in the research needed to do so, would likely have a deeply transformative impact for people with long-term chemical dependency issues.

Expand Affordable and Accessible Housing, Including Housing First Options

The increase in housing instability and homelessness is one of the most pressing problems in twenty-first-century America. Homelessness is an important social problem in its own right, but it also makes addressing issues like substance misuse exponentially more difficult. In fact, it is nearly impossible for people to address harmful drug use while they are living unsheltered, for several reasons. First, as many Co-LEAD and JustCARE participants have explained in interviews, living unsheltered is extraordinarily stressful and uncomfortable. In the context of living outdoors, drugs can provide a functional benefit, at least in the short term: they can help people stay awake to guard their property, help them to sleep during the day when their belongings are less likely to be stolen, and generally relieve the stress, misery, and boredom that accompanies homelessness. Accessing treatment and, for that matter, any kind of healthcare is much more difficult when people lack access to regular schedules, calendars, and transportation. Meaningfully addressing homelessness is thus crucial to efforts to reduce the harm associated with drug use among the most vulnerable members of society.

The rise of homelessness is inextricably bound up with recent economic transformations, most notably the shift to a postindustrial economy.[90] As the manufacturing sector declined in the United States, so did the factory jobs that once provided a reasonably comfortable existence for low-skilled workers. Service jobs became more prominent, but these were bifurcated. Those who worked largely with information—in the finance and high-tech sectors, for example—drew hefty salaries, while those who worked in the lower rungs of the service sector—in retail or restaurants—earned the minimum wage. In the 1980s, more than three-quarters of new jobs paid the minimum wage.[91] This wage level typically fails to generate sufficient income to escape poverty.[92]

As changes in the job market and reduced earnings increased poverty and income inequality, shifts in the housing market made acquiring inexpensive shelter more and more difficult. A key dynamic in many urban housing markets is the rise of gentrification. City neighborhoods experiencing gentrification witnessed infusions of both capital and young professionals as residents.[93] Multiple factors fueled gentrification: the enforcement of growth limits that reduced suburban home availability, the desire of urban professionals to avoid long commutes by living near their downtown workplaces, and the opportunity to generate significant home equity by sharply increasing the value of previously declining properties.

Gentrification also depletes the stock of affordable housing. The displacement of single-room occupancy (SRO) hotels in the face of gentrification offers an important example. Indeed, their loss decreased the stock of inexpensive housing by about one million units in urban America between 1970 and 1982.[94] SROs were replaced by apartments or condominiums that are beyond the means of low-income people. This process generated a shortfall of affordable housing that persists today.[95] By 2012, more than one in four (27 percent) of all renters paid more than 50 percent of their income in rent. These "burdened renters" are at heightened risk of eviction and hence homelessness.[96]

In addition to these recent economic shifts, the fraying of the public social safety net also fueled housing instability and homelessness. Federal support for housing assistance dropped precipitously in the 1980s, as did funding for other forms of social support. This trend was part of a broader movement to reduce government services and supports for those at the bottom of the economic ladder. These neoliberal policies emaciated federal support for low-income people. In the three-year period from 1982 to 1985 alone, federal programs targeted to the poor were cut by $57 billion.[97] Housing assistance was particularly hard-hit. From 1978 to 1983, the portion of the federal Housing and Urban Development budget dedicated to low-income housing declined from $83 billion to $18 billion. Not surprisingly, federal authorizations for housing shifted from 7 percent of the federal budget in 1978 to 0.7 percent by 1988.[98] The resulting decline in government-built public housing was dramatic. In the six years between 1976 and 1982, HUD built more than 755,000 public housing units. In the twenty-two years between 1983 and 2005, it built only a third that number—256,000 units.[99] Federal support for low-income housing remains at historically low levels.

Instead of building public housing, the federal government shifted to providing vouchers for those deemed sufficiently poor to require housing assistance. Those granted vouchers were then required to enter the private market to secure housing. This approach is consistent with neoliberalism's emphasis on private markets as the solution to complex social problems. Yet vouchers failed to provide the same level of housing security relative to inclusive public housing.[100] In particular, people with addiction histories and criminal records are often unable to secure housing on the private market.

Although homeless shelters have proliferated and help keep some people off the streets, they do not represent a comprehensive solution to the need for housing, for several reasons. For one thing, there are almost never a sufficient number of shelter beds. Moreover, even if people can access a shelter bed, some are unable to comply with the shelter's many restrictions. Many shelters are noisy, disease-prone, and crowded and cannot ensure the safety of the people they house or the security of their belongings.[101] Clients are invariably required to abstain from the use of illicit drugs or alcohol and may be required to attend church services, to perform chores, or to arrive before their other obligations permit. And as the COVID-19 pandemic has made abundantly clear, the inadequate and crowded housing of congregate shelters is not conducive to mental well-being or to public health. The solution shelters provide is, by definition, limited and temporary.

Affordable housing, including units that are open to people with criminal records and who use drugs, is clearly needed to address this problem. Currently, vouchers are the main policy response to the need for affordable housing, but private landlords have little incentive to rent to people they consider to be "high risk," especially in tight housing markets. In fact, private landlords continue to engage in a variety of discriminatory practices and rely on screening procedures that have the effect of reducing housing access for historically marginalized groups and protected classes, particularly in tight housing markets. This is true even where "Ban the Box" policies that restrict landlords' ability to ask about applicants' criminal records are intended to prevent this from happening.[102]

Two other options exist. First, the federal government could elect to reverse the budget cuts that decimated local housing assistance efforts in the 1980s and 1990s. Federal authorities could also make sure that people with criminal records have access to some of this housing by conditioning receipt of federal housing dollars on landlords' willingness to house people with criminal records. Another option is for states and localities to invest in all types of affordable housing, including Housing First facilities. The Housing First approach stresses the importance of permanent housing, without which, people are less likely to respond favorably to any social service intervention. From this perspective, housing is a basic need that deserves to be met regardless of any potentially harmful behavior, such as heavy alcohol or drug use. In the best-case scenario, permanent housing is accompanied by supportive services where they are needed, all geared toward helping individuals and families to attain stability.

Housing First has attracted considerable attention among contemporary American policymakers. It is now embraced by the U.S. Department of Housing and Urban Development and is a centerpiece of many cities' "ten-year plans" to end homelessness.[103] To date, however, this growing recognition of the need for Housing First approaches has not translated into the fiscal investments to make the approach a reality.

Although harm reduction and Housing First are distinct, they are highly complementary, as their coexistence in Co-LEAD and JustCARE suggests. Both approaches accept the need to address the wide array of challenges faced by many people experiencing homelessness. Both recognize the need to develop comprehensive plans to help people stabilize. Both accept the fact that eradication of all risky behaviors is unlikely but that nonetheless significant harms may be reduced. Both also recognize the negative impact of criminal legal intervention. Most fundamentally, harm reduction and Housing First recognize that improving the quality of life of all urban residents requires improving the lives of the most disadvantaged.

One place where these two philosophies have met for years is in a building on the northeast edge of downtown Seattle, 1811 Eastlake. Run by the Downtown Emergency Services Center, which oversees a wide array of shelters for disadvantaged people in Seattle, 1811 is sometimes described as "wet" housing, meaning that residents are allowed to drink on the premises. Here, especially chronic and impoverished alcoholics are provided with subsidized housing and have access to on-site staff who can assist them with various forms of support and services. This is the definition of harm reduction in action. Initiatives like 1811 Eastlake are highly cost-effective.[104] And, unsurprisingly, the residents are healthier than when they were unsheltered, and many reduce their drinking substantially over time.[105] It is clear that expanding this kind of housing option would also promote the health and well-being of those who have used illicit substances for long periods of time and for whom more conventional treatment options have not been effective.

Summary

Although the war on drugs is not the primary driver of mass incarceration, it has contributed importantly to the expansion of prisons and jails and to the emergence of "mass supervision." It also constitutes an unjust and ineffective response to the problem of unmanaged addiction and unregulated drug markets, thus exacerbating rather than alleviating human suffering and intensifying racial and socioeconomic inequalities. Unfortunately, the most popular drug reforms, including drug courts and other forms of court-based diversion and supervision, do not represent a meaningful solution to these problems, as was discussed in chapter 4.

In this chapter, I have argued that ending criminal legal system involvement in the lives of people who use drugs is an important first step toward reducing the harm caused by the drug war. However, decriminalization statutes in the United States generally maintain criminal or civil sanctions for drug possession (and drug distribution), and thus do not go far enough. Ultimately, legalization and regulation of drug markets is needed. Although legalization could, in theory, be accomplished by state and federal lawmakers, this seems unlikely to occur in the near or medium term. In the meantime, therefore, greater investment in a variety of harm reduction initiatives, including alternative response frameworks such as LEAD 2.0 and JustCARE, can create the conditions in which drug possession is legalized in practice for the most vulnerable drug users, many of whom would otherwise cycle repeatedly in and out of jail. Such initiatives also provide long-term emotional and social support, helping people navigate complex bureaucracies, secure identification, access benefits and healthcare, apply for housing, quash warrants, reconnect with family, and address outstanding legal issues. Importantly, frameworks such as JustCARE also address the public safety concerns of people who live and work in neighborhoods in which outdoor drug markets are concentrated; left unaddressed, these concerns are likely to motivate high demand for emergency services via 911 and could well sustain calls for policies and practices associated with the war on drugs. These harm reduction models thus interrupt public demand for crackdowns on people who use and sell drugs in public, do not rely on either criminal or civil sanctions, and help to reduce the policeability of substance use.

A variety of social investments would dramatically enhance the impact of these kinds of harm reduction interventions. In particular, expanding access to all forms of treatment, especially MAT, and affordable housing (with and without supportive services) would greatly reduce the individual- and neighborhood-level harm associated with substance abuse, illegal drug markets, and extreme poverty. While such initiatives would require significant expenditures, there is compelling evidence that these investments would yield remarkable returns: improvements in health and well-being, reductions in crime and violence, and reduced criminal legal involvement and expenditures. The adoption of these and other harm reduction measures in the United States is long overdue.

8

Reimagining Public Safety

Between the time I began working on this book in 2018 and its completion, "abolition" became a household word. In the summer of 2020, mobilization by Black Lives Matter protestors intensified and activists called on local governments across the country to defund the police.[1] For some advocates, the goal was not total defunding or complete abolition, but rather reallocation of significant monies from police departments to social services, housing, education, child care, and community-based organizations.

In this context, activists' insistence on the need to reimagine public safety received an unprecedented degree of attention. And, as if on cue, a vast array of other crises—the pandemic, rising poverty and joblessness, and projections of an unprecedented wave of evictions—further underscored the importance of broadening our understanding of and approach to public safety.

In the introduction to this book, I argued that the ascendance of a narrow definition of public safety that recognizes just one threat to public safety—the risk of interpersonal violence—was the result of an eminently useful political strategy employed by conservative (and, increasingly, liberal) political actors over several decades. Yet the institutional expression of this political strategy—mass incarceration—has been an overwhelming and devastating policy failure. Mass incarceration does not make us safer. In fact, by consuming scarce public resources, substituting for meaningful assistance for people who have experienced crime and violence, and reinforcing poverty and racial inequality, mass incarceration has failed us all. It has particularly failed communities of color and low-income families by ensnaring, traumatizing, and stigmatizing millions.

The chapters in the first part of this book identified and analyzed three dynamics that help to explain the persistence of mass incarceration in the context of falling crime rates and the widespread enactment of (ostensibly) decarcerative reforms. In chapter 2, I argued that our collective unwillingness to question widespread assumptions about the nature and causes of violence constitutes a crucial and, so far, insurmountable barrier to transformative change. The myth of monstrosity is deeply embedded in our history, our culture, and our politics. At the same time, this mythology reinforces racial and other stereotypes regarding the nature and causes of violence and is in tension with a wide body of psychological and sociological research showing that a variety of social conditions fuel interpersonal violence.[2] This mythology also ignores the human capacity for maturation and growth, despite studies showing remarkably low recidivism rates among people who had been convicted of comparatively serious crimes, including homicide, after spending long periods of time behind bars.[3]

Consistent with the constraints created by the myth of monstrosity, the vast majority of recent reform measures have been limited to the least serious offenses, especially drug possession. Analysis of media coverage showed that many advocates justify these quite limited reforms by calling for the heightened punishment of "real criminals" and "predators." This bifurcated approach to criminal legal reform draws a sharp but misleading line between people who are involved with drugs (or who commit other, less serious offenses) and those who are convicted of a violent act. It also ignores the fact that the proliferation of long and life sentences, which are mainly imposed in cases involving violence, is a fundamental driver of mass incarceration, and that limiting reforms to the most minor offenses will also limit the degree to which we are able to reduce mass incarceration. Our failure to critically interrogate the myth of monstrosity and to allow this mythology to so radically limit the ways we transform our response to punishment has meant that the tepid reforms we have adopted in recent years have failed to meaningfully reduce mass incarceration.

In chapter 3, I described a second dynamic that helps to explain the persistence of mass incarceration: changes in the geography of punishment. Criminal legal outcomes in urban and nonurban counties are increasingly divergent. Specifically, while many urban prosecutors and judges are rethinking the drug war and the overuse of incarceration for minor crimes, rural and suburban officials continue to rely heavily on jails and prisons. In fact, the criminal legal response to all types of crime is comparatively strong and has continued to intensify in nonurban areas. Statistical analysis shows that other characteristics, especially political conservatism, the size of the Black population, and social disadvantage, help explain heightened punitiveness at the county level. Even after controlling for all of these factors as well as crime and drug arrests, though, ruralness and suburbanness are significantly associated with heightened punishment. Curbing the propensity to punish in nonurban areas will require replacing statutory maximums with statutory minimums. It will also require addressing the intensification of poverty and social disadvantage and the unhelpful ways that authorities in these increasingly conservative jurisdictions are responding to that trend.

In chapter 4 I explored a third factor that helps to explain the persistence of mass incarceration: the limited nature of mainstream drug policy reforms. While drug policy reform is important and necessary on social justice and racial equity grounds, most reforms enacted to date fail to meaningfully transform the societal response to addiction or drug markets. They also fail to keep people out of the criminal legal system, for several reasons. First, by limiting attention to those who use (rather than distribute) drugs, many drug policy reforms fail to meaningfully address mass incarceration and carceral state power. Because only a small fraction—fewer than 1 in 28—people are in prison for drug possession, such reforms cannot have much of an impact on prison populations, though they can have slightly more significant effects on jail and probation populations. To be more impactful, drug reforms need to also reduce confinement for people who distribute drugs (often to support their own use of drugs). But recent legislation often does the opposite. In fact, calls to treat drug sales as a violent crime and prosecutions for drug-induced homicide have proliferated. If unabated, this trend will greatly constrain the impact of drug policy reforms aimed exclusively at drug possession offenses.

In addition, many jurisdictions have created and/or expanded drug courts. While these courts may be intended to reduce reliance on jail or prison, the evidence suggests that they fail to reduce the amount of time people arrested on drug charges spend behind bars as a result of tight eligibility requirements and strict sanctions for noncompliance.[4] Moreover, the existence of drug courts appears to increase the number of drug arrests.[5] Even when people are "successfully" diverted, drug courts often subject participants to extended and intensive court supervision and rest on an outdated and ineffective approach to addiction. Truly transformative drug reforms will need to meaningfully reduce criminal legal system involvement while also addressing the harm caused by unmanaged addiction, an unregulated drug supply, and illicit markets that generate a great deal of violence. Sadly, research indicates that mainstream drug policy reforms, including drug courts, do not achieve these ends.

In chapters 5, 6, and 7, I identified changes that are desperately needed if we are to bring about truly transformative penal and social change. My decision to focus on these particular changes was guided by a number of factors, including my belief that changes that enhance the well-being of marginalized and vulnerable people while also reducing the size and scope of the carceral state and racial inequities in it are needed. In chapter 5, I focused on the need to end excessive sentencing, which in turn requires tackling the myth of monstrosity. The United States is a global outlier in its use of life sentences: one in seven prisoners, and one in five Black prisoners, is serving a life sentence.[6]

Long sentences have also become far more common.[7] Comprehensive sentencing reform is needed to end the routine imposition of excessive sentences and to create the possibility for more humane and viable approaches to violence prevention. Toward these ends, the adoption of a twenty-year maximum sentence would help to reduce mass incarceration—especially the incarceration of the elderly.[8] It would also reduce the magnitude of the "trial penalty," which has grown ever larger as a result of recent sentencing trends. The creation and expansion of postconviction review processes are also essential: they will enable the release of people who were previously sentenced to very long or life sentences and are thus central to the development of a more humane and effective justice system.[9]

The widespread imposition of long and life sentences is sustained by widespread acceptance of the myth of monstrosity, or what Craig Haney calls the "master crime narrative."[10] This myth assigns sole responsibility for violence to the allegedly irredeemable, evil, and corrupt souls who commit it at one point in their lives. By contrast, the life stories of Christopher Blackwell, Jeff Foxx, Ray Williams, Anthony Wright, and Eugene Youngblood—and so many others—who are serving long or life sentences illustrate powerfully the remarkable capacity for maturation and growth that many incarcerated people exhibit despite their history of abuse and long-term confinement in dehumanizing institutions. Securing the passage of needed policy changes will require rejection of the seemingly indestructible myth of monstrosity. Expanding opportunities for defendants to present evidence of mitigating circumstances, amplifying the voices of formerly incarcerated people and of violence survivors who do not favor the current approach to public safety, and the enactment of policies that recognize that the system-involved have also experienced significant trauma may help us begin to chip away at this mythology.

In chapter 6, I argued for the expansion of restorative justice alternatives that can empower and facilitate healing for people who have been harmed, as well as for people who have caused harm. Restorative justice also offers a non-confinement-based method of holding people who cause harm accountable for their actions. Increased awareness of the human costs of mass incarceration and its failure to meet the needs of many survivors of crime and violence has led some to consider restorative justice as an alternative or supplement to the traditional criminal legal process. Yet most programs in the United States exclude cases involving violent crime, and few divert people who have caused harm from prison. Paradoxically, studies show that restorative justice interventions are most effective in cases involving interpersonal violence.[11] Moreover, insofar as the majority of people who are convicted of a violent crime have often been a victim of violence in the past,[12] addressing the trauma of those who have caused harm is crucial.

In short, diversionary, restorative justice programs that include cases involving violence are desperately needed and have the potential to meaningfully reduce reliance on prisons. In the long run, the development and implementation of these and other alternative, nonviolent ways of holding accountable people who harm others, and enabling them to address the conditions that facilitated their harmful actions, will reduce the violence associated with both interpersonal aggression and mass incarceration.

In chapter 7, I argued that expanding harm-reduction-based alternative responses to harmful forms of drug use would dramatically reduce the suffering associated with unmanaged addiction and the violence associated with illicit drug markets while also limiting the reach of the criminal legal system. These alternative models respond to low-level crimes that stem from unmanaged substance abuse without the use of sanctions of any sort. Drawing on the example of newer adaptations of LEAD, including JustCARE, I showed that alternative response frameworks based on harm reduction principles and trauma-informed practice create spaces in which drug use and associated behaviors are effectively decriminalized, and services, care, medication-assisted treatment, and other opportunities can be provided. These interventions thus show, in real time, what a shift toward legalization and social investment might look like.

Such responses offer a more meaningful opportunity to reduce suffering than drug courts or even statutory decriminalization alone. Whereas the latter generally involves reliance on (reduced) criminal or civil sanctions, alternative response models such as LEAD 2.0 and JustCARE entail de facto decriminalization, and do not rely on police as gatekeepers or employ sanctions of any sort. When accompanied by the other initiatives and investments described in this chapter, these alternative response models represent a means of bridging the gap between the failed drug war and more radical alternatives such as regulated legalization coupled with targeted social investments. While these alternative response frameworks do require significant resources, there is compelling evidence that these investments would yield remarkable returns: improvements in health and well-being, reductions in crime and violence, and reduced criminal legal involvement and expenditures. At the same time, the long-term success and viability of such approaches will depend on increased investments in low-income housing, substance abuse treatment (including the provision of medication-assisted treatment), and healthcare, as well as the development of alternative approaches to drug distribution itself.

Conclusion

As I write this conclusion in early 2021, more than half a million people have died from COVID-19 in the United States alone. Sadly, these numbers will be greater by the time this book is published. People of color, the elderly, the unhoused, and the poor will be disproportionately represented among the pandemic's victims. These fatalities will also include a devastatingly large number of people who were confined in prisons, jails, and detention centers during the pandemic.

It didn't take long for incarcerated people, their loved ones, reform advocates, health experts, and others to realize that the virus would spread rapidly in overcrowded institutions of confinement, and with devastating consequences. Chronic diseases such as asthma, heart disease, hypertension, diabetes, and other medical conditions that increase the risk of death from COVID-19 are unusually common among incarcerated people. In fact, 40 percent of prisoners and jail inmates have a chronic medical condition.[13] Moreover, the number of older people serving time has increased dramatically. As of 2017, nearly 170,000 people fifty-five or older were incarcerated in state prisons alone.[14]

The risk of serious illness and death stemming from COVID-19 in prison and jail is compounded by the inadequacies of jail and prison healthcare systems, restrictions on life-saving protections, and the impossibility of social distancing in jails, prisons, and detention centers.[15] As the pandemic spread, many prisoners reported that effective cleaning materials and hand sanitizers that contain alcohol (which is necessary to kill the virus) were unavailable.[16] In many prisons and jails, quarantine has also meant lockdown in close proximity with others who were infected, restricted mobility, and an inability to access fresh air. In some prisons and jails, people who fall ill are being placed in solitary confinement or shipped to newly erected "micro-prisons" that mimic the conditions of solitary confinement.[17] Together, these circumstances mean that COVID-19 is having especially devastating effects on those who live and work in detention centers, jails, and prisons.[18] To date, the age-adjusted COVID death rate among prisoners is three times higher than in the general population.[19]

Despite widespread calls for the emergency release of vulnerable prisoners, and lawsuits aimed at the same, governors and the federal government had, at the time of this writing, done little to alleviate overcrowding and improve the safety of prisoners across the country. As of March 2021, there have been 275,000 confirmed cases of COVID-19 in U.S. prisons, though the actual number is likely much higher.[20] These tragic events render visible an important truth about prisons: they are places in which human beings are caged and deprived of the means to ensure their own basic needs for safety and security. In short, incarceration is a form of violence.

Although varied, local officials' response to the pandemic in jails has been slightly more encouraging. Some jails, like the one in Cook County, Illinois, released few of the detained despite very high levels of infection.[21] In other counties, though, local officials have accepted the idea that people who are in jail for minor offenses or technical violations, or are awaiting adjudication for such issues, can and should be released. And in a number of locales, local law enforcement officials booked hotel and motel rooms to ensure that people who are released from jail in the context of the pandemic have somewhere to go and safely self-isolate.[22] Unfortunately, though, recent data suggest that jail populations had begun to rebound, despite the ongoing nature of the pandemic and in the absence of widespread vaccination, by winter of 2021.[23]

Pandemics cause untold devastation, loss, and suffering. But, as *Slate* writer Dan Kois notes, they also help reveal the "bullshit" nature of common policies and practices that punish people, make lives more rather than less difficult, and ensure that money flows upward, to those who need it least. Prior to the pandemic, innumerable policies and practices of this sort—turning off the water supply to those who cannot afford to pay, forcing sick employees to work while ill or go hungry by depriving them of sick leave, allowing hundreds of thousands to sleep on the streets and in unsafe shelters in the richest country on earth, jailing people who do not pose a threat to public safety, including elderly and medically frail people—were accepted as unavoidable. As Kois points out, the pandemic has the potential to produce massive policy change because

> once a policy is revealed as bullshit, it gets a lot harder to convince smart, engaged citizens to capitulate to it. That's one reason why activists are agitating to end cash bail in the coronavirus crisis, or fighting to ensure that coronavirus tests and any eventual vaccine are available to all. Not only would those measures save or better countless lives during the pandemic, but in their common-sense wisdom, they expose the absurdity of the opposing view. What kind of ghoul would argue that we shouldn't vaccinate everyone against a pandemic threatening the health of our nation? The same kind of ghoul, perhaps, who thinks that cancer treatment, or insulin, should only be available for those lucky enough to be able to pay for them.[24]

As many observers have noted, the events of 2020 have shone an especially bright light on long-standing inequalities and injustices across the globe and within the United States. Without a doubt, mass incarceration in the United

States is among the gravest of these injustices. The futility of seeking to protect public safety and enhance our collective well-being by putting more and more people in cages has been revealed. There is, then, hope in the midst of devastating darkness. In seeking to end mass incarceration, our efforts to reduce the state's power to punish must be tethered to policies and practices that reduce and ameliorate all forms of injustice, harm, and suffering. True public safety requires no less.

Legislative Reforms: Data and Methods

Information about recent statutory reforms presented in chapter 2 draws on work I conducted with Lindsay Beach, Anna Reosti, and Emily Knaphus-Soran[1] and was taken from the *State Sentencing and Corrections Legislation* data set compiled by the National Conference of State Legislatures (NCSL). Information about measures enacted from 2007 to 2009 comes from *Significant State Sentencing and Corrections Legislation* reports published annually by NCSL; descriptions of session laws implemented between 2010 and 2014 were obtained through NCSL's searchable online database. We also accessed the final bill online to determine its intent and focus. These sources were cross-checked against and supplemented with a number of synthetic reports published by the Vera Institute that summarize developments in criminal justice legislation. I have updated the analysis to include data from 2015 and 2016. These data encompass all fifty states.

Once the database was compiled, provisions that appear to have been intended to reduce or enhance prison sentences or time served were identified. (In states with combined prison/jail systems, measures intended to alter jail sentences or stays were also included.) For example, legislation that prohibits registered sex offenders from obtaining licenses that allow them to own and operate ice-cream trucks was not included in the analysis; legislation that expands inmates' capacity to earn credits toward early release was classified as a "back-end" measure intended to reduce time served. In order to render the scope of the analysis manageable, we included measures that were intended to affect the length of prison sentences and stays for felony (but not misdemeanor) crimes. Many provisions included in the analysis may or may not have an impact on prison sentences or time served. For example, many recent sentencing reforms authorized, but did not require, judges to impose more lenient sentences for nonviolent offenses. Similarly, some back-end reforms authorized parole board members to *consider* parole applicants' involvement in educational and other programming for those serving time for nonviolent crimes. Because we do not seek to assess the quantitative impact of these legislative provisions, but rather are interested in their intent, the uncertain impact of these measures on outcomes is not a concern.

Legislative provisions aimed at reducing sentences or time served were coded as decarcerative; provisions intended to enhance sentences or time served were coded as incarcerative. Measures that seek to affect the sentences imposed by judges were coded as front-end, while provisions that pertain to prison release and parole revocation decisions, and therefore may impact time served, were classified as back-end. We also coded the type of offense(s) to which the legislation pertains in order to compare trends in the violent and nonviolent categories. The unit of analysis is the legislative provision rather than the session law, as the majority of enacted laws contained multiple and substantively distinct provisions, often with diverse purposes. For example, Minnesota's 2013 Senate Bill 671 simultaneously expanded release opportunities for drug offenders and created a new mandatory minimum sentence for repeat sex offenders. Each distinct provision was coded according to the nature and direction of the reform implemented. In this case, the former provision was coded as "Decarcerative—Back End—Drug," while the latter provision was coded as "Incarcerative—Front End—Sex."

Drug Law Reforms

The analysis of recent trends in drug sentencing policy presented in chapter 4 draws on work I conducted with Marco Brydolf-Horwitz and includes state-level drug sentencing statutes passed between 2010 and 2016. The NCSL database of *Statewide Sentencing and Corrections Legislation* was used to identify these reforms. This comprehensive database is provided by the NCSL in partnership with the Pew Center on the States and is currently available for 2010–16. The database provides a description of each law, which we used to create a list of bills with any mention of controlled substances, drug-related crimes, drug courts, or court supervision. Significant criminal justice reform efforts such as omnibus crime bills and state budgets were also included in this first sweep, even if controlled substances did not appear in the title or description. This list was then cross-checked against databases compiled by researchers at the Vera Institute of Justice, the Drug Policy Alliance, an open-access list organized by *Vox* journalist German Lopez, and the NCLS's reports on drug sentencing trends. The list was further refined during the coding process as we identified substantive changes to sentencing or court supervision policies.

Once the pertinent bills were identified, the full text of each statute was accessed through the NCLS database for 2015–16 and through state legislative websites for 2010–14. The relevant provisions of each law were then coded to reflect whether they shifted drug penalties in a lenient, punitive, or mixed direction. Laws that reduced confinement time were coded as lenient, while those that increased confinement sentences were coded as punitive. In a relatively small number of cases, legislative provisions modified sentencing rules in a way that reduced confinement time in cases involving relatively small quantities of drugs but increased penalties for cases involving larger amounts of the same substance. For example, Kansas House Bill 2318 (2012) added graduated weight classifications to its criminal code for sale of a controlled substance, thereby reducing the penalty for sale of less than 1 gram of certain substances but increasing sentence length for weights over 100 grams. We coded these kinds of provisions as "mixed." The coding protocol did not require that the coder predict the magnitude of the impact legislative shifts would have on jail or prison populations. Instead, the results are used to enable a qualitative assessment of the direction of drug sentencing reforms adopted by U.S. states.

Laws that affect eligibility for and requirements of drug courts and court supervision more generally were also recorded. These results are presented separately. Insofar as drug and other therapeutic courts ostensibly seek to divert people from prison and jail, we considered coding provisions that expand access to drug courts or court-supervised treatment as "lenient." However, as Tiger[2] points out, drug courts, and coercive treatment more generally, rest on a unique blend of medicalization and criminalization and often extend the degree to which courts retain control over people's lives. There is also compelling evidence that drug courts entail net-widening.[3] For these reasons, these findings are presented separately.

The unit of analysis is the legislative provision rather than the session law, as the latter often contains multiple and distinct provisions that address different types of drug law violations and may shift sentences in opposite directions. A provision, as we define it, is a portion of a bill that substantively changes state law regarding drug sentencing, drug courts, or court supervision related to drug offenses. Each distinct provision in each session law was coded according to the nature and direction of the change enacted and, when available, the associated crime(s) and the substance(s). Legislative changes that applied to different levels of severity, crimes, and/or substances but moved in the same direction were coded as a single provision. For example, Minnesota Senate Bill 3481 (2016) increased weight thresholds that define cocaine and methamphetamine offenses in the first and second degrees, thereby reducing the number of cases that would be eligible for the more severe sanctions that first- and second-degree violations entail. We coded these changes as a single, lenient provision pertaining to cocaine and methamphetamine. That same law also set mandatory minimum sentences for sale and possession of more than 100 grams of certain controlled substances, which we coded as a single, punitive provision. By coding multiple changes that move penalties in the same direction as one provision, we capture the direction and type of legislative change without giving undue weight to states whose criminal codes are comparatively differentiated.

Criminal Case Processing: Data and Methods

The analyses of criminal case processing outcomes presented in chapter 3 draw on work I conducted with Lindsey Beach and identify local variation in admissions to state prisons, where the majority of U.S. inmates reside.[1] Because many felony convictions result in a sentence of probation or jail time rather than a prison admission, the proportion of felony arrests that result in a prison sentence is widely treated as an indicator of penal intensity. Given interest in local, county-level differences in the use of prisons, the analysis focuses on prison admissions over which county officials have influence, that is, admissions stemming from the commission of felony offenses or violations of probation sentences. Admissions stemming from technical parole violations are determined by state correctional authorities and are therefore not included in our analyses.[2] Prison admissions involving persons sentenced to twelve months or more of confinement time, most—but not all—of whom serve these sentences in state prison, are included.[3]

Data Sources

Data pertaining to prison admissions are taken from the National Corrections Reporting Program (NCRP), which provides individual-level, administrative data collected by the Bureau of Justice Statistics that include offense type, length of sentence imposed, county of sentencing, type of admission, and type of release. The collection began in 1983 and is available through the Inter-University Consortium for Political and Social Research at the University of Michigan. NCRP data are available for counties in thirty-eight states from 2011 to 2013, and for notably fewer states in 2014. In order to ensure a larger and more inclusive sample, average prison admission rates from 2011 to 2013 were used as a window onto recent dynamics. In a separate analysis, we also analyze NCRP data from 2001 to 2003 in order to ascertain whether the patterns observed in the most recent period mark a break with the recent past.[4] For these earlier years, NCRP data are available for counties in twenty-one states.

The Centers for Disease Control and Prevention's (CDC) National Center for Health Statistics' detailed categorization scheme was used to identify urban, suburban, and rural counties. This categorization scheme includes total population and density measures, as well as information about counties' metropolitan/nonmetropolitan status, the size of the surrounding metropolitan or micropolitan statistical area, and demographic and socioeconomic information. Although large, central metropolitan (i.e., urban) counties and large, fringe metropolitan (suburban) counties may have similar population sizes, the social characteristics of these counties differ significantly. We therefore include large, central metropolitan counties in our urban category, and classify large fringe, medium, and small metropolitan counties as suburban. Micropolitan and non-core (i.e., rural) counties have smaller population centers and are neither economically nor socially connected to larger metropolitan areas. To be sure that this three-category classification system was not unduly influencing the results, we also ran the models using a four-category measurement system in which large fringe and medium metro counties were classified as large suburban counties, and small metro counties were classified as small suburban counties. The findings of stepwise models that included all four geographic categories were similar in size, direction, and significance as those reported here.

Crime and arrest data are taken from the FBI's Uniform Crime Reports (UCR)[5] for 2010–12 in order to create a one-year lag vis-à-vis prison admissions. These data are aggregated by the National Archive of Criminal Justice Data to the county level. UCR data identify twenty-eight offenses, eight of which are considered comparatively serious. Of these "index crimes," four (murder and nonnegligent manslaughter, rape, aggravated assault, and robbery) are categorized by UCR as violent, while another four (burglary, larceny-theft, motor vehicle theft, and arson) are classified as property crimes. We focus on these comparatively serious index crimes, all of which have the potential to become felony criminal cases and therefore to trigger prison admission. We also analyze data for all drug arrests other than marijuana possession (because marijuana possession arrests rarely result in prison admission), as well as weapons violations, which can also trigger felony charges. Crime rates are calculated as the number of crimes known to the police per 100,000 residents.

The majority of counties now report data to the UCR. For example, in 2012 the law enforcement agencies participating in the UCR program represented more than 270 million U.S. inhabitants—85.4 percent of the total population. To ensure the quality and reliability of UCR data, counties with fully imputed data and/or where the difference in sampled populations between offense and arrest data was greater than 10 percent were dropped from the analysis. Our sample for the more recent time period includes 2,366 counties (84 percent of all U.S. counties): 50 urban, 835 suburban, and 1,479 rural. The thirty-eight states in which these counties are located are regionally diverse and highly varied in terms of population size and density. Our sample for the earlier time period includes 1,329 counties—26 urban, 449 suburban, and 854 rural—in twenty-four states, a total of 42.3 percent of all U.S. counties. The sample includes counties in states located in all regions, of varying sizes and levels of urbanization, and with quite different population demographics.[6]

Other data regarding independent variables included in the hierarchical linear modeling (HLM) analysis are drawn from a variety of sources. We employ a variety of socioeconomic indicators to measure social disadvantage. These include the share of the population with incomes below the poverty threshold, the proportion of the population that has not completed high school, the percentage of households that are female-headed, the proportion of the labor force that is unemployed, and the age-adjusted premature mortality rate. These data are taken from the U.S. Census Bureau's 2012 Small Area Income and Poverty Estimates, the 2012 American Community Survey, and the CDC. These measures are included in a single concentrated disadvantage index derived using principal component analysis. Analysis confirms the emergence of a single factor that explains 62 percent of the variance. All index variables load positively on the component, ranging from a factor loading of 0.5 for percentage of the population in poverty and 0.33 for percentage of the labor force that is unemployed. High values for the concentrated disadvantage index indicate that a county is experiencing high levels of poverty and related problems; small or negative values indicate that a small share of the county population is experiencing concentrated disadvantage. In addition, two CDC measures of the extent of drug use are included: the opioid prescription rate in 2012 (per 100 residents) and the drug-poisoning mortality rate in 2008–12 (per 100,000 residents).[7]

Information about county-level demographics, including race, ethnicity, total population size, and nativity, are taken from the American Community Survey and the U.S. Census. Given the potential importance of recent changes in the distribution of the immigrant population, we used the change in the percentage of the population that identifies as non-Hispanic and White from 2000 to 2012 as indicators of racial threat. We also include the share of the population identified as Black in our models given previous findings regarding the potential impact of this variable. Information regarding the local political climate is measured by the 2012 presidential election results, specifically as the share of the county population that voted for the Republican presidential nominee, Mitt Romney. These data were compiled by the *Guardian*.[8] We supplemented these sources with voting data provided by CNN. Missing data for independent variables were limited and replaced using multiple imputation methods with predictive mean matching.

The HLM sample includes 2,366 counties—50 urban, 835 suburban, and 1,479 rural—in thirty-eight states, for a total of 84 percent of all U.S. counties. Table B.1 shows the descriptive statistics associated with this sample.

Table B.1 Descriptive Statistics (Mean, Standard Deviation, and Range) for HLM Analysis of Predictors of Prison Admissions by County Type

Variable	Time Period	Urban	Suburban	Rural
Prison Admission Rate (logged)	2013	4.8 (.56) 3.4–5.8	4.8 (.64) 2.4–6.6	4.9 (.75) 1.89–7.1
Crime Rate	2010–12	4,412 (1,528) 2,350–9,868	2,738 (1,223) 16.5–7,214	2,127 (1,329) 0–15,927
Drug Arrest Rate (logged)	2010–12	5.7 (.58) 4.49–7.53	5.1 (.72) 0–8.42	4.9 (1.11) 0–8.28
Arrest-to-Offense Ratio	2010–12	.18 (.09) .06–.42	.19 (.08) 0–.9	.21 (.13) 0–1.95
Disadvantage Index	2012	.65 (1.47) −2.51–5.03	−.27 (1.49) −3.55–5.15	.16 (1.85) −3.43–6.99
Drug-Related Death Rate (logged)	2008–12	2.63 (.42) 1.75–3.42	2.59 (.43) 1.11–3.96	.2.72 (.47) 1.4–4.61
Opioid Prescribing Rate	2012	74.04 (24.01) 28.8–141.2	92.58 (41.5) .5–335.1	98.69 (50.55) 4.9–387.2
% Black	2012	22.05 (13.8 1.6–63.7	9.31 (12.14) 0–74	6.89 (13.51) 0–84.5
Change in % Non-Hispanic White	2000 & 2012	−6.03 (3.32) −13.1–1.95	−3.86 (3.5) −31.39–6.34	−2.71 (3.03) −38.96–6.16
% Republican Presidential Vote	2012 (Romney)	37.02 (14.34) 8.3–65.1	54.72 (14.56) 9.2–90.9	59.94 (15.82) 11.6–95.9
Sample Size		*50*	*835*	*1,479*

Methods

We employed HLM to examine the association of county-level covariates with the logged average prison admission rate. Due to interest in county-level variation in the use of prisons, we control for the effects of state differences but do not seek to identify state-level drivers of prison admissions. A two-level hierarchical linear model "nests" cases (counties) within groups (states) to statistically account for the clustering due to state differences in the prison admission rate. HLM accounts for this clustering in standard errors, providing more useful comparisons between counties in differing states than alternative methods. (We also address this state clustering of prison admission rates in using random intercepts for each state $[\beta 0_j]$.) In addition, HLM enables the estimation of county-level effects related to variation in prison admissions by accounting for the error structure at each level. This helps to correct downward-biased estimates of standard errors due to nesting. To ensure that this methodological choice did not unduly influence the results, we also ran OLS regressions with state-level dummies. These results are very similar to those obtained using HLM.[9]

Consistent with our theoretical framework, we sequentially introduce variables to the base random-intercept model. The first set of control variables includes jurisdiction-type (β_1County Type$_{ij}$), and the second set includes crime and policing variables: β_2Offense Rate$_{ij}$, $\beta_3$log(Drug Arrest Rate)$_{ij}$, and β_4Arrest:Offense$_{ij}$. We then introduce the disadvantage index and measures of drug abuse in the third model—β_5Con. Dis. Index$_{ij}$, $\beta_6$log(Drug-related Death Rate)$_{ij}$, and β_7Opioid Prescribing Rate$_{ij}$—followed by county-level measures for the racial threat hypothesis (β_8% Black$_{ij}$, β_9% Black)$^2_{ij}$, and β_9Change White$_{ij}$), and the political ideology variable (β_{10}% Republican Vote$_{ij}$) in the final model. For county i in state j, we fit the following regression to the log prison admission rate:

$$
\begin{aligned}
log\left(\text{Prison Admission Rate}\right)_{ij} = {} & \beta_{0j} + \beta_1\text{County Type}_{ij} + \beta_2\text{Offense Rate}_{ij} \\
& + \beta_3 log(\text{Drug Arrest Rate})_{ij} + \beta_4\text{Arrest: Offense}_{ij} \\
& + \beta_5\text{Con. Dis. Index}_{ij} \\
& + \beta_6 log\left(\text{Drug-related Death Rate}\right)_{ij} \\
& + \beta_7\text{Opioid Prescribing Rate}_{ij} \\
& + \beta_8\% \text{ Black}_{ij} + \beta_9\text{Change White}_{ij} \\
& + \beta_9\% \text{ Black})^2_{ij}, + \beta_{10}\% \text{Republican Vote}_{ij}
\end{aligned}
$$

and

$$
\beta_{0j} = \gamma_{00} + \mu_{0j}
$$

Here, γ_{00} is the average log prison admission rate for the sample population, μ_{0j} is the state-specific effect on the log prison admission rate, and ε_{ij} is the level-1 (state) residuals.

Restricted maximum likelihood methods were used in all models. Highly skewed variables were transformed where appropriate, and assessments of multi-collinearity (measured through variable inflation factor tests) informed model selection. Leverage tests were conducted to ensure potential outlying counties did not significantly impact our overall estimates. Z-score transformations were performed (mean = 0, standard deviation = 1) to compare effects across all explanatory variables and to standardize variables with divergent scales. Due to variable scaling and the logged transformation of the dependent variable, regression coefficients are interpreted as the percent change in the logged prison admission rate for a one standard deviation increase in a predictor, holding all other variables constant.

Poisson and negative binomial model specifications for a county count of prison admissions were also explored for basic and final model specifications. Both specifications performed significantly less well than the final linear model. To test for possible spatial autocorrelation within states, we compared two basic models: M1 with no correction for within-class correlation and M2 with the correlation matrix specified with a compound symmetry structure (corresponding to a constant correlation). The log likelihood for both models was calculated, subtracted (M2–M1), and multiplied by 2 to calculate the G^2 statistic, which was not statically significant when analyzed using a x^2 distribution. For this reason, spatial lags are not included in the models.

County-Level Determinants of Prison Admissions

	County Type		Crime		Poverty		Race		Politics	
	(S.E.)	p	(S.E.)	p	(S.E.)	p	(S.E.)	p	(S.E.)	p
Fixed effects:										
(Intercept)	4.750 (.112)	***	4.444 (.108)	***	4.544 (.101)	***	4.528 (.102)	***	4.629 (.100)	***
County Type (Urban)	—		—		—		—		—	
Rural	.003 (.083)	.970	.346 (.081)	***	.235 (.079)	**	.261 (.082)	**	.171 (.083)	*
Suburban	-.039 (.083)	.639	.241 (.080)	**	.227 (.079)	**	.243 (.080)	**	.172 (.080)	*
Felony Offense Rate	—		.172 (.014)	***	.107 (.015)	***	.108 (.015)	***	.119 (.015)	***
Felony Drug Arrest Rate (logged)	—		.109 (.014)	***	.092 (.014)	***	.085 (.014)	***	.086 (.014)	***
Arrest-to-Offense Ratio	—		.046 (.013)	***	.021 (.012)	.091	.018 (.012)	.138	.018 (.012)	.147
Concentrated Disadvantage Index	—		—		.151 (.017)	***	.184 (.019)	***	.210 (.019)	***
Drug-Related Death Rate (logged)	—		—		.006 (.013)	.644	.006 (.013)	.670	-.0003 (.013)	.979
Opioid Prescribing Rate	—		—		.093 (.001)	***	.081 (.018)	***	.070 (.014)	***
% Black	—		—		—		.086 (.039)	*	.085 (.039)	*
% Black (squared)	—		—		—		-.140 (.032)	***	-.135 (.032)	***
Change in % Non-Hispanic White	—		—		—		-.014 (.012)	.242	-.009 (.012)	.417
% Romney Vote	—		—		—		—		.099 (.016)	***

Random effects:

State Intercept Variance (S.D.)	.227 (.476)	.209 (.457)	.160 (.400)	.158 (.397)	.137 (.370)
Residual Variance (S.D.)	.322 (.568)	.282 (.531)	.267 (.516)	.263 (.513)	.260 (.510)
REML Criterion	4120.3	3833.5	3710.4	3696.8	3665
AIC	4130.281	3849.486	3732.402	3724.807	3695.003
BIC	4159.055	3895.525	3795.706	3805.375	3781.327
N–Counties	2,333	2,333	2,333	2,333	2,333
N–States	38	38	38	38	38

p-values: *** < .001, ** <.01, * <.05

Notes

Chapter 1

1. Wapner, "Covid-19."
2. Berman, *Give Us the Ballot*; Pérez, "7 Years of Gutting Voting Rights."
3. U.S. Bureau of Labor Statistics, "Employment Situation Summary."
4. Benfer et al., *The Covid-19 Eviction Crisis.*
5. Healy, Nicas and Baker, "A Line of Fire."
6. Beckett, *Making Crime Pay*; Carter, *The Politics of Rage*; Flamm, *Law and Order*; Haney-Lopez, "How the GOP Became the White Man's Party"; Weaver, "Frontlash."
7. "Goldwater's Acceptance Speech to GOP Convention," *New York Times*, July 17, 1964, cited in Beckett, *Making Crime Pay*, 31.
8. Brown and Socia, "Twenty-First Century Punitiveness"; Drakulich, "The Hidden Role of Racial Bias"; Unnever and Cullen, "The Social Sources of American's Punitiveness."
9. Gilens, *Why Americans Hate Welfare.*
10. Mendleberg, *The Race Card.*
11. Davis, "GOP Finds an Unexpectedly Potent Line of Attack."
12. Even before the election of 2020, it was far from clear whether Trump's effort to highlight the law-and-order issue in the middle of the pandemic and the worst economic collapse since the Great Depression would be successful. See Burns and Martin, "Trump Onslaught."
13. In 1980, governments (federal, state, and local) spent roughly the same amount on social control (including police, courts, and corrections) as on cash welfare. Today governments spend more than twice as much on social control spending than on Temporary Assistance for Needy Families, food stamps, and supplemental social security combined (Saez and Zucman, *The Triumph of Injustice*). While total per capita welfare spending—including both social insurance and means-tested programs—has increased since the 1970s, state aid increasingly prioritizes social services over cash support and depends on contracts with for-profit firms and nonprofit organizations to deliver social services aimed at fixing broken people. See Brydolf-Horwitz and Beckett, "Welfare, Punishment, and Social Marginality."
14. Gould and Wething, "U.S. Poverty Rates Higher"; Organisation for Economic Co-operation and Development, "Income Inequality Update."
15. Western, *Punishment and Inequality.*
16. Haney, *Criminality in Context*, ch. 6; Western, *Homeward.*
17. Liebertz and Bunch, "Examining the Externalities"; Savage and Vila, "Changes in Child Welfare."
18. Beckett and Evans, *About Time*; Tonry, *Sentencing Fragments*; Travis, Western, and Redburn, *The Growth of Incarceration*; Western, *Punishment and Inequality.*
19. Roeder, "A Million People."
20. Kaeble and Cowhig, *Correctional Populations*, table 1; Pew Center on the States, *One in 100*; Sabol, *Survey of State Criminal History Information Systems.*

21. Kassie, "Detained." Over the course of 2019, nearly half a million immigrants were detained.
22. Kang-Brown, Montagnet, and Heiss, *People in Jail and Prison in 2020*. Incarceration rates did drop further during the pandemic, but these declines stem mainly from delayed court-processes rather than policy changes and are therefore likely to be temporary.
23. Walmsley, *World Prison Population List*. Figures are for 2021.
24. Garland, *Mass Imprisonment*, 2.
25. Beckett and Harris, "On Cash and Conviction"; Lee et al., "A Heavy Burden?; Harris, Evans, and Beckett, "Drawing Blood from Stones"; Pettit, *Invisible Men*; Pettit and Western, "Mass Imprisonment"; Travis, Western, and Redburn, *The Growth of Incarceration*; Wakefield, Lee, and Wildeman, "Tough on Crime"; Wakefield and Wildeman, *Children of the Prison Boom*; Western, *Punishment and Inequality*; Western, "The Impact of Incarceration."
26. Harris, Evans, and Beckett, "Drawing Blood from Stones"; Sewell and Jefferson, "Collateral Damage"; Travis, Western, and Redburn, *The Growth of Incarceration*; Western, *Punishment and Inequality*; Western, "The Impact of Incarceration."
27. Comfort, *Doing Time Together*; Lee et al., "A Heavy Burden?"; Sykes and Pettit, "Mass Incarceration"; Wakefield and Wildeman, *Children of the Prison Boom*; Wakefield, Lee, and Wildeman, "Tough on Crime."
28. Alexander, *The New Jim Crow*; Clear, *Imprisoning Communities*; Lee et al., "Racial Inequalities"; Pettit and Western, "Mass Imprisonment."
29. Lee et al., "Racial Inequalities."
30. Garland, *Punishment and Modern Society*, 18.
31. Maruschak and Minton, *Correctional Populations*.
32. Halushka, "The Runaround"; Kohler-Hausmann, *Misdemeanorland*; Miller, "Devolving the Carceral State."
33. See, for example, Brayne, "Surveillance and System Avoidance"; Harris, *A Pound of Flesh*; Harris, Evans, and Beckett, "Drawing Blood from Stones"; Napatoff, "Misdemeanors."
34. Pager, *Marked*; Pager, Western, and Bonikowski, "Discrimination in Low Wage Labor Markets."
35. Beckett and Herbert, *Banished*; Geller et al., "Aggressive Policing"; Lerman and Weaver, *Arresting Citizenship*.
36. Sewell, Jefferson, and Lee, "Living under Surveillance."
37. Kohler-Hausmann, *Misdemeanorland*.
38. Flores, *Caught Up*; Lerman and Weaver, *Arresting Citizenship*; Stuart, *Down, out and under Arrest*.
39. Lara-Millan, "Public Emergency."
40. Brayne, "Surveillance and System Avoidance."
41. Beckett and Harris, "On Cash and Conviction"; Harris, *A Pound of Flesh*; Harris, Evans, and Beckett, "Drawing Blood from Stones."
42. Greenberg, Meredith, and Morse, "The Growing and Broad Nature of Legal Financial Obligations."
43. Hagar, "Your Kid Goes to Jail."
44. Small, "Cause for Trepidation."
45. Doob and Webster, "Countering Punitiveness"; Tonry and Farrington, "Punishment and Crime"; Zimring, *The Great American Crime Decline*.
46. Pew Charitable Trusts, *Prisons and Crime*. See also Lofstrom and Raphael, "Prison Downsizing."

47. For an excellent overview of this literature, see Haney, *Criminality in Context*, 151–53, 196–99.
48. Travis, Western, and Redburn, *The Growth of Incarceration*; Lofstrom and Raphael, "Incarceration and Crime"; Sundt, Salisbury, and Harmon, "Is Downsizing Prisons Dangerous?"
49. Beckett, Reosti, and Knaphus, "The End of an Era"; Opportunity Agenda, *An Overview of Public Opinion*.
50. Dagan and Telles, "Locked In?," 70; see also Dagan and Telles, *Prison Break*.
51. Dagan and Telles, "Locked In?," 270.
52. Beckett, "Media Depictions of Drug Abuse."
53. Simon, *Governing through Crime*.
54. Opportunity Agenda, *An Overview of Public Opinion*, 3.
55. Beckett, Reosti, and Knaphus, "The End of an Era."
56. Ramirez, "Americans' Changing Views."
57. Beckett et al., "U.S. Criminal Justice Policy."
58. Greene and Mauer, *Downscaling Prisons*.
59. Ibid.; Subramanian and Moreno, *Drug War Détente*.
60. Lopez, "The New War on Drugs"; Netherland and Hansen, "The Drug War That Wasn't"; Shaw, "Photos Reveal"; Stone, "Is There 'Hope.'"
61. Gramlich, *America's Incarceration Rate*.
62. Maruschak and Minton, *Correctional Populations*.
63. Pew Charitable Trusts, "Issue Brief."
64. Beckett et al., "U.S. Criminal Justice Policy."
65. Ibid. The increase in the proportion of felony arrests that resulted in a prison sentence may stem from changes in the exercise of prosecutorial discretion, judicial decision-making, or some combination of these (and potentially other) factors.
66. The results of this analysis indicate that the increased intensity of the penal response to crime did not stem from changes in policing. While the share of known property crimes that resulted in arrest did increase, this trend was offset by a decline in drug arrests. Beckett et al., "U.S. Criminal Justice Policy."
67. See also Sabol, Johnson, and Caccavale, *Trends in Correctional Control*.
68. Carson, *Prisoners in 2018*; West and Sabol, *Prisoners in 2007*.
69. Travis, Western, and Redburn, *The Growth of Incarceration*, ch. 6.
70. Kupchik, *Homeroom Security*; Schram, Soss, and Fording, "Deciding to Discipline."
71. Gottschalk, *Caught*.
72. Beckett et al., "U.S. Criminal Justice Policy."
73. Tonry, *Sentencing Fragments*; see also Gottschalk, *Caught*.
74. Streiker and Streiker, "Judicial Developments."
75. Butler, "The System Is Working."
76. Cruz, "Smart Sentencing Act."
77. Tonry, *Sentencing Fragments*.
78. For an overview of the bail reform movement and the progress it has made, see Wykstra, "Bail Reform." See also Pinto, "Bailing Out."
79. See especially Alexander, *The New Jim Crow*; Muhammad, *The Condemnation of Blackness*.
80. Lee et al., "A Heavy Burden?"; Harris, Evans, and Beckett, "Drawing Blood from Stones"; Pettit, *Invisible Men*; Pettit and Western, "Mass Imprisonment"; Travis, Western, and Redburn, *The Growth of Incarceration*; Wakefield, Lee, and Wildeman, "Tough on

Crime"; Wakefield and Wildeman, *Children of the Prison Boom*; Western, *Punishment and Inequality*; Western, "The Impact of Incarceration."

81. Sen, "Development as Capability Expansion."
82. Jonathan Simon has written eloquently and persuasively about the right to dignity. See, for example, *Mass Incarceration on Trial*.
83. Gottschalk, "America Needs a Third Reconstruction."
84. Gould and Wething, "U.S. Poverty Rates"; Ho, "The Contemporary American Drug Overdose Epidemic"; Organisation for Economic Co-operation and Development, "Income Inequality Update."
85. For an overview and response, see Goldstein, "How to Cut the Prison Population."
86. U.S. government support for low-income housing trails far behind its counterparts in Europe. In England and France, for instance, publicly owned or financed housing accounts for more than 40 percent of the housing market. In the United States, it accounts for 1 percent. See Wacquant, *Urban Outcasts*. On the extremity of poverty-related problems in the United States more generally, see Ho, "The Contemporary American Drug Overdose Epidemic"; Organisation for Economic Co-operation and Development, "Income Inequality Update"; Smeeding, "Poor People."
87. Herring, "Complaint-Oriented Policing."
88. Austin et al., *Ending Mass Incarceration*.
89. Berger, Kaba, and Stein, "What Abolitionists Do."
90. Legal scholar Paul Butler provides one chilling example of an apparent reform that masked a darker reality: in Los Angeles, perceptions of the fairness of the police department improved after a pattern and practice investigation conducted by the U.S. Department of Justice, while use of force incidents actually increased. See Butler, "The System Is Working."
91. Berger, Kaba, and Stein, "What Abolitionists Do"; see also Kushner, "Are Prisons Necessary?"
92. Berger, Kaba, and Stein, "What Abolitionists Do"; Schenwar and Law, *Prison by Any Other Name*.
93. Gottschalk, *Caught*.
94. Butler, "The System Is Working," 1460.
95. Haney, *Criminality in Context*.
96. Jaggi et al., "The Relationship"; Neller et al., "The Relationship"; Western, "Lifetimes of Violence"; Western, *Homeward*; Wolff, Jing, and Siegel, "Patterns of Victimization."
97. For an excellent overview of much of this research, see Haney, *Criminality in Context*.
98. As of 2017, just 3.5 percent of all state prisoners were behind bars as a result of a drug possession conviction (Bronson and Carson, *Prisoners in 2017*, table 12). However, drug violations were the most serious conviction charge for nearly one in four (24 percent) of probationers (Kaeble, *Probation and Parole*, appendix table 4).
99. Lilley, "Did Drug Courts Lead"; Lilley, Stewart, and Tucker-Gail, "Drug Courts"; Sevigny, Pollack, and Reuter, "Can Drug Courts Help"; Walch, *Addicted to Courts*.
100. Tonry, *Sentencing Fragments*. See also Renaud, *Eight Keys to Mercy*, showing that the number of state prisoners who had been behind bars for at least ten years tripled from 1999 and 2015. By 2015, one in six state prisoners had been locked up for ten or more years.
101. Mauer and Nellis, *The Meaning of Life*.
102. See Pfaff, *Locked In*, for the explication of this argument.

103. Happily, Eugene Youngblood was released from prison on March 5, 2021, by Governor Jay Inslee after receiving a unanimous vote in favor of clemency from the Washington State Clemency and Pardons Board in 2019. Eugene is currently working with the Freedom Project to support youth.

104. Zehr, *Little Book*.

105. Angel et al., "Short-Term Effects"; Sherman et al., "Are Restorative Justice Conferences."

106. Sered, *Until We Reckon*; see also Haney, *Criminality in Context*; Jaggi et al., "The Relationship"; Neller et al., "The Relationship"; Western, "Lifetimes of Violence"; Western, *Homeward*.

Chapter 2

1. Seitz-Wald and Izadi, "Criminal Justice Reform."

2. Dagan and Telles, "Locked In?," 268.

3. Petersilia and Cullen, "Liberal but Not Stupid," 12.

4. Gottschalk, *Caught*.

5. Indeed, it is conceivable that the reform process itself has deepened the collective commitment to severely punishing people who were convicted of violent or sex offenses, as Gottschalk argues. However, I argue later in this chapter that we simply don't know whether rhetoric that legitimates reforms aimed only at the "nons" renders meaningful transformation of the criminal legal system less likely.

6. Pierson, "Increasing Returns."

7. Barkow, *Prisoners of Politics*; Campbell, "Ornery Alligators"; Campbell and Schoenfeld, "The Transformation of America's Penal Order"; Gottschalk, *Caught*; Page, *The Toughest Beat*.

8. Gottschalk, *Caught*; Justice Policy Institute, *For Better or for Profit*; Page, *The Toughest Beat*; Page, "Prisoners Officer Unions"; Petersilia and Cullen, "Liberal but Not Stupid."

9. Thorpe, "Perverse Politics."

10. Barkow, *Prisoners of Politics*; Davis, "The American Prosecutor." Barkow convincingly argues that the staunch opposition of prosecutor organizations to many reform efforts stems primarily from prosecutors' desire to retain the tough sentencing laws that enhance their leverage in plea negotiations, thereby enabling them to avoid going to trial in the vast majority of cases. On the power of prosecutorial associations, see also Campbell, "Ornery Alligators"; Lynch, *Hard Bargains*; Pfaff, *Locked In*.

11. Page, *The Toughest Beat*; Page, "Prisoners Officer Unions."

12. Barkow, *Prisoners of Politics*, 7.

13. In California, this occurred in the wake of the U.S. Supreme Court's 2011 *Brown v. Plata* ruling, which mandated that California significantly reduce its prison population. In this context, voters eventually approved several decarcerative reforms despite the opposition of the California Correctional Peace Officers Association and many law enforcement groups.

14. Porter, *Repurposing*.

15. Ibid., 1.

16. Hernandez, "New Jersey Eliminates"; Wiggins, "Bail Reform." In New York, bail reform was enacted but interest groups, including the New York Police Department, continue to seek to undermine it. McKinley, "The Bail Reform Backlash."

17. Barkow, *Prisoners of Politics,* 7.

18. Ibid; Davis, "Reimagining Prosecution."

19. Beckett, Reosti, and Knaphus, "The End of an Era"; Green, "U.S. Penal-Reform Catalysts."

20. Garland, *Punishment and Modern Society.*

21. Muhammad, *The Condemnation of Blackness.*

22. Eberhardt et al., "Seeing Black."

23. Edelman, *The Symbolic Uses of Politics.*

24. See Gottschalk, *Caught.*

25. Seeds, "Bifurcation Nation."

26. Ibid.

27. These findings appear in Beckett et al., "U.S. Criminal Justice Policy."

28. A majority of these decarcerative reforms pertain to drug possession.

29. Seeds, "Bifurcation Nation."

30. At the federal level, too, recent drug reforms have drawn a sharp line between people convicted of drug offenses and those convicted of more serious offenses. Specifically, the First Step Act reduces sentences for many people convicted of a drug crime and enables some prisoners to earn time off their sentence by participating in certain kinds of programming. Yet it also prohibits prisoners serving time for dozens of other offenses from earning additional time-off credits. Lopez, "The First Step Act, Explained."

31. Beckett, Reosti, and Knaphus, "The End of an Era."

32. Horswell, "A New Approach."

33. "A Sensible Call."

34. Rankin, "Drug Court Grads."

35. Wenger, "Sanford Backs Prison Reform."

36. "Reform Sentencing."

37. "Prison Sentences Revised."

38. Wade, "Governor Kasich."

39. Toda, "Something's Got to Give."

40. Haney, *Criminality in Context.*

41. Arthur Longworth's writings can be accessed at this website, http://www.arthurlongworth.com/.

42. This information was provided by Art's sister, Dawn, at Art's clemency hearing. See also Martin, "Writer's World."

43. In 2019, the O.K. Boy's Ranch settled a lawsuit filed by fourteen survivors. See Matassa, Murakami, and Postman, "O.K. Boys Ranch."

44. Mauer and Nellis, *The Meaning of Life.*

45. Ibid.

46. I am indebted to Craig Haney, whose discussion of the "myth of demonic agency" in the context of capital cases inspired my use of the phrase "myth of monstrosity." See Haney, "The Social Context."

47. Pilgrim, "The Brute Caricature."

48. Adamson, "Punishment after Slavery"; Alexander, *The New Jim Crow*; Blackmon, *Slavery by Another Name.*

49. Smiley and Fakunle, "From 'Brute' to 'Thug.'"

50. Pilgrim, "The Brute Caricature."

51. Muhammad, *The Condemnation of Blackness.*

52. Cohen, "Jim Crow's Drug War."

53. Chiricos and Eschholz, "The Racial and Ethnic Typification"; Devine and Elliot, "Are Racial Stereotypes Really Fading?"; Drakulich, "The Hidden Role"; Eberhardt et al., "Seeing Black."

54. Haney, *Criminality in Context*.

55. Kempf-Leonard, "Offense Specialization/Expertise."

56. Jaggi et al., "The Relationship"; Neller et al., "The Relationship"; Western, "Lifetimes of Violence"; Western, *Homeward*; Wolff, Jing, and Siegel, "Patterns of Victimization."

57. Reuter, "Systemic Violence."

58. Arkowitz, "Once a Sex Offender."

59. For example, the California Department of Corrections and Rehabilitation recently reported, "Examination of lifer parolee recidivism rates for a fiscal year cohort that was followed for a period of three years from release to parole shows that lifer parolees receive fewer new convictions within three years of being released to parole (4.8 vs. 51.5 percent, respectively). They also have a markedly lower return to prison recidivism rate than non-lifer parolees (13.3 vs. 65.1 percent, respectively)" (*Lifer Parole Recidivism Report*, 9). See also Weisberg, Mukamal, and Segall, *Life in Limbo*.

60. Truman and Langton, *Criminal Victimization*, table 7.

61. Centers for Disease Control and Prevention, *Injury Prevention and Control*.

62. Harrell et al., *Household Poverty*.

63. U.S. Department of Justice, *Crimes against Persons with Disabilities*.

64. Hanson et al., "The Impact of Crime Victimization"; Kilpatrick and Acierno, "Mental Health Needs"; Langton and Truman, *Socio-Emotional Impact*; Simmons, "Getting By."

65. Sledjeski, Speisman, and Dierker, "Does Number of Lifetime Traumas."

66. Vallas, *Disabled behind Bars*.

67. Clear, *Imprisoning Communities*.

68. Uggen, Manza, and Thompson, "Citizenship, Democracy."

69. Pettit and Western, "Mass Imprisonment."

70. Western, "Lifetimes of Violence"; Western, *Homeward*.

71. Jaggi et al., "The Relationship"; Neller et al., "The Relationship"; Wolff, Jing, and Siegel, "Patterns of Victimization."

72. Jaggi et al., "The Relationship."

73. See, for example, Smith, "England and Wales."

74. Ciaramella, "House Passes Bill." Many inferred that their primary motivation for doing so was to ensure the deportation of as many noncitizens as possible.

75. Hager, "When 'Violent Offenders' "; Kopp, "Is Burglary a Violent Crime?"

76. Kopp, "Is Burglary a Violent Crime?"

77. Ibid., 664.

78. Hager, "When 'Violent Offenders.' "

79. Ibid.

80. Smith and Merolla, "Black, Blue, and Blow."

81. Eberhardt et al., "Seeing Black."

82. Hofstader, "Introduction," 7.

83. Dvorak, "America's Missing Slave Memorials." The opening of the National Museum of African American History and Culture in Washington, D.C., in 2016 and the National Memorial for Peace and Justice in Montgomery, Alabama, in 2018 represent important steps toward more complete recognition of this history.

84. Madley, *An American Genocide*.

85. Centers for Disease Control and Prevention, "Preventing Intimate Partner Violence" defines intimate partner violence as "physical violence, sexual violence, stalking, or psychological harm by a current or former partner or spouse."
86. According to the Centers for Disease Control and Prevention, "Preventing Child Abuse and Neglect" "At least 1 in 7 children have experienced child abuse and/or neglect in the past year, and this is likely an underestimate."
87. Ibid.
88. Haney, *Criminality in Context*, ch. 4.
89. Sabik, "The Dangerous Shortage."
90. U.S. Department of Health and Human Services, *The AFCARS Report*.
91. The term "structural violence" is thought to have originated with sociologist Johan Galtung, "Violence, Peace, and Peace Research." See also Farmer, "On Suffering."
92. Gould and Wething, "U.S. Poverty Rates."
93. For example, of the thirty-three OECD member countries, only Chile, Turkey, Israel, and Mexico have higher poverty rates than the United States; only Turkey, Mexico, and Chile have higher levels of inequality as measured by the Gini coefficient. Organisation for Economic Co-operation and Development, Statistics Directorate, "Income Inequality Update."
94. "In most rich countries, the relative child poverty rate is 10 percent or less; in the United States, it is 21.9 percent" (Smeeding, "Poor People," 86).
95. Hagan and Petersen, "Criminal Inequality," 34; Sampson, *Toward a Theory*.
96. Grinshteyn and Hemenway, "Violent Death Rates."
97. Zimring and Hawkins, *Crime Is Not the Problem*; Hepburn and Hemenway, "Firearm Availability."
98. In more recent years, Alexander has emphasized the degree to which our response to violence must also be reimagined. See, for example, Alexander, "Reckoning with Violence."
99. Forman, "Racial Critiques"; Gottschalk, *Caught*; Pfaff, *Locked In*.
100. Carson, *Prisoners in 2018*. Alexander has argued that this measure of the import of the drug war ignores its broader significance: "Some people get caught up in the prison data. . . . They lose sight of the fact that the drug war was a game-changer culturally and politically. . . . The declaration and escalation of the war on drugs marked a moment in our history when a group of people defined by race and class was defined as the 'enemy.' A literal war was declared on them, leading to a wave of punitiveness that affected every aspect of our criminal justice system. . . . Counting heads in prison and jails often obscures that social and political history" (quoted in Hagar and Keller, "Everything You Think You Know").
101. As I argue in chapter 8, however, initiatives that address both addiction and the criminal legal response to drug use have greater potential to reduce the scope of the penal system.
102. Dagan and Telles, "Locked In?," 272.
103. Data provided by the Prison Policy Institute indicate that 41.5 percent of all incarcerated people (including jail inmates as well as state and federal prisoners) were behind bars due to a violent crime, and 19 percent for a drug crime, in 2016. See Wagner and Rabuy, *Mass Incarceration*.
104. PEW Center on the States, *Time Served*, appendix A.
105. National Conference of State Legislatures, *Drug Sentencing Trends*.

Chapter 3

1. Gramlich, *America's Incarceration Rate.*
2. Over the course of 2020, in the context of the pandemic, the number of people in prison and especially jails declined from approximately 2.1 to 1.8 million. However, there is reason to believe that much of this drop will be reversed, for two main reasons. First, prison populations declined in 2020 mainly because many courts ceased operations and a backlog of felony cases accrued. Most of these cases remain pending. The jail population has already begun rebounding as of winter 2021, as law enforcement activities resume some semblance of normalcy and jail managers return to pre-pandemic policies and practices (Kang-Brown, Montagnet, and Heiss, *People in Jail*). It thus appears likely that the impact of the pandemic on prison and jail populations will prove to have been temporary.
3. Calculations based on data from the Bureau of Justice Statistics Correctional Populations series and FBI, *Uniform Crime Reports* show that index crimes fell by 25 percent, while the incarcerated population dropped by just 8 percent from 2008 to 2018.
4. Nellis, *No End in Sight.*
5. For an overview of this movement, see Davis, "Reimagining Prosecution."
6. Medina, "The Progressive Prosecutors"; Nichanian, "Voters."
7. Kang-Brown et al., *The New Dynamics*; Subramanian, Henrichson and Kang-Brown, *In Our Own Backyard*; Oppel, "A Cesspool of a Dungeon."
8. Keller and Pearce, "This Small Indiana County."
9. Pfaff, *Locked In*, 72.
10. Lynch, *Hard Bargains.*
11. Many thanks to Lindsey Beach for her excellent and substantive contributions to this analysis.
12. Of the 2.2 million people incarcerated in the United States in 2014, 63.7% were housed in state prisons, while 26.7% and 9.6% were housed in local jails and federal prisons, respectively. Kaeble et al., *Correctional Populations,* table 1.
13. These include admissions stemming from the commission of felony offenses or violations of probation sentences. Admissions stemming from technical parole violations are determined by state correctional authorities and are therefore not included in our analyses. See also Blumstein and Beck, "Population Growth"; Raphael and Stoll, *Why*; Travis, Western, and Redburn, *The Growth of Incarceration.*
14. For more information about the data and methods used in this analysis, see appendix B.
15. Keller and Pearce, "This Small Indiana County."
16. Pfaff, *Locked In,* 72.
17. For an extended critique of the data and methods upon which Pfaff bases this claim, see Beckett, "Mass Incarceration."
18. Halliday et al., "Street-Level Bureaucracy"; Lipsky, *Street-Level Bureaucracy*; Silbey and Sarat, "Critical Traditions."
19. Davis, "The American Prosecutor"; Lynch, *Hard Bargains*; Pfaff, *Locked In*; Stuntz, *The Collapse.*
20. Ghandnoosh, *Delaying a Second Chance*; Gottschalk, *Caught.*
21. Local norms and organizational practices also powerfully shape discretionary decision-making and hence case outcomes. Bowers, "Integrity of the Game"; Chen, "In the Furtherance of Justice"; Lynch, *Hard Bargains*; Lynch and Omori, "Legal Change"; Sutton,

"Symbol and Substance"; Ulmer and Johnson, "Organizational Conformity"; Verma, "The Law-Before."
22. Lynch, *Hard Bargains*; see also Bazelon, *Charged*.
23. Brown and Jolivette, *A Primer*.
24. Bowers, "Integrity of the Game"; Chen, "In the Furtherance of Justice"; Sutton, "Symbol and Substance."
25. Mauer and Nellis, *The Meaning of Life*; Nellis, *Still Life*; Nellis, *No End in Sight*.
26. Lynch, *Hard Bargains*.
27. Owens, "Truthiness in Punishment."
28. In a handful of states, the punishment rates found in urban and nonurban counties are similar. In Massachusetts, the rural punishment rate in 2013 was .0144, the suburban rate was .0137, and urban rate was .0142. New Jersey follows a similar pattern, with a suburban rate of .036 and an urban rate of .037 (there are no rural counties in the state). In Maryland and Rhode Island, the rural punishment rate is lower than the urban rate (.039 vs. .057 and .02 vs. .028, respectively). In most locales, however, nonurban counties send a notably larger share of arrestees to prison, as Table 3.1 shows.
29. Weidner and Frase, "A County-Level Comparison"; Weidner and Frase, "Legal and Extralegal Determinants." Our analysis similarly suggests that roughly half of the variation in the use of prisons across counties is explained by state-level factors.
30. Beckett and Beach, "The Place of Punishment."
31. Kang-Brown et al., *The New Dynamics*; Subramanian, Henrichson, and Kang-Brown, *In Our Own Backyard*; Oppel, "A Cesspool of a Dungeon."
32. Grusky, Western, and Wimer, *The Great Recession*; Mather and Jarosz, *Poverty and Inequality*.
33. Kneebone, *The Changing Geography*; Kneebone and Berube, *Confronting Suburban Poverty*.
34. Edsall, "Reaching Out"; Kron, "Red State, Blue City."
35. Sampson and Loeffler, "Punishment's Place"; Sampson, *Great American City*.
36. Sampson and Loeffler, "Punishment's Place"; Sampson, *Great American City*; Sampson, "Criminal Justice Processing"; see also Simes, "Place and Punishment."
37. Sampson and Loeffler, *Great American City*, 28.
38. Simes, "Place and Punishment."
39. Lichter, Parisi, and Tacquino, "The Geography of Exclusion."
40. Mather and Jarosz, *Poverty and Inequality*.
41. Lichter, Parisi, and Tacquino, "The Geography of Exclusion."
42. Edsall, "Reaching Out."
43. Farrigan, *Poverty and Deep Poverty*.
44. Ibid.
45. Burton et al., "Inequality."
46. Ibid.
47. Ibid.
48. Ibid.
49. Myers et al., "Safety in Numbers."
50. Kneebone, *The Changing Geography*.
51. Kneebone and Berube, *Confronting Suburban Poverty*.
52. Lacy, "The New Sociology."
53. Raphael and Stoll, *Job Sprawl*.

54. Quinones, *Dreamland*; Reding, *Methland*.
55. Beckett and Western, "Governing Social Marginality"; Garland, *Punishment and Modern Society*.
56. Garland, *Punishment and Modern Society*, 134.
57. Beckett, *Making Crime Pay*; Davey, *The Politics of Prison Expansion*; Jacobs and Jackson, "On the Politics of Imprisonment"; Weaver, "Frontlash."
58. Beckett, *Making Crime Pay*; Beckett and Western, "Governing Social Marginality"; Kohler-Hausmann, *Getting Tough*; Soss, Fording, and Schram, *Disciplining the Poor*; Weaver, "Frontlash."
59. Drakulich, "The Hidden Role"; Unnever and Cullen, "The Social Sources."
60. For a recent discussion and iteration of this argument, see Beckett and Francis, "The Origins of Mass Incarceration." Comparative studies suggest that race, politics, and racial politics are especially likely to affect penal outcomes in the United States, which is characterized by a decentralized, federalist, and two-party system in which elites are incentivized to attempt to shape and respond to public opinion and where the sentiments of electorally important segments of the public may have undue weight. See Jacobs and Klebans, "Political Institutions"; Savelsberg, "Knowledge."
61. Jacobs and Carmichael, "The Politics of Punishment."
62. Beckett and Western, "Governing Social Marginality"; Jacobs and Carmichael, "The Politics of Punishment"; Jacobs and Helms, "Toward a Political Sociology"; Jacobs and Jackson, "On the Politics of Imprisonment"; Smith, "The Politics of Punishment"; Western, *Punishment and Inequality*.
63. Kron, "Red State, Blue City."
64. Badger, Bui, and Pearce, "The Election."
65. Brown and Socia, "Twenty-First Century Punitiveness"; Unnever and Cullen, "The Social Sources."
66. Helms and Jacobs, "The Political Context"; see also Sutton, "Symbol and Substance."
67. Of the 2.2 million people incarcerated in the United States in 2014, 63.7% were housed in state prisons, while 26.7% and 9.6% were housed in local jails and federal prisons, respectively (Kaeble et al., *Correctional Populations*, table 1).
68. For more information about the data and methods used in this analysis, see appendix B.
69. In this counterfactual analysis, we include observed felony crimes and drug arrests for each county type but manipulated the punishment rate to match that observed in large urban counties.
70. Kang-Brown et al., *The New Dynamics*; Subramanian, Henrichson, and Kang-Brown, *In Our Own Backyard*; Oppel, "A Cesspool of a Dungeon."

Chapter 4

1. Alexander, *The New Jim Crow*, 60.
2. These dynamics include bipartisan competition among elected officials seeking to establish their tough-on-drug credentials in the 1980s and 1990s; the enactment of asset forfeiture laws that incentivize drug law enforcement; the complicity of the news media in the reproduction of information and images that engender support for punitive drug policies (especially those focused on crack cocaine); and the enhancement of bureaucracies with a vested interest in the perpetuation of the drug war. See Alexander, *The New Jim Crow*; Baum,

Smoke and Mirrors; Beckett, "Media Depictions"; Beckett, *Making Crime Pay*; Benavie, *How the Drug War*; Gordon, *The Return of the Dangerous Classes*; Provine, *Unequal under the Law*; Reinarman and Levine, "Crack in Context."

3. Duster, "Pattern, Purpose"; Provine, *Unequal under the Law*; Reeves and Campbell, *Cracked Coverage*; Reinarman and Levine, "The Crack Attack."

4. Alexander, *The New Jim Crow*; Lynch, *Hard Bargains*; Reinarman and Levine, "The Crack Attack."

5. Beckett et al., "Drug Use"; Beckett, Nyrop, and Pfingst, "Race, Drugs and Policing"; Lynch and Omori, "Crack as Proxy."

6. Snyder, Cooper, and Mulako-Wangota, "Arrests in the United States." Because the majority of Latinx people are classified as White in the Uniform Crime Report arrest data, this is likely a conservative estimate of the degree to which the Black drug arrest rate outstrips the White arrest rate.

7. Katz and Goodnough, "The Opioid Crisis."

8. Lopez, "When a Drug Epidemic's Victims"; Netherland and Hansen, "The Drug War"; Shaw, "Photos Reveal"; Stone, "Is There 'Hope.'"

9. Netherland and Hansen, "White Opioids"; Netherland and Hansen, "The Drug War"; Stone, "Is There 'Hope.'"

10. Ghandnoosh and Anderson, *Opioids*.

11. This figure is based on analysis of data from the Bureau of Justice's Prisoners Series.

12. Unfortunately, the available data do not enable assessment of whether the number of people in jail as a result of a drug arrest has declined, as the most recent jail survey data that include information about offense type are for 2002. Thus, estimates of the share of the jail population generated since that time assume that the proportion of jail inmates who are behind bars as a result of a drug law violation have not changed. See Sawyer and Wagner, *Mass Incarceration*.

13. Consistent with the findings presented in chapter 3 regarding the geography of punishment in the contemporary United States, Blacks have benefited most from this decline in the use of prisons for drug law violations. Whereas the number of White and Latinx people in state prison for a drug charge fell by 12.4 and 34 percent, respectively, the number of Black people in state prisons as a result of a drug conviction fell most dramatically—by 53.5 percent. Beckett and Brydolf-Horwitz, "A Kinder, Gentler Drug War?" Of course, significant disparities in drug-related incarceration persist despite this recent trend.

14. Subramanian and Moreno, *Drug War Détente*.

15. Stellin, "Is the Drug War Over?"

16. Bronson and Carson, *Prisoners*, table 12.

17. For example, as of 2002, the most recent year for which data are available, 10.8 percent of all (convicted and unconvicted) jail inmates were confined as a result of drug charges. James, *Profile of Jail Inmates*, table 3.

18. Beletsky, "America's Favorite Antidote"; Boecker, "Charging Drug Sellers"; Goldensohn, "They Shared Drugs"; LaSalle, *An Overdose Death*; Shuler, "Overdose and Punishment."

19. Bennett and Holloway, "The Causal Connection."

20. Reuter, "Systemic Violence"; Reuter, "On the Multiple Sources."

21. Many thanks to Marco Brydolf-Horwitz for his excellent research assistance and thoughtful collaboration in this project.

22. A small number of drug courts allow participation of people arrested for delivery of small quantities of drugs on the premise that many low-level drug dealers and couriers engage in this behavior to support their drug habit.

23. Recent data indicate that more than half—54 percent—of those in state prisons are behind bars as a result of a violent offense; 11.5 percent are imprisoned as a result of a drug distribution or manufacture charge. Just 3.5 percent are confined due to a drug possession conviction. Bronson and Carson, *Prisoners,* table 12.

24. Bennett and Walters, "Drug Dealing."

25. LaSalle, *An Overdose Death.*

26. Drug Policy Alliance, *Drug Courts Are Not the Answer,* 2.

27. Beletsky, "America's Favorite Antidote."

28. Ibid., 870–71.

29. LaSalle, *An Overdose Death*, 2.

30. Data available at https://www.healthinjustice.org/drug-induced-homicide.

31. Beletsky, "America's Favorite Anecdote."

32. Ibid.

33. Ibid.

34. LaSalle, *An Overdose Death*, 2. Research on the question of whether these prosecutions will deter users from calling 911 when others overdose is limited. One recent study found that drug users' fear of summoning authorities persists even after the enactment of a Good Samaritan law among drug users. See Latimore and Bergstein, " 'Caught with a Body.' "

35. Lassiter, "Impossible Criminals."

36. Seeds, "Bifurcation Nation."

37. Casteel, "A Crackdown"; Hoffer and Alam, " 'Copping' in Heroin Markets."

38. Beckett and Beach, "The Place of Punishment."

39. Boerner, "Prosecution in Washington State," 202. More recently released data show that just 11 percent of the state's total drug possession arrests stem from King County. On the other hand, the overrepresentation of Black people in these cases is especially pronounced in King County. See Smith, "New Data Analysis."

40. Boerner, "Prosecution in Washington State," table 6.

41. Ibid., 205–6.

42. Beckett, "The Uses and Abuses"; see also Satterberg, "My Sister's Drug Addiction."

43. Beckett, "The Uses and Abuses."

44. See Lead National Support Bureau, available at https://www.leadbureau.org/.

45. Bazelon, *Charged.*

46. PEW Charitable Trusts, *Prisons and Crime.*

47. Maynard, "Kentucky Incarceration Rate Surges."

48. Kang-Brown et al., *The New Dynamics.*

49. Wolfson, "Unequal Justice."

50. Ibid.

51. Beckett et al., "U.S. Criminal Justice Policy", tables 1–4.

52. The literature on these courts is now quite large. Useful introductions include Berman, Feinblatt, and Glazer, *Good Courts*; Dorf and Fagan, "Problem-Solving Courts"; Hora, Schma, and Rosenthal, "Therapeutic Jurisprudence"; Nolan, *Reinventing Justice.*

53. Kaye, *Enforcing Freedom.*

54. Drug Policy Alliance, *Moving Away from Drug Courts.*

55. Gowan and Whetstone, "Making the Criminal Addict"; Kaye, *Enforcing Freedom*; Whetstone and Gowan, "Diagnosing the Criminal Addict."

56. Substance Abuse and Mental Health Services Administration, *Key Substance Use*.

57. Gowan and Whetstone, "Making the Criminal Addict"; Kaye, *Enforcing Freedom*; Marlowe, DeMatteo, and Festinger, "A Sober Assessment"; Tiger, *Judging Addicts*; Whetstone and Gowan, "Diagnosing the Criminal Addict."

58. Rottman and Casey, "Therapeutic Jurisprudence."

59. Ibid.

60. Ibid.

61. Tiger, *Judging Addicts*.

62. Stuart, *Down, out and under Arrest*.

63. Aos and Drake, "Evidence-Based Public Policy"; Latimer, Morton-Bourgon, and Chrétien, *A Meta-Analytic Examination*; Lowenkamp, Holsinger, and Latessa, "Are Drug Courts Effective"; Mitchell et al., "Assessing the Effectiveness"; Rossman et al., *The Multi-Site Adult Drug Court Evaluation*; Shaffer, "Looking inside the Black Box"; Wilson, Mitchell, and MacKenzie, "A Systematic Review."

64. Rempel et al., "Multi-Site Evaluation," 157.

65. Bowen and Whitehead, *Problem-Solving Courts*; Csete and Tomasini-Joshi, *Drug Courts*; Drug Policy Alliance, *Drug Courts Are Not the Answer*; Drugs, Security and Democracy Program, *Drug Courts in the Americas*; Walch, *Addicted to Courts*; King and Pasquarella, *Drug Courts*.

66. Drug Policy Alliance, *Drug Courts Are Not the Answer*, 66.

67. DeMatteo et al., "Outcome Trajectories."

68. Shah et al., "Addiction Severity Index Scores," 1271.

69. Rossman et al., *The Multi-Site Adult Drug Court Evaluation*, 80. See also Sevigny, Fuleihan, and Ferdik, "Do Drug Courts Reduce."

70. Sevigny, Fuleihan, and Ferdik, "Do Drug Courts Reduce"; Gallagher et al., "Further Evidence"; Csete, "Drug Courts in the United States."

71. U.S. Government Accountability Office, *Adult Drug Courts*.

72. Lilley, "Did Drug Courts Lead"; Lilley, Stewart, and Tucker-Gail, "Drug Courts and Net-Widening."

73. Lilley, DeVall, and Tucker-Gail, "Drug Courts and Arrest."

74. Ibid.

75. Ibid.; Marlowe, "Achieving Racial and Ethnic Fairness"; Howard, "Race, Neighborhood."

76. Møllmann and Mehta, *Neither Justice nor Treatment*, 3.

77. Lipari, Park-Lee, and Van Horn, *America's Need*.

78. Walch, *Addicted to Courts*.

79. Most of the people who are believed to suffer from a substance abuse disorder do not believe that they need treatment. However, nearly a million such people who desired such treatment in 2015 were unable to access it. Lipari, Park-Lee, and Van Horn, *America's Need*.

80. Tiger, *Judging Addicts*; see also Stone, "Is There 'Hope.'"

81. Beckett, Bell, and Stuart, "Dignity."

82. See Fagan, "Dignity Is the New Legitimacy"; Simon, *Mass Incarceration*; Simon, "The Second Coming of Dignity." Some legal scholars have argued that the weakness of the dignity principle in U.S. law enabled the emergence of mass incarceration and that efforts to tame the excesses of U.S. criminal law and limit the brutality of its penal systems will necessarily require incorporation of the dignity principle into its jurisprudence.

83. See especially Burns and Peyrot, "Tough Love"; Gowan and Whetstone, "Making the Criminal Addict"; Kaye, "Rehabilitating"; Kaye, *Enforcing Freedom*; Murphy, *Illness or Deviance?*; Tiger, "Race Class"; Tiger, *Judging Addicts*; Whetstone and Gowan, "Diagnosing the Criminal Addict."

84. On the importance of narrative autonomy, see Simon and Rosenbaum, "Dignifying Madness."

85. National Association of Drug Court Professionals, Drug Court Standards Committee, *Defining Drug Courts*.

86. Burns and Peyrot, "Tough Love"; Kaye, *Enforcing Freedom*; Whetstone and Gowan, "Diagnosing the Criminal Addict."

87. Burns and Peyrot, "Tough Love"; Kaye, *Enforcing Freedom*; Whetstone and Gowan, "Diagnosing the Criminal Addict."

88. National Association of Drug Court Professionals, Drug Court Standards Committee, *Defining Drug Courts*, 11–12.

89. Burns and Peyrot, "Tough Love"; Kaye, *Enforcing Freedom*; Whetstone and Gowan, "Diagnosing the Criminal Addict."

90. Forman, "Racial Critiques"; Gottschalk, *Caught*; Pfaff, *Locked In*.

Chapter 5

1. This phrase is taken from the concurring opinion signed by three Washington State Supreme Court justices in *State of Washington v. Anthony Allen Moretti* (No. 95263-9). The full sentence in which this phrase appears is as follows: "We should join the national movement favoring release upon a showing of rehabilitation and inject into our sentencing practices the exercise of mercy, compassion, and the fact that we know not a person's capacity to change" (38).

2. Herbert, *Too Easy to Keep*.

3. See Blumstein and Beck, "Population Growth"; Neal and Rick, "The Prison Boom"; Pfaff, *Locked In*; Raphael and Stoll, *Why*; Tonry, *Sentencing Fragments*; Western, *Punishment and Inequality*; Travis, Western, and Redburn, *The Growth of Incarceration*.

4. Raphael and Stoll, *Why*, 70.

5. Western, *Punishment and Inequality*, 44.

6. Blumstein and Beck, "Population Growth"; Pfaff, *Locked In*; Raphael and Stoll, *Why*; Tonry, *Sentencing Fragments*; Western, *Punishment and Inequality*; Travis, Western, and Redburn, *The Growth of Incarceration*.

7. Sentences of one year or more of confinement are typically served in prison rather than jail.

8. Blumstein and Beck, "Population Growth"; Raphael and Stoll, *Why*; Travis, Western, and Redburn, *The Growth of Incarceration*; Tonry, *Sentencing Fragments*; Western, *Punishment and Inequality*. For the opposite view, see Pfaff, "The Myths and Realities"; Pfaff, "Micro and Macro Causes"; Pfaff, *Locked In*.

9. See Patterson and Preston, "Estimating." Indeed, PEW Center on the States in *Time Served* concluded that in 2009, the observed measure underestimates time served for people convicted of violent offenses by an average of about two years.

10. See, for example, Raphael and Stoll, *Why*.

11. Ibid., 51.

12. Western, *Punishment and Inequality*, 45.

13. Travis, Western, and Redburn, *The Growth of Incarceration*.
14. Beckett et al., "U.S. Criminal Justice Policy," table 3.
15. Tonry, *Sentencing Fragments*.
16. Ghandnoosh, *Delaying a Second Chance*.
17. A recent Sentencing Project report shows that parole boards have become increasingly reluctant to release lifers on parole, despite low recidivism rates among this population. This trend has notably contributed to the growth of the lifer population. See Ghandnoosh, *Delaying a Second Chance*.
18. Pfaff, "The Myths and Realities"; Pfaff, "Micro and Macro Causes"; Pfaff, *Locked In*.
19. Pfaff, *Locked In*, 72.
20. Elsewhere, I suggest that Pfaff's use of the observational method and his failure to analyze time served by offense category may have contributed to his finding that time served did not increase. See Beckett, "Mass Incarceration."
21. Pfaff, *Locked In*, 55–56.
22. Chen, "In the Furtherance of Justice"; Lynch, *Hard Bargains*.
23. Brown and Jolivette, *A Primer*.
24. Ibid.
25. Horwitz, "Justice Department Set."
26. Gottschalk, "No Way Out?"; Mauer and Nellis, *The Meaning of Life*; Seeds, "Bifurcation Nation"; Nellis, *No End in Sight*.
27. Zimring and Hawkins, *The Scale of Imprisonment*; see also Raphael and Stoll, *Why*.
28. Ditton and Wilson, *Truth in Sentencing*.
29. Tonry, *Sentencing Fragment*, 78–83.
30. Lynch, *Hard Bargains*.
31. See, for example, Enns, *Incarceration Nation*; Lacey and Soskice, "American Exceptionalism"; Miller, *The Myth of Mob Rule*.
32. Miller, *The Myth of Mob Rule*, 8.
33. Van Dijk and van Kesteren, "The Prevalence."
34. While the U.S. homicide rate is notably higher than rates in other industrialized countries, it is far lower than the rates found in many parts of the world. Thus, while the United States is a world leader in incarceration, it is not among the countries with the highest homicide rates. International homicide data are compiled by the United Nations Office on Drugs and Crime.
35. Papachristos and Bastomski, "Connected in Crime."
36. Davey, *The Politics of Prison Expansion*; Zimring and Hawkins, *The Scale of Imprisonment*.
37. Centers for Disease Control and Prevention mortality data show that the Black homicide rate in 1950, for example, was more than eleven times higher than the White homicide rate (56.2 vs. 5 per 100,000 residents). See Grove and Hetzel, *Vital Statistics Rates*.
38. The homicide rate increased from under 2 per 100,000 residents in the early 1900s to 9.7 in 1933. *Sourcebook of Criminal Justice Statistics Online*, table 6.28.2012.
39. Imprisonment rates reached their pre–World War II peak in 1939, when 139 of every 100,000 residents lived behind bars. *Sourcebook of Criminal Justice Statistics* online, table 6.28.2012.
40. Both Uniform Crime Report data based on crimes known and the policy and victimization survey data show that the incidence of violent crime fell dramatically in the United States in recent decades. Zimring, *The Great American Crime Decline*.

41. Specifically, more conservative jurisdictions and those with larger Black populations tend to have higher incarceration rates. Jacobs and Carmichael, "The Politics of Punishment"; Jacobs and Helms, "Toward a Political Sociology"; Jacobs, and Klebans, "Political Institutions"; Jacobs and Jackson, "On the Politics of Imprisonment"; Smith, "The Politics of Punishment"; Western, *Punishment and Inequality*; Weidner and Frase, "Legal and Extralegal Determinants."
42. Ibid.
43. Changes to bail practices that require more defendants to stay in jail while they await adjudication have also contributed to the expansion of the jail population. A secular increase in the average number of prior convictions possessed by defendants may also contribute to the growth of jail and prison populations.
44. Lynch, *Hard Bargains*; Oppel, "Sentencing Shift"; Rakoff, "Why Innocent People Plead Guilty"; Weiser, "Trial by Jury."
45. Lynch, *Hard Bargains.*
46. Schauffler et al., "Court Statistics Project DataViewer."
47. Analysis of records included in the National Registry of Exonerations as of July 16, 2018, indicate that 398 of the 2,246 (17.7 percent) of registered exonerations involved cases in which defendants pled guilty, presumably for fear of the consequences of being convicted at trial.
48. Rakoff, "Why Innocent People Plead Guilty."
49. Beckett and Evans, *About Time.*
50. Travis, Western, and Redburn, *The Growth of Incarceration,* 101–2.
51. Ibid., 155.
52. Nagin, "Deterrence," 199.
53. Travis, Western, and Redburn, *The Growth of Incarceration,* 156.
54. Ibid., 143–45.
55. Farrington, "Developmental and Life-Course Criminology."
56. Sampson and Laub, "Life Course Desisters?"
57. Sered, *Until We Reckon.*
58. Travis, Western, and Redburn, *The Growth of Incarceration,* 155–56.
59. Ibid., 345.
60. Doob and Webster, "Countering Punitiveness"; Tonry and Farrington, "Punishment and Crime"; Zimring, *The Great American Crime Decline.*
61. PEW Charitable Trusts, *Prisons and Crime.* See also Lofstrom and Raphael, "Prison Downsizing"; Lofstrom and Raphael, "Incarceration and Crime"; Sundt, Salisbury, and Harmon, "Is Downsizing Prisons Dangerous?"
62. Ibid.
63. PEW Charitable Trusts, *Imprisonment.*
64. Tonry, *Sentencing Fragments.*
65. Center for Law and Global Justice, *Cruel and Unusual,* 25; Mauer and Nellis, *The Meaning of Life.*
66. Center for Law and Global Justice, *Cruel and Unusual.*
67. Appleton and Grover, "The Pros and Cons."
68. Mauer and Nellis, *The Meaning of Life.*
69. Ibid.
70. Carson and Sabol, *Aging.*
71. See National Institute of Corrections, *Correctional Health Care.*

72. Psick et al., "Baby Boomers."
73. See, for example, Ghandnoosh, *The Next Step*; Leigh et al., *A Matter of Time*; Mauer and Nellis, *The Meaning of Life*; Tonry, *Sentencing Fragments*.
74. Ghandnoosh, *U.S. Prison Decline*.
75. Frase, *Just Sentencing*.
76. American Law Institute, *Model Penal Code*.
77. Rhine, Petersilia, and Reitz, "Improving Parole Release."
78. Travis, Western, and Redburn, *The Growth of Incarceration*, ch. 12.
79. Tonry, *Sentencing Fragments*.
80. Beckett, Reosti, and Knaphus, "The End of an Era."
81. Ghandnoosh, *The Next Step*; Leigh et al., *A Matter of Time*; Mauer and Nellis, *The Meaning of Life*; Travis, Western, and Redburn, *The Growth of Incarceration*.
82. Mauer and Nellis, *The Meaning of Life*; Nellis, *No End in Sight*.
83. Leigh et al., *A Matter of Time*, 2.
84. See Ghandnoosh, "Minimizing the Maximum"; Mauer, "A Twenty Year Maximum."
85. For instance, the maximum allowable sentence in Norway is twenty-one years (Mauer, "A Twenty-Year Maximum"). The U.S. homicide rate (at 5 per 100,000 residents) is roughly eight times higher than the homicide rate in Norway (.6 per 100,000 residents) (United Nations Office on Drugs and Crimes, International Homicide Statistics Database). In Canada, the maximum allowable sentence is life with mandatory parole eligibility after twenty-five years; the homicide rate in Canada is 1.8 per 100,000 compared to 5 per 100,000 in the United States.
86. Nellis, *No End in Sight*.
87. Stuntz, *The Collapse*.
88. Martinson, "New Findings."
89. Travis, Western, and Redburn, *The Growth of Incarceration*, 192.
90. Drake, *Inventory*.
91. Heckman et al., *Understanding the Mechanisms*.
92. Travis, Western, and Redburn, *The Growth of Incarceration*, 345.
93. In states that have parole, parole boards have long served this function. As a result of recent U.S. Supreme Court decisions, some groups have the right to postconviction review even though their state has largely abolished parole.
94. Kuziemko, "How Should Inmates Be Released."
95. Renaud, *Grading the Parole Release Systems*.
96. Weisberg, Mukamal, and Segall, *Life in Limbo*.
97. The California Department of Corrections and Rehabilitation concluded, "Examination of lifer parolee recidivism rates for a fiscal year cohort that was followed for a period of three years from release to parole shows that lifer parolees receive fewer new convictions within three years of being released to parole (4.8 vs. 51.5 percent, respectively). They also have a markedly lower return to prison recidivism rate than non-lifer parolees (13.3 vs. 65.1 percent, respectively)", (*Lifer Parole Recidivism Report*, 9).
98. Ghandnoosh, *Delaying a Second Chance*. Ghandnoosh identifies a number of factors that explain this trend: parole boards' tendency to focus on the original offense rather than what the petitioner has accomplished since their conviction; legislative changes that extend the amount of time people must wait for subsequent hearings after being denied parole; gubernatorial appointments to parole boards that are intended to reduce parole grants; and the narrowing of petitioner's rights in the parole process.

99. Mitchell and Williams, "Compassionate Release Policy Reform."

100. Ibid.

101. Warner and Lucas, *Release Options*.

102. Washington State Department of Corrections, "Extraordinary Medical Placement."

103. Mitchell and Williams, "Compassionate Release Policy Reform."

104. Drinan, "Clemency in a Time of Crisis."

105. Ibid.

106. Ibid.

107. Robina Institute of Criminal Law and Criminal Justice, "New Model Penal Code."

108. Drake, *Inventory*; Kuziemko, "How Should Inmates Be Released."

109. Ghandnoosh, *Delaying a Second Chance*.

110. Rhine, Petersilia, and Reitz, "Improving Parole Release."

111. Robina Institute of Criminal Law and Criminal Justice, "New Model Penal Code."

112. Ibid., 98.

113. Rhine, Petersilia, and Reitz, "Improving Parole Release," 2.

114. Muhammad, *The Condemnation of Blackness*.

115. Sarat, *The Killing State*, 267.

116. See Haney, *Criminality in Context* for an extended discussion of the tension between the assumptions regarding individual agency and the large body of social scientific evidence that casts doubt upon this emphasis.

117. Haney, "The Social Context," 591.

118. See Haney, *Criminality in Context*, 290–312 for an extended discussion of the empirical weaknesses of the "not everybody" fallacy.

119. Haney, "Condemning the Other."

120. Lynch and Haney, "Looking across the Empathic Divide."

121. Ibid.

122. For an overview of this issue, see Gohara, "Grace Notes."

123. See Haney, *Criminality in Context*, 322–35 for a thoughtful argument for these measures.

124. National Association of Criminal Defense Lawyers, *The Trial Penalty*.

125. O'Hear and Wheelock, "Violent Crime."

126. Ibid.

127. I did not seek documentary evidence regarding childhood and early life experiences, but did obtain documentation of certain claims regarding the facts of legal cases. These are on file with the author.

128. Rakoff, "Why Innocent People Plead Guilty"; Reimer and Sabelli, "The Tyranny of the Trial Penalty."

129. Currently in Washington State, most prisoners are not eligible for parole. Instead, the Institutional Sentencing Review Board (ISRB) makes decisions regarding discretionary release for three relatively small groups of prisoners: (1) those who were sentenced prior to 1984; (2) those sentenced to more than twenty years for an offense they committed prior to the age of eighteen; and (3) those sentenced under the Determinate Plus Sentencing statute, which stipulates that people convicted of certain sex offenses receive a maximum life with the possibility of parole sentence. People falling outside of these categories do not have the opportunity to present a case for release to the ISRB, though they may petition the Washington State Clemency and Pardons Board to request commutation of their sentence (i.e., clemency). For clemency to occur, a petitioner must be granted a hearing, the Board must recommend commutation, and the governor must accept this recommendation.

This happens quite rarely. For example, the Board grants a hearing regarding roughly one-fourth of the petitions it receives; from 2013 to 2017, it recommended and the governor granted clemency in just twenty-two cases, an average of fewer than five cases per year. To put this number in context: 41 percent of all Washington State prisoners—nearly eight thousand people—are currently serving a sentence of ten years or more. As is true in other states, being granted clemency is akin to winning the lottery; the commutation system simply does not provide a meaningful relief valve. See Beckett and Evans, *About Time*.

130. Weisberg, Mukamal, and Segall, *Life in Limbo*; California Department of Corrections and Rehabilitation, *Lifer Parole Recidivism Report*, 9.
131. Herbert, *Too Easy to Keep*.
132. This description of the crime is taken from the plea agreement signed by Chris, his attorney, and the prosecuting attorney (document on file with the author).
133. Examples of his writing can be found on the website of the Marshall Project. See, e.g., https://www.themarshallproject.org/2020/05/28/in-prison-even-social-distancing-rules-get-weaponized.
134. For more about Chris's wedding, see Block, "Grateful for a Wedding in Prison."
135. In March of 2021, the Washington State Supreme Court invalidated the mandatory LWOP sentences imposed on two men who were nineteen and twenty years old at the time they committed aggravated murder, ruling that failure to consider the youthfulness of defendants younger than twenty-one is unconstitutional. As a result, an estimated fifty people serving LWOPs for crimes committed at the age of eighteen, nineteen, or twenty—including Jeff—are eligible for re-sentencing. The decision in this case can be accessed at https://documentcloud.adobe.com/link/review?uri=urn:aaid:scds:US:c978e861-e7df-401a-8737-cd96cfc92b49#pageNum=1.
136. In the letter describing the prosecutor's plea offer, Anthony's attorney wrote that the prosecutor was willing to stipulate that Anthony did not shoot the child if Anthony accepted the plea offer. Letter on file with the author.
137. Quoted in Marez, "Youngblood, Bailey Guilty of Murder." An attorney who represented Eugene in his appeal until April 1, 1998, later wrote in a letter to the Washington State Bar Association, "Although a great deal of testimony was presented showing the rancorous prior relationship between co-defendants Campbell and Bailey and the two victims and establishing that the victims were last seen alive leaving for their home in the company of Campbell and Bailey shortly before the murders, no such testimony was presented as to Eugene. To the contrary, the evidence showed he was not present when the victims were killed and had indeed never even met them. In the end, of the many dozens of witnesses who testified at trial, the state's case against Eugene was premised on the testimony of a single witness. This was Barbara Davis, a crack cocaine addict. During her original police interviews, Davis had not mentioned Eugene. Three months after the murders, however, when Davis was in custody on nine separate charges which would have resulted in a standard sentencing range of 108–144 months, Davis claimed to have seen Youngblood the night of the murders and heard him brag about committing them. In exchange for her testimony, the state allowed Davis to plead guilty to a single charge with a standard sentence of 51–64 months. Davis's testimony was directly contradicted by other witnesses."
138. Haney, "The Social Context." See also Haney, "Psychological Secrecy."
139. National Institute of Corrections, *Correctional Health Care*.
140. The majority of crime survivors do not receive the services they need even if they do report their victimization to authorities. Violence survivors who are poor and/or of color

are especially unlikely to receive needed services following victimization. See Alliance for Safety and Justice, *Crime Survivors Speak*; Herman, *Parallel Justice*; Sered, *Until We Reckon*; Stillman, "Black Wounds Matter."

Chapter 6

1. Centers for Disease Control and Prevention, *Injury Prevention and Control*; Harrell et al., *Household Poverty*; Truman and Langton, *Criminal Victimization*, table 7; U.S. Department of Justice, *Crimes against Persons with Disabilities*.
2. Hertz, "The Debate."
3. Hanson et al., "The Impact of Crime Victimization"; Kilpatrick and Acierno, "Mental Health Needs"; Langton and Truman, *Socio-emotional Impact of Violent Crime*.
4. Simmons, "Getting By."
5. Cutler, Lleras-Muney, and Vogl, "Socio-economic Status and Health"; Flett et al., "Traumatic Events"; Sledjeski, Speisman, and Dierker, "Does Number of Lifetime Traumas"; Ullman and Siegel, "Traumatic Events."
6. Corso et al., "Medical Costs"; Hanson et al., "The Impact of Crime Victimization"; Kilpatrick and Acierno, "Mental Health Needs"; Langton and Truman, *Socio-emotional Impact of Violent Crime*.
7. Travis, "Summoning the Superheroes."
8. Sered, *Until We Reckon*.
9. Herman, *Parallel Justice*.
10. Sered, *Until We Reckon*.
11. Bennett, Goodman, and Dutton, "Systemic Obstacles"; Orth, "The Effects of Legal Involvement"; Parsons and Bergin, "The Impact of Criminal Justice Involvement."
12. Englebrecht, Mason and Adams, "The Experience."
13. Alliance for Safety and Justice, *Crime Survivors Speak*.
14. Ibid.
15. Stillman, "Black Wounds Matter."
16. For example, consider the Alliance for Safety and Justice, which you can read about here: https://allianceforsafetyandjustice.org/.
17. Jaggi et al., "The Relationship"; Neller et al., "The Relationship"; Western, "Lifetimes of Violence"; Western, *Homeward*; Wolff, Jing, and Siegel, "Patterns of Victimization."
18. Jaggi et al., "The Relationship."
19. Heckman et al., *Understanding the Mechanisms*.
20. Quoted in Ghandnoosh, "Minimizing the Maximum," 150.
21. Drake, *Inventory*.
22. Sharkey, Torrats-Espinosa, and Takyar, "Community and the Crime Decline."
23. Zehr, *Little Book of Restorative Justice*.
24. Ibid.
25. Ibid.
26. Llewellyn and Howse, *Restorative Justice*.
27. Zehr, *Little Book of Restorative Justice*.
28. Daly and Immarigeon, "The Past, Present, and Future."
29. Zehr, *Changing Lenses*.
30. Pranis, "Restorative Justice."
31. Umbreit et al., "Restorative Justice in Action."

32. Daly and Immarigeon, "The Past, Present, and Future."
33. Stuart, *Building Community Justice Partnerships.*
34. Griffiths, "Sanctioning and Healing," 201.
35. Pranis, "Restorative Justice."
36. Sliva and Lambert, "Restorative Justice Legislation."
37. Karp and Frank, "Anxiously Awaiting."
38. For example, Sered reports in *Until We Reckon* that more than 90 percent of the survivors offered a restorative justice alternative to the traditional legal process accepted that offer.
39. Umbreit and Armour, *Restorative Justice Dialogue.*
40. Umbreit et al., "Restorative Justice in Action"; Wilson, Olaghere, and Kimbrell, *Effectiveness of Restorative Justice Principles.*
41. Umbreit et al., "Restorative Justice in Action."
42. Angel et al., "Short-Term Effects."
43. Wilson, Olaghere, and Kimbrell, *Effectiveness of Restorative Justice Principles*, 2.
44. Beven et al., "Restoration or Renovation?"
45. Ibid.
46. Umbreit et al., "Restorative Justice in Action."
47. Sered, *Until We Reckon.*
48. Umbreit et al., "Restorative Justice in Action."
49. Sherman et al., "Are Restorative Justice Conferences Effective," 1.
50. Bradshaw and Roseborough, "Restorative Justice Dialogue."
51. Umbreit et al., "Restorative Justice in Action."
52. Wilson, Olaghere, and Kimbrell, *Effectiveness of Restorative Justice Principles.*
53. Umbreit, Vos, and Coates, *Restorative Justice Dialogue.*
54. Wilson, Olaghere, and Kimbrell, *Effectiveness of Restorative Justice Principles.*
55. Sherman et al., "Are Restorative Justice Conferences Effective."
56. McCold and Wachtel, *Restorative Policing Experiment.*
57. See also Sered, *Until We Reckon.*
58. Beckett and Kartman, *Violence, Mass Incarceration, and Restorative Justice.*
59. Ibid.
60. Bloch, "Reconceptualizing Restorative Justice."
61. Greenwood and Umbreit, *National Survey*; Center for Health and Justice, *No Entry.*
62. Wood, "Why Restorative Justice."
63. Angel et al., "Short-Term Effects"; McCold and Wachtel, *Restorative Policing Experiment*; Sherman et al., "Are Restorative Justice Conferences."
64. Sered, *Until We Reckon.*
65. Payne and Welch, "Restorative Justice in Schools."
66. Travis, Western, and Redburn, *The Growth of Incarceration.*
67. Herman, *Parallel Justice.*

Chapter 7

1. Sawyer and Wagner, "Mass Incarceration." These figures have undoubtedly changed as a result of the pandemic, though it is difficult to know if these changes will be lasting.
2. Kaeble, *Probation and Parole,* appendix table 4. As of 2016, 24 percent of probationers were under supervision as a result of a drug law violation.

3. Alexander, *The New Jim Crow*; Duster, "Pattern, Purpose and Race"; Lynch, "Crack Pipes and Policing"; Lynch, *Hard Bargains*.

4. Snyder, Cooper, and Mulako-Wangota, "Arrests in the United States." Because the majority of Latinx people are classified as White in the Uniform Crime Report arrest data, this is likely a conservative estimate of the degree to which the Black drug arrest rate outstrips the White.

5. Nearly 66 percent of all prisoners meet the medical criteria for an alcohol or drug disorder. Of these, only 10 percent receive any kind of professional treatment while behind bars. While 22.7 percent of incarcerated people with substance use disorders participate in mutual support/peer counseling, and 14.2 percent receive drug education, these programs have not been found to produce long-term behavioral changes among those in need of treatment. See National Center on Addiction and Substance Abuse at Columbia University, *Behind Bars II*.

6. Ranapurwala et al., "Opioid Overdose Mortality."

7. Keck and Correa-Cabera, "U.S. Drug Policy." In recent years, for example, highly potent fentanyl analogues and methamphetamine have flooded the market, despite decades of enhanced border control and supply reduction efforts. See, for example, Goodnough, "A New Drug Scourge."

8. Travis, Western, and Redburn, *The Growth of Incarceration*.

9. Reuter, "Systemic Violence."

10. Substance Abuse and Mental Health Services Administration, *Key Substance Use*. An additional 12 million struggle with alcohol dependence.

11. Ghandnoosh and Anderson, *Opioids*.

12. Ho, "The Contemporary American Drug Overdose Epidemic."

13. Centers for Disease Control and Prevention, *Opioid Overdose*.

14. Engel, "This Chart"; Goldstein, "The Drugs/Violence Nexus"; Reuter, "Systemic Violence"; Reuter, "On the Multiple Sources."

15. Bennett and Holloway, "The Causal Connection."

16. Bronson et al., *Drug Use*.

17. Fischer et al., "Heroin Assisted Treatment"; Killiasand and Aebi, "The Impact of Heroin Prescription"; Löbmann and Verthein, "Explaining the Effectiveness." For a fascinating illustration of how this might work, listen to the podcast *Cited: The Heroin Clinic* (Episode 41, March 9, 2017).

18. It is worth noting, though, that Oregon voters elected in November 2020 to decriminalize possession of small amounts of all illicit drugs and legalize psychedelic mushrooms for use in therapeutic settings. Acker, "Oregon Becomes First State."

19. Hughes and Stevens, "What Can We Learn."

20. Ibid.

21. Shade, "HB 1269."

22. Kohler-Haussmann, *Misdemeanorland*; Maruna, "Commentary."

23. Beckett and Harris, "On Cash and Conviction"; Harris, *A Pound of Flesh*; Harris, Evans, and Beckett, "Drawing Blood."

24. Beckett and Harris, "On Cash and Conviction"; Harris, *A Pound of Flesh*; Harris, Evans, and Beckett, "Drawing Blood."

25. Roussell and Gascón, "Defining 'Policeability'"; Gascón and Roussell, *The Limits of Community Policing*.

26. Human Rights Watch, *Every 25 Seconds*.

27. Vitale, *The End of Policing*.
28. Lennard, "Oregon's Decriminalization Vote."
29. Shepherd, "Portlanders Call 911."
30. Herring, "Complaint-Oriented Policing"; see also Beckett and Herbert, *Banished*; Stuart, *Down, out and under Arrest*.
31. NENA: The 9-1-1 Association, *9-1-1 Statistics*.
32. King County, *Familiar Faces*.
33. Travis, Western, and Redburn, *The Growth of Incarceration*.
34. Dobbie, Goldin, and Yang, "The Effects of Pretrial Detention."
35. Couloute, *Nowhere to Go*.
36. Pettit and Sykes, *State of the Union 2017: Incarceration*
37. Crowley and Chung, *Congress Can Lead*.
38. See the LEAD National Bureau website, https://www.leadbureau.org/.
39. I collected and analyzed a variety of data sources in the course of evaluation. These include foundational documents, such as LEAD's Memorandum of Understanding, protocol, and concept paper; observations of LEAD-affiliated SPD and Department of Corrections officers and sergeants and case managers as they conducted LEAD-related work; observation of the LEAD operations work group and policy group meetings; and interviews with LEAD stakeholders and participants. I collected and analyzed these data during the summer and fall of 2013. This process evaluation was funded by the Ford Foundation.
40. This research has involved ninety-nine interviews with JustCARE participants, as well as approximately fifty interviews with stakeholders, outreach responders, leadership, and community partners. It includes analysis of administrative data provided by participating organizations. Many thanks to Marco Brydolf-Horwitz, Devin Collins, Allison Goldberg, and Aliyah Turner for their illuminating and thoughtful contributions to this project.
41. Although Seattle's White arrest rate was not unusually high, the Black drug arrest rate was far higher than the national average. See Beckett, *Race and Drug Law Enforcement,* tables 1 and 10.
42. Beckett, *Race and Drug Law Enforcement*.
43. See Beckett et al., "Drug Use, Drug Possession Arrests"; Beckett, Nyrop, and Pfingst, "Race, Drugs and Policing"; Beckett, *Race and Drug Law Enforcement*.
44. For general overviews of harm reduction, see Marlatt, *Harm Reduction*; Nadelmann, "Thinking Seriously"; MacCoun, "Toward a Psychology of Harm Reduction."
45. Law Enforcement Assisted Diversion (LEAD). *Referral and Diversion Protocol,* November 2018.
46. Malm, Perrone, and Magaña, *Law Enforcement Assisted Diversion (LEAD) External Evaluation*.
47. For general overviews of harm reduction, see Marlatt, *Harm Reduction*; Nadelmann, "Thinking Seriously"; MacCoun, "Toward a Psychology of Harm Reduction."
48. Interview with Lisa Daugaard, director of the Public Defender Association, June 21, 2013.
49. Evans, "Lessons from Seattle."
50. Law Enforcement Assisted Diversion (LEAD). *Referral and Diversion Protocol*.
51. Malm, Perrone, and Magaña, *Law Enforcement Assisted Diversion (LEAD) External Evaluation*.
52. Clifasefi, Lonczak, and Collins, "Seattle's Law Enforcement Assisted Diversion (LEAD) Program."

53. Malm, Perrone, and Magaña, *Law Enforcement Assisted Diversion (LEAD) External Evaluation.*

54. Collins, Longczak, and Clifasefi, "Seattle's Law Enforcement Assisted Diversion (LEAD)."

55. Kroman, "Seattle's Arrest Alternative."

56. LEAD continues to function independently in other neighborhoods outside of the JustCARE context.

57. O'Connor, *The Hidden Disaster of State.*

58. Tiger, *Judging Addicts.*

59. Kaye, *Enforcing Freedom*; Tiger, *Judging Addicts.*

60. While LEAD participants may be subject to arrest and incarceration for committing other offenses while participating in LEAD, they are not subjected to compliance requirements by LEAD and are not incarcerated for ongoing drug use.

61. DeMatteo et al., "Outcome Trajectories in Drug Court"; Shah et al., "Addiction Severity Index Scores."

62. Although case managers may discuss clinical issues with other stakeholders in operational workgroup meetings, prosecutors sign an operating agreement that they won't use what they hear at those meetings as evidence against somebody in a prosecution.

63. Fedders, "Opioid Policing."

64. Purnell and Stahly-Butts, "The Police Can't Solve the Problem."

65. Clifasefi, Lonczak, and Collins, "Seattle's Law Enforcement Assisted Diversion (LEAD) Program."

66. Roberts, "LEAD Us Not into Temptation."

67. Ibid.

68. Fedders, "Opioid Policing," 439. More generally, Fedders's treatment of LEAD as a form of "opioid policing" is difficult to reconcile with its origins in race-based litigation that demonstrated massive racial disparities in Seattle drug law enforcement stemmed from its overwhelming focus on people who used and sold crack cocaine.

69. Data for Seattle LEAD are cited earlier in this chapter. See also Malm, Perrone, and Magaña, *Law Enforcement Assisted Diversion (LEAD) External Evaluation.*

70. See the LEAD National Bureau website, https://www.leadbureau.org/.

71. Substance Abuse and Mental Health Services Administration, *Key Substance Use.*

72. Frakt, "Spend a Dollar."

73. Ghandnoosh and Anderson, *Opioids.*

74. Ibid.

75. Wen, Druss, and Cummings, "Effect of Medicaid Expansions."

76. National Center on Addiction and Substance Abuse at Columbia University, *Behind Bars II.* This study found that 1.5 million of the 2.3 million people who were incarcerated at the time of the study met the strict *DSM-IV* medical criteria for addiction. Another 458,000 did not, but had histories of substance use issues and were under the influence of alcohol or another substance at the time of their crime, committed their offense to get money to buy drugs, were incarcerated for an alcohol or drug law violation, or shared some combination of these characteristics. This report also found that only 11.2 percent of the 64.5 percent of prison and jail inmates who met clinical diagnostic criteria for a substance use disorder in 2006 had received any type of professional treatment since admission. Of those who do receive treatment, few receive evidence-based services.

77. Ghandnoosh and Anderson, *Opioids.*

78. Ibid.

79. Ibid. Just 0.2 percent had received pharmacological (i.e., medication-assisted) treatment.
80. Christie et al., *The President's Commission*; Kilmer et al., *Considering Heroin-Assisted Treatment*; National Academies of Sciences, Engineering and Medicine, *Medications for Opioid Use Disorder*.
81. Kilmer et al., *Considering Heroin Assisted Treatment,* viii; see also Fischer et al., "Heroin Assisted Treatment."
82. For an extended discussion of the implications of this finding for the medical model of addiction, see Hari, *Chasing the Scream*.
83. Quoted in Ghandnoosh and Anderson, *Opioids,* 11.
84. Killias and Aebi, "The Impact of Heroin Prescription"; Kilmer et al., *Considering Heroin Assisted Treatment*; Löbmann and Verthein, "Explaining the Effectiveness."
85. Reuter and Schnoz, *Assessing Drug Problems*; European Monitoring Centre for Drugs and Drug Addiction, *New Heroin Assisted Treatment*.
86. Killias and Aebi, "The Impact of Heroin Prescription"; Kilmer et al., *Considering Heroin Assisted Treatment*; Löbmann and Verthein, "Explaining the Effectiveness"; Reuter and Schnoz, *Assessing Drug Problems*; European Monitoring Centre for Drugs and Drug Addiction, *New Heroin Assisted Treatment*.
87. Boyd et al., "Telling Our Stories." For an excellent account of the impact of the opening and subsequent closure of the first heroin clinic in British Columbia, listen to the podcast *Cited: The Heroin Clinic* (Episode 41, March 9, 2017).
88. Kilmer et al., *Considering Heroin Assisted Treatment*.
89. Kampman, "The Treatment of Cocaine Use Disorder."
90. Barak, *Gimme Shelter*; Harvey, *The Condition of Postmodernity*; Wolch and Dear, *Landscapes of Despair*.
91. Wolch and Dear, *Landscapes of Despair*.
92. The federal minimum wage remained at $3.35 an hour between 1980 and 1990. Consequently, the real value of the minimum wage fell by about 30 percent over the decade. See Morris and Western, "Inequality"; Burt, *Over the Edge*.
93. Hackworth, *The Neoliberal City*; Lees and Wyly, *Gentrification*; Smith, *The New Urban Frontier*.
94. Wolch and Dear, *Malign Neglect*.
95. Joint Center for Housing Studies of Harvard University, *The State of the Nation's Housing 2003*.
96. Ibid.
97. Wolch and Dear, *Malign Neglect*.
98. Western Regional Advocacy Project, *Without Housing*.
99. U.S. government support for low-income housing trails far behind that in Europe. In England and France, for instance, publicly owned or financed housing accounts for more than 40 percent of the housing market. In the United States, it accounts for 1 percent. See Wacquant, *Urban Outcasts*.
100. Gilderbloom and Applebaum, *Rethinking Rental Housing*; National Low Income Housing Coalition, *The Crisis*.
101. Blasi, "Policing Our Way."
102. Brydolf-Horwitz, "Risk, Property Rights"; Reosti, "We Totally Go Subjective."
103. National Alliance to End Homelessness, *A Plan*.
104. Larimer et al., "Health Care and Public Service Use."
105. Collins et al., "Project-Based Housing First."

Chapter 8

1. These protests may have involved record-setting numbers of people. Buchanan, Bui, and Patel, "Black Lives Matter."
2. For an excellent overview of much of this research, see Haney, *Criminality in Context*.
3. California Department of Corrections and Rehabilitation, *Lifer Parole Recidivism Report*; Weisberg, Mukamal, and Segall, *Life in Limbo*.
4. Lilley, "Did Drug Courts Lead"; Sevigny, Pollack and Reuter, "Can Drug Courts Help"; Walch, *Addicted to Courts*.
5. Lilley, Stewart, and Tucker-Gail, "Drug Courts."
6. Mauer and Nellis, *The Meaning of Life*.
7. Tonry, *Sentencing Fragments*.
8. Mauer and Nellis, *The Meaning of Life*.
9. Alternatively, the enactment of a twenty-year maximum sentence could be made retroactive.
10. Haney, *Criminality in Context*.
11. Angel et al., "Short-Term Effects"; Sherman et al., "Are Restorative Justice Conferences Effective."
12. Haney, *Criminality in Context*; Jaggi et al., "The Relationship"; Neller et al., "The Relationship"; Western, "Lifetimes of Violence"; Western, *Homeward*.
13. Maruschak and Berzofsky, *Medical Problems*.
14. Calculation based on data presented in Bronson and Carson, *Prisoners in 2017*, table 8.
15. Gonnerman, "How Prisons and Jails Can Respond"; Rich, Allen, and Nimoh, "We Must Release Prisoners."
16. Blackwell and Longworth, "What Coronavirus Quarantine Looks Like."
17. Unlock the Box, *Solitary Confinement Is Never the Answer*.
18. These issues are succinctly summarized in National Academies of Sciences, Engineering and Medicine, *Decarcerating Correctional Facilities during COVID-19*. See also Saloner et al., "COVID-19 Cases and Deaths." For updates about the impact of Covid-19 in U.S. prisons and jails, see Dolovich and Littman, COVID-19 Behind Bars Data Project and Marshall Project, "A State by State Look."
19. Saloner et al., "COVID-19 Cases and Deaths."
20. Many departments of correction are not testing people who show symptoms, and many are not investigating the cause of death when an imprisoned person dies, thus ensuring that the official numbers are a dramatic undercount. See Schwartzapfel, Park, and Demillo, *One in Five Prisoners in the United States Has Had Covid-19*.
21. Ibid.
22. Vansickle, "A New Tactic."
23. Kang-Brown, Montagnet, and Heiss, *People in Jail and Prison*.
24. Kois, "America Is a Sham."

Appendix A

1. Beckett et al., "U.S. Criminal Justice Policy."
2. Tiger, "Race, Class"; Tiger, *Judging Addicts*.
3. Lilley, "Did Drug Courts Lead"; Lilley, Stewart, and Tucker-Gail, "Drug Courts"; Walch, *Addicted to Courts*.

Appendix B

1. Of the 2.2 million people incarcerated in the United States in 2014, 63.7% were housed in state prisons, and 26.7% and 9.6% were housed in local jails and federal prisons, respectively. Kaeble et al., *Correctional Populations*, table 1.

2. See Blumstein and Beck, "Population Growth"; Raphael and Stoll, *Why Are So Many Americans*; Travis, Western, and Redburn, *The Growth of Incarceration.*

3. In most states, people sentenced to less than one year of confinement serve their sentence in jail, while those sentenced to a year or more serve their time in prison. However, in a few states with combined jail/prison systems, everyone serves their sentence in a state facility. Moreover, as our case studies make plain, an increasing number of people sentenced to more than one year of confinement are held in county jails. To make the data comparable across states, we include only admissions that involve twelve or more months of confinement. See also Raphael and Stoll, *Why Are So Many Americans*; Western, *Punishment and Inequality.*

4. Beckett and Beach, "The Place of Punishment."

5. County-level UCR arrest data were unavailable for Florida and Illinois. For these states, arrest data from state police departments were used instead.

6. Studies that rely on NCRP data are unable to include all states due to data limitations; those that focus on more recent years are able to include more. Recent studies include a number of findings similar to those presented here. For example, the PEW Center on the States, *Time Served* study of trends in time served draws on data from thirty-five states; Raphael and Stoll, *Why Are So Many Americans* utilize a sample of thirty-four states. Because the states that do provide usable data are quite varied, these and other researchers use NCRP data to draw inferences about the national pattern.

7. See Monnat, "Factors," for more information about these measures.

8. Rodgers and Cage, "Full US 2012 Election."

9. See Beckett and Beach, "Understanding the Place," appendix D.

Bibliography

Acker, Lizzy. "Oregon Becomes First State to Legalize Psychedelic Mushrooms." *Oregonian*, November 4, 2020. https://www.oregonlive.com/politics/2020/11/oregon-becomes-first-state-to-legalize-psychedelic-mushrooms.html.

Adamson, Christopher. "Punishment after Slavery: Southern State Penal Systems, 1865–1890." *Social Problems* 30, no. 5 (1983): 555–69.

Alexander, Michelle. *The New Jim Crow: Mass Incarceration in the Age of Colorblindness.* New York: New Press, 2010.

Alexander, Michelle. "Reckoning with Violence." *New York Times,* March 3, 2019.

Alliance for Safety and Justice, *Crime Survivors Speak: The First-Ever National Survey of Victims' Views of Safety and Justice.* https://allianceforsafetyandjustice.org/wp-content/uploads/documents/Crime%20Survivors%20Speak%20Report.pdf.

American Law Institute, Model Penal Code: Sentencing, Draft No. 1, Section 1.02, 2, 2007.

Angel, Caroline M., Lawrence W. Sherman, Heather Strang, Barak Ariel, Sarah Bennett, Nova Inkpen, Anne Keane, and Therese S. Richmond. "Short-Term Effects of Restorative Justice Conferences on Post-Traumatic Stress Symptoms among Robbery and Burglary Victims." *Journal of Experimental Criminology* 10, no. 3 (2014): 291–307.

Aos, Steve, Marna Miller, and Elizabeth Drake. "Evidence-Based Public Policy Options to Reduce Future Prison Construction, Criminal Justice Costs, and Crime Rates: Individual State Developments." *Federal Sentencing Reporter* 4 (2006): 275–90.

Appleton, Catherine, and Brent Grover. "The Pros and Cons of Life without Parole." *British Journal of Criminology* 47 (2007): 597–615.

Arkowitz, Hal. "Once a Sex Offender, Always a Sex Offender? Maybe Not." *Scientific American,* April 1, 2008.

Austin, James, Eric Cadora, Todd Clear, Kara Dansky, Judith Greene, Vanita Gupta, Marc Mauer, Nicole Porter, Susan Tucker, and Malcolm Young. *Ending Mass Incarceration: Charting a New Justice Reinvestment.* New York: Justice Strategies, 2015.

Badger, Emily, Quoctrung Bui, and Adam Pearce. "The Election Highlighted Growing Rural-Urban Split." *New York Times,* November 11, 2016.

Barak, Gregg. *Gimme Shelter: A Social History of Homelessness in Contemporary America.* Westport, CT: Praeger, 1992.

Barkow, Rachel Elise. *Prisoners of Politics: Breaking the Cycle of Mass Incarceration.* Cambridge, MA: Harvard University Press, 2019.

Bazelon, Emily. *Charged: The New Movement to Transform American Prosecution and End Mass Incarceration.* New York: Penguin Random House, 2019.

Baum, Dan. *Smoke and Mirrors: The War on Drugs and the Politics of Failure.* Boston: Little, Brown, 1996.

Beckett, Katherine. *Making Crime Pay: Law and Order in Contemporary American Politics.* New York: Oxford University Press, 1997.

Beckett, Katherine. "Mass Incarceration and Its Discontents." *Contemporary Sociology: A Journal of Reviews* 47, no. 1 (2018): 11–23.

Beckett, Katherine. "Media Depictions of Drug Abuse: The Impact of Official Sources." *Journal of Research in Political Sociology* 7 (1995): 161–82.

Beckett, Katherine. "The Politics, Peril and Promise of Criminal Justice Reform in the Context of Mass Incarceration." *Annual Review of Criminology* 1 (2018): 235–59.

Beckett, Katherine. *Race and Drug Law Enforcement in Seattle.* Report Prepared for the ACLU Drug Law Reform Project and the Defender Association, 2008.

Beckett, Katherine. "The Uses and Abuses of Police Discretion: Toward Harm Reduction Policing." *Harvard Law & Policy Review* 10 (2016): 77–100.

Beckett, Katherine, and Lindsey Beach. "The Place of Punishment in 21st Century America: Understanding the Persistence of Mass Incarceration." *Law and Social Inquiry* 46, no. 1 (2021): 1–31.

Beckett, Katherine, and Lindsey Beach. "Understanding the Place of Punishment: Disadvantage, Politics and the Geography of Imprisonment in 21st Century America." *Law & Policy* 43 (2021): 5–29.

Beckett, Katherine, Lindsey Beach, Anna Reosti, and Emily Knaphus. "U.S. Criminal Justice Policy and Practice in the 21st Century: Toward the End of Mass Incarceration?" *Law & Policy* 40, no. 4 (2018): 321–45.

Beckett, Katherine, Monica Bell, and Forrest Stuart. "Dignity and the Management of Addiction." Unpublished manuscript.

Beckett, Katherine, and Marco Brydolf-Horwitz. "A Kinder, Gentler Drug War? Race, Drugs, and Punishment in 21st Century America." *Punishment and Society* 22, no. 4 (2020): 509–33.

Beckett, Katherine, and Heather Evans. *About Time: How Long and Life Sentences Fuel Mass Incarceration in Washington State.* Seattle: ACLU of Washington, 2020.

Beckett, Katherine, and Megan Ming Francis. "The Origins of Mass Incarceration: The Racial Politics of Crime and Punishment in the Post–Civil Rights Era." *Annual Review of Law and Social Sciences* 16 (2020): 433–52.

Beckett, Katherine, and Alexes Harris. "On Cash and Conviction: Monetary Sanctions as Misguided Policy." *Criminology and Public Policy* 10, no. 3 (2011): 509–37.

Beckett, Katherine, and Steve Herbert. *Banished: The New Social Control in Urban America.* New York: Oxford University Press, 2010.

Beckett, Katherine, and Martina Kartman. *Violence, Mass Incarceration and Restorative Justice: Promising Possibilities.* Seattle: University of Washington Center for Human Rights and West Coast Poverty Center, 2016.

Beckett, Katherine, and Naomi Murakawa. "Mapping the Shadow Carceral State: Toward an Institutionally Capacious Approach to Punishment." *Theoretical Criminology* 16, no. 2 (2012): 221–44.

Beckett, Katherine, Kris Nyrop, and Lori Pfingst. "Race, Drugs and Policing: Understanding Disparities in Drug Delivery Arrests." *Criminology* 44, no. 1 (2006): 105–38.

Beckett, Katherine, Kris Nyrop, Lori Pfingst, and Melissa Bowen. "Drug Use, Drug Possession Arrests, and the Question of Race: Lessons from Seattle." *Social Problems* 52, no. 3 (2005): 419–41.

Beckett, Katherine, Anna Reosti, and Emily Knaphus. "The End of an Era: Understanding the Contradictions of Criminal Justice Reform." *Annals of the American Academy of Political and Social Sciences* 664 (2016): 238–59.

Beckett, Katherine, and Bruce Western. "Governing Social Marginality: Welfare, Incarceration, and the Transformation of State Policy." *Punishment and Society* 3, no. 1 (2001): 43–59.

Beekman, Daniel, and Asia Fields. "Seattle Council Wants to Expand Program That Keeps Low-Level Offenders Out of Jail, Getting Help They Need." *Seattle Times,* November 25, 2019.

Beletsky, Leo. "America's Favorite Antidote: Drug-Induced Homicide in the Age of the Overdose Crisis." *Utah Law Review* 4 (2019): 833–90.

Benavie, Arthur. *How the Drug War Ruins American Lives.* Santa Barbara, CA: Praeger, 2016.

Benfer, Emily, David Bloom Robinson, Stacy Butler, Lavar Edmonds, Sam Gilman, Katherine Lucas McKay, Zach Neumann, Lisa Owens, Neil Steinkamp, and Diane Yentel. *The*

Covid-19 Eviction Crisis: An Estimated 30–40 Million People Are at Risk. Washington, DC: Aspen Institute, 2020.

Bennett, Lauren, Lisa Goodman, and Mary Ann Dutton. "Systemic Obstacles to the Criminal Prosecution of a Battering Partner: A Victim Perspective." *Journal of Interpersonal Violence* 14 (1999): 761–72.

Bennett, Trevor, and Katy Holloway. "The Causal Connection between Drug Misuse and Crime." *British Journal of Criminology* 49, no. 4 (2009): 513–31.

Bennett, William J., and John P. Walters. "Drug Dealing Is a Violent Crime." *Washington Examiner*, May 9, 2016.

Berger, Dan, Miriame Kaba, and David Stein. "What Abolitions Do." *Jacobin*, August 24, 2017.

Berman, Ari. *Give Us the Ballot: The Modern Struggle for Voting Rights in America.* New York: Farrar, Straus & Giroux, 2015.

Berman, Greg, John Feinblatt, and Sarah Glazer. *Good Courts: The Case for Problem-Solving Justice.* New York: Free Press, 2005.

Bernstein, Nell. *All Alone in the World: Children of the Incarcerated.* New York: New Press, 2007.

Beven, Jamie P., Guy Hall, Irene Froyland, Brian Steels, and Dorothy Goulding. "Restoration or Renovation? Evaluating Restorative Justice Outcomes." *Psychiatry, Psychology & Law* 12 (2005): 194–206.

Blackmon, Douglas A. *Slavery By Another Name: The Reenslavement of Black Americans from the Civil War to World War II.* New York: Anchor Books, 2008.

Blackwell, Christopher, and Arthur Longworth. "What Coronavirus Quarantine Looks Like in Prison." *Marshall Project*, March 18, 2020.

Blalock, Hubert M. *Toward a Theory of Minority Group Relations.* New York: Wiley, 1967.

Blasi, Gary. *Policing Our Way Out of Homelessness? The First Year of the Safer Cities Initiative on Skid Row.* Los Angeles: USC Center for Sustainable Cities, 2007.

Bloch, Kate. "Reconceptualizing Restorative Justice." *Hastings Race and Poverty Law Journal* 2010 (2010): 201–21.

Block, Jenny. "Grateful for a Wedding in Prison." *New York Times,* October 22, 2020.

Blumstein, Alfred, and Allen J. Beck. "Population Growth in U.S. Prisons, 1980–1996." *Crime and Justice* 26 (1999): 17–61.

Boecker, Kaitlyn. *Charging Drug Sellers with Murder If Someone Dies from Overdose Will Ruin Lives, Save None.* Washington, DC: Drug Policy Alliance, 2015.

Boerner, David. "Prosecution in Washington State." *Crime and Justice* 41, no. 1 (2012): 167–210.

Bowen, Phil, and Stephen Whitehead. *Problem-Solving Courts: An Evidence Review.* London: Centre for Justice Innovation, 2016.

Bowers, Joshua E. "Integrity of the Game Is Everything: The Problem of Geographic Disparity in Three Strikes." *New York University Law Review* 76 (2001): 1164–202.

Boyd, Susan, Dave Murray, SNAP, and Donald MacPherson. "Telling Our Stories." *Harm Reduction Journal* 14 (2017): 27–37.

Bradshaw, William, and David J. Roseborough. "Restorative Justice Dialogue: The Impact of Mediation and Conferencing on Juvenile Recidivism." *Federal Probation* 69, no. 2 (2005): 15–21.

Brayne, Sarah. "Surveillance and System Avoidance: Criminal Justice Contact and Institutional Attachment." *American Sociological Review* 79, no. 3 (2014): 367–91.

Bronson, Jennifer, and Ann E. Carson. *Prisoners in 2017.* Washington, DC: Bureau of Justice Statistics, 2018.

Bronson, Jennifer, Jessica Stroop, Stephanie Zimmer, and Marcus Berzofsky. *Drug Use, Dependence and Abuse among State Prisoners and Jail Inmates, 2007–2009.* Washington, DC: Bureau of Justice Statistics, 2017.

Brown, Brian, and Greg Jolivette. *A Primer: Three Strikes—The Impact after More Than a Decade.* Sacramento: California Legislative Analyst's Office, 2005.

Brown, Elizabeth K. "Toward Refining the Criminology of Mass Incarceration: Group-Based Trajectories of U.S. States, 1977–2010." *Criminal Justice Review* 45, no. 1 (2020): 45–63.

Brown, Elizabeth K., and Kelly M. Socia. "Twenty-First Century Punitiveness: Social Sources of Punitive American Views Reconsidered." *Journal of Quantitative Criminology* 33 (2017): 935–59.

Brydolf-Horwitz, Marco. "Risk, Property Rights, and Antidiscrimination Law in Rental Housing: Toward a Property-in-Action Framework." *Law and Social Inquiry* 45, no. 4 (2020): 875–901.

Brydolf-Horwitz, Marco, and Katherine Beckett. "Welfare, Punishment, and Social Marginality: Understanding the Connections." *Research in Political Sociology* 28 (in press).

Buchanan, Larry, Quoctrung Bui, and Jugal K. Patel. "Black Lives Matter May Be the Largest Movement in U.S. History." *New York Times*, July 3, 2020. https://www.nytimes.com/interactive/2020/07/03/us/george-floyd-protests-crowd-size.html.

Bureau of Justice Statistics. *National Prisoner Statistics Program*. Washington, DC: Department of Justice.

Bureau of Justice Statistics. *Correctional Populations in the United States*. Washington, DC: Department of Justice.

Burns, Alexander, and Jonathan Martin. "Trump Onslaught against Biden Falls Short of a Breakthrough." *New York Times*, September 12, 2020.

Burns, Stacy Lee, and Mark Peyrot. "Tough Love: Nurturing and Coercing Responsibility and Recovery in California Drug Courts." *Social Problems* 50, no. 3 (2003): 416–38.

Burt, Martha. *Over the Edge: The Growth of Homelessness in the 1980s*. New York: Russell Sage Foundation, 1992.

Burton, Linda M., Daniel T. Lichter, Regina S. Baker, and John M. Eason. "Inequality, Family Processes, and Health in the 'New' Rural America." *American Behavioral Scientist* 57, no. 8 (2013): 1128–51.

Butler, Paul. "The System Is Working the Way It Is Supposed To: The Limits of Criminal Justice Reform." *Georgetown Law Journal* 104, no. 6 (2016): 1419–79.

California Department of Corrections and Rehabilitation. *Lifer Parole Recidivism Report*. Sacramento, CA: CDCR, 2013.

Campbell, Michael. "Ornery Alligators and Soap on a Rope: Texas Prosecutors and Punishment Reform in the Lone Star State." *Theoretical Criminology* 16, no. 3 (2012): 289–311.

Campbell, Michael C., and Heather Schoenfeld. "The Transformation of America's Penal Order: A Historicized Political Sociology of Punishment." *American Journal of Sociology* 118, no. 5 (2013): 1375–423.

Campbell, Michael C., Matt Vogel, and Joshua Williams. "Historical Contingencies and the Evolving Importance of Race, Violent Crime, and Region in Explaining Mass Incarceration in the United States." *Criminology* 53 (2015): 180–203.

Carson, E. Ann. *Prisoners in 2018*. Washington, DC: Bureau of Justice Statistics, 2016.

Carson, E. Ann, and William J. Sabol. *Aging of the State Prison Population, 1993–2013*. Washington, DC: Bureau of Justice Statistics, 2016.

Carter, Dan T. *The Politics of Rage: George Wallace, the Origins of the New Conservatism, and the Transformation of American Politics*. New York: Simon & Schuster, 1995.

Case, Anne, and Angus Deaton. "Rising Morbidity and Mortality in Midlife among White Non-Hispanic Americans in the 21st Century." *Proceedings of the National Academy of Science* 112, no. 49 (2015): 15078–83.

Casey, Pamela, and David Rottman. "Therapeutic Jurisprudence in the Courts." *Behavioral Sciences and the Law* 18 (2000): 445–57.

Casteel, Kathryn. "A Crackdown on Drug Dealers Is Also a Crackdown on Drug Users." *FiveThirtyEight*, April 5, 2018.

Center for Health and Justice. *No Entry: A National Survey of Criminal Justice Diversion Programs and Initiatives.* Chicago: Center for Health and Justice, 2014.

Center for Law and Global Justice. *Cruel and Unusual: U.S. Sentencing Practices in a Global Context.* San Francisco: University of California at San Francisco Law School, 2012.

Centers for Disease Control and Prevention. *Injury Prevention and Control: Data & Statistics.* Washington, DC: CDC, 2011.

Centers for Disease Control and Prevention. "Opioid Overdose: Fentanyl." Accessed April 21, 2021. https://www.cdc.gov/drugoverdose/opioids/fentanyl.html.

Centers for Disease Control and Prevention. "Preventing Child Abuse and Neglect." Accessed April 29, 2021. https://www.cdc.gov/violenceprevention/childabuseandneglect/fastfact. html.

Centers for Disease Control and Prevention. "Preventing Intimate Partner Violence." Accessed April 29, 2021. Centers for Disease Control and Prevention. https://www.cdc.gov/ violenceprevention/intimatepartnerviolence/fastfact.html.

Chen, Elsa Y. "In the Furtherance of Justice, Injustice, or Both? A Multilevel Analysis of Courtroom Context and the Implementation of Three Strikes." *Justice Quarterly* 31 (2014): 257–86.

Chiricos, Ted, and Sarah Eschholz. "The Racial and Ethnic Typification of Crime and the Criminal Typification of Race and Ethnicity in Local Television News." *Journal of Research in Crime and Delinquency* 39 (2002): 400–442.

Christie, Chris, Charlie Baker, Roy Cooper, Patrick J. Kennedy, and Pam Bondi. *The President's Commission on Combatting Drug Addiction and the Opioid Crisis.* Washington, DC, November 2017.

Ciaramella, C. J. "House Passes Bill to Reclassify Dozens of Offenses as 'Crimes of Violence.'" *Reason,* September 7, 2018.

Clear, Todd R. *Imprisoning Communities: How Mass Incarceration Makes Disadvantaged Communities Worse.* Oxford: Oxford University Press, 2007.

Clear, Todd, and James Austin. "Reducing Mass Incarceration: Implications of the Iron Law of Prison Populations." *Harvard Law & Policy Review* 307 (2009).

Clifasefi, S. L., H. S. Lonczak, and S. E. Collins. "Seattle's Law Enforcement Assisted Diversion (LEAD) Program: Within-Subjects Changes on Housing, Employment and Income/Benefits Outcomes and Associations with Recidivism." *Crime & Delinquency* 63 (2017): 429–45.

Cohen, Michael M. "Jim Crow's Drug War: Race, Coca Cola and the Southern Origins of Drug Prohibition." *Southern Cultures* 12, no. 3 (2006): 55–79.

Cole, David. "Turning the Corner on Mass Incarceration?" *Ohio State Journal of Criminal Law* 9 (2011): 27–51.

Collins, Susan E., Heather S. Lonczak, and Seema L. Clifasefi. "Seattle's Law Enforcement Assisted Diversion (LEAD): Program Effects on Recidivism Outcomes." *Evaluation and Program Planning* 64 (2019): 49–56.

Collins, Susan E., Daniel K. Malone, Seema L. Clifasefi, Joshua A. Ginzler, Michelle D. Garner, Bonnie Burlingham, Heather S. Lonczak, Elizabeth A. Dana, Megan Kirouac, Kenneth Tanzer, William G. Hobson, G. Alan Marlatt, and Mary E. Larimer. "Project-Based Housing First for Chronically Homeless Individuals with Alcohol Problems: Within-Subjects Analyses of 2-Year Alcohol Trajectories." *American Journal of Public Health* 102, no. 3 (2012): 511–19.

Comfort, Megan. *Doing Time Together: Love and Family in the Shadow of the Prison.* Chicago: University of Chicago Press, 2007.

Corso, Phaedra S., James A Mercy, Thomas R. Simon, and Eric A. Finkelstein. "Medical Costs and Productivity Losses Due to Interpersonal and Self-Directed Violence in the United States." *American Journal of Preventative Medicine* 32, no. 6 (2007): 474–82.

Couloute, Lucius. *Nowhere to Go: Homelessness among Formerly Incarcerated People.* Northampton, MA: Prison Policy Initiative, 2018.

Crowley, Mike, and Ed Chung. *Congress Can Lead on Criminal Justice Reform Through Funding Choices.* Washington, DC: Center for American Progress, 2017.

Crutchfield, Robert, and David Pettinicchio. "'Cultures of Inequality': Ethnicity, Immigration, Social Welfare, and Imprisonment." *Annals of the American Academy of Political and Social Science* 623, no. 1 (2009): 134–47.

Cruz, Ted. "Smart Sentencing Act Is Common Sense." Press release. February 12, 2015. https://www.cruz.senate.gov/?p=press_release&id=2184.

Csete, Joanne. "Drug Courts in the United States: Punishment for 'Patients'?" In *Rethinking Drug Courts: International Experiences of a US Policy Export,* edited by John Collins, Winifred Agnew-Pauley, and Alexander Soderholm. London: London Publishing Partnership, 2019.

Csete, Joanne, and Denise Tomasini-Joshi. *Drug Courts: Equivocal Evidence on a Popular Intervention.* New York: Open Societies Foundation, 2015.

Cutler, David M., Adriana Lleras-Muney, and Tom Vogl. "Socio-economic Status and Health: Dimensions and Mechanisms." In *The Oxford Handbook of Health Economics,* edited by Sherry Glied and Peter C. Smith. New York: Oxford University Press, 2011.

Dagan, David, and Steven M. Telles. "Locked In? Conservative Reform and the Future of Mass Incarceration." *Annals of the American Academy of Political and Social Science* 651, no. 1 (2014): 266–76.

Dagan, David, and Steven M. Telles. *Prison Break: Why Conservatives Turned against Mass Incarceration.* New York: Oxford University Press, 2016.

Daly, Kathleen, and Russ Immarigeon. "The Past, Present, and Future of Restorative Justice: Some Critical Reflections." *Contemporary Justice Review* 1, no. 1 (1998): 21–45.

Davey, Joseph D. *The Politics of Prison Expansion: Winning Elections by Waging War on Crime.* Westport, CT: Praeger, 1998.

Davis, Angela J. "The American Prosecutor: Power, Discretion and Misconduct." *Criminal Justice* 1 (2008): 24–37.

Davis, Angela J. "Reimagining Prosecution: A Growing Progressive Movement." *UCLA Criminal Justice Law Review* 3, no. 1 (2019): 1–27.

Davis, Julie Hirschfeld. "GOP Finds an Unexpectedly Potent Line of Attack: Immigration." *New York Times,* October 14, 2018.

DeMatteo, David, Kirk Heilbrun, Alice Thornewill, and Shelby Arnold. *Problem-Solving Courts and the Criminal Justice System.* Oxford: Oxford University Press, 2019.

DeMatteo, David, Douglas B. Marlowe, David S. Festinger, and Patricia L. Arabia. "Outcome Trajectories in Drug Court: Do All Participants Have Serious Drug Problems?" *Criminal Justice and Behavior* 36, no. 4 (2009): 354–68.

Devine, Patricia G., and Andrew J. Elliot. "Are Racial Stereotypes Really Fading? The Princeton Trilogy Revisited." *Personality and Social Psychology Bulletin* 11 (1995): 1139–50.

Ditton, Paula M., and Doris James Wilson. *Truth in Sentencing in State Prisons.* Washington, DC: Bureau of Justice Statistics, 1999.

Dobbie, Will, Jacob Goldin, and Crystal S. Yang. "The Effects of Pretrial Detention on Conviction, Future Crime, and Employment: Evidence from Randomly Assigned Judges." *American Economic Review* 108, no. 2 (2018): 201–40.

Dolovich, Sharon, and Aaron Littman. UCLA COVID-19 Behind Bars Data Project. Accessed April 21, 2021. https://docs.google.com/spreadsheets/d/1X6uJkXXS-O6eePLxw2e4JeRtM41uPZ2eRcOA_HkPVTk/edit#gid=1641553906.

Donato, Katharine M., Charles Tolbert, Alfred Nucci, and Yukio Kawana. "Changing Faces, Changing Places: The Emergence of New Nonmetropolitan Immigrant Gateways." In *New Faces in New Places: The Changing Geography of American Immigration,* edited by Douglas S. Massey. New York: Russell Sage, 2008.

Donziger, Steven R., ed. *The Real War on Crime: The Report of the National Criminal Justice Commission.* New York: Harper Perennial, 1996.

Doob, Anthony, and C. Webster. "Countering Punitiveness: Understanding Stability in Canada's Imprisonment." *Law & Society Review* 40, no. 2 (2006): 325–67.

Dorf, Michael, and Jeffrey Fagan. "Problem-Solving Courts: From Innovation to Institutionalization." *American Criminal Law Review* 40 (2003): 1501–12.

Drake, Elizabeth. *Inventory of Evidence-Based and Research-Based Programs for Adult Corrections.* Olympia: Washington State Institute for Public Policy, 2013.

Drakulich, Kevin M. "The Hidden Role of Racial Bias in Support of Policies Related to Inequality and Crime." *Punishment and Society* 17, no. 5 (2015): 541–74.

Drinan, Carla H. "Clemency in a Time of Crisis." *Georgia State University Law Review* 28, no. 4 (2012): 1123–60.

Drug Policy Alliance. *Drug Courts Are Not the Answer: Toward a Health-Centered Approach to Drug Use.* New York: Drug Policy Alliance, 2011.

Drug Policy Alliance. *Moving Away from Drug Courts.* New York: Drug Policy Alliance, 2014.

Drugs, Security and Democracy Program. *Drug Courts in the Americas.* New York: Social Science Research Council, 2018.

Duster, Troy. "Pattern, Purpose and Race in the Drug War: The Crisis of Credibility in Criminal Justice." In *Crack in America: Demon Drugs and Social Justice,* edited by Craig Reinarman and Harry G. Levine. Berkeley: University of California Press, 1997.

Dvorak, Petula. "America's Missing Slave Memorials: It's Time to Truly Acknowledge Our Bloody Past." *Washington Post,* August 28, 2017.

Eberhardt, Jennifer L., Phillip Atiba Goff, Valerie J. Purdie, and Paul G. Davies. "Seeing Black: Race, Crime and Visual Processing." *Journal of Personality and Social Psychology* 87, no. 6 (2004): 876–93.

Eason, Jason. *Big House on the Prairie.* Chicago: University of Chicago Press, 2017.

Eason, John M., Danielle Zucker, and Christopher Wildeman. "Mass Imprisonment across the Rural-Urban Interface." *Annals of the American Academy of Political and Social Sciences* 372 (2017): 202–16.

Edelman, Murray. *The Symbolic Uses of Politics.* Champaign: University of Illinois Press, 1985.

Edsall, Thomas. "Reaching Out to the Voters the Left Behind." *New York Times,* April 13, 2017.

Engel, Pamela. "This Chart Shows Incredibly High Markups on Illegal Drugs." *Business Insider,* May 7, 2014.

Englebrecht, Christine, Derek T. Mason, and Margaret J. Adams. "The Experience of Homicide Victims' Families with the Criminal Justice System: An Exploratory Study." *Violence and Victims* 29, no. 3 (2014): 407–21.

Enns, Peter K. *Incarceration Nation: How the United States Became the Most Punitive Democracy in the World.* New York: Cambridge University Press, 2016.

Essig Alan. "Five Categories That Cry Out for Reform." *Atlanta Journal-Constitution,* January 8, 2012.

European Monitoring Centre for Drugs and Drug Addiction. *New Heroin Assisted Treatment.* Lisbon, Portugal, 2012. Accessed February 5, 2021. https://www.emcdda.europa.eu/publications/insights/heroin-assisted-treatment_en

Evans, Erica. "Lessons from Seattle: How This Alternative to Jail May Be a Solution for Utah." *Desert News,* December 26, 2017.

Fagan, Jeffrey. "Dignity Is the New Legitimacy." In *The New Criminal Justice Thinking,* edited by Sharon Dolovich and Alexandra Natapoff. New York: New York University Press, 2017.

Farmer, Paul. "On Suffering and Structural Violence: A View from Below." *Daedalus* 125, no. 1 (1996): 261–83.

Farmer, Paul, Bruce Nizeye, Sara Stulac, and Salmman Keshavjee. "Structural Violence and Clinical Medicine." *PLOS Medicine* 3, no. 10 (2006). Online.

Farrigan, Tracey. *Poverty and Deep Poverty Increasing in Rural America*. Washington, DC: U.S. Department of Agriculture, 2014.

Farrington, David P. "Developmental and Life-Course Criminology: Key Theoretical and Empirical Issues." *Criminology* 41 (2003): 221–55.

Federal Bureau of Investigation. *Uniform Crime Reports*. Washington, DC: Department of Justice.

Fedders, Barbara. "Opioid Policing." *Indiana Law Journal* 94, no. 2 (2019): 389–450.

Fischer, Benedikt, Jurgen Rehm, Maritt Kirst, Miguel Cases, Wayne Hall, Michael Krausz, Nicky Metrebian, Jean Reggers, Ambros Uchtenhagen, Wim Van den Brink, and Jan M. Van Ree. "Heroin Assisted Treatment as a Response to the Public Health Problem of Opiate Dependence." *European Journal Public Health* 12 (2002): 228–34.

Flamm, Michael W. *Law and Order: Street Crime, Civil Unrest, and the Crisis of Liberalism in the 1960s*. New York: Columbia University Press, 2005.

Flett, Ross A., Nikolaos Kazantizis, Nigel R. Long, Carol MacDonald, and Michelle Millar. "Traumatic Events and Physical Health in a New Zealand Community Sample." *Journal of Traumatic Stress* 15, no. 4 (2002): 303–12.

Flores, Jerry. *Caught Up: Girls, Surveillance, and Wraparound Incarceration*. Berkeley: University of California Press, 2016.

Forman, James, Jr. *Locking Up Our Own*. New York: Farrar, Straus and Giroux, 2017.

Forman, James, Jr. "Racial Critiques of Mass Incarceration: Beyond the New Jim Crow." *New York Law Review* 87, no. 1 (2012): 101–46.

Frakt, Austin. "Spend a Dollar on Drug Treatment, Save More on Crime Reduction." *New York Times*, April 24, 2017.

Frase, Richard S. *Just Sentencing: Principles and Procedures for a Workable Sentencing System*. New York: Oxford University Press, 2012.

Gallagher, John Robert, Elizabeth A. Wahler, and Elyse Lefebvre. "Further Evidence of Racial Disparities in Drug Court Outcomes: Enhancing Service-Delivery to Reduce Criminal Recidivism Rates for Non-White Participants." *Journal of Social Service Research* 46, no. 3 (2020): 406–15.

Galtung, Johan. "Violence, Peace, and Peace Research." *Journal of Peace Research* 6, no. 3 (1969): 167–91.

Garfinkel, Harold. "Conditions of Successful Degradation Ceremonies." *American Journal of Sociology* 6 (1956): 420–24.

Garland, David. *Mass Imprisonment: Social Causes and Consequences*. Beverley Hills, CA: Sage, 2001.

Garland, David. *Punishment and Modern Society*. Chicago: University of Chicago Press, 1990.

Gascón, Daniel, and Aaron Roussell. *The Limits of Community Policing: Civilian Power and Police Accountability in Black and Brown Los Angeles*. New York: NYU Press, 2019.

Geller, Amanda, Jeffrey Fagan, Tom T. Tyler, and Bruce G. Link. "Aggressive Policing and the Mental Health of Young Urban Men." *American Journal of Public Health* 104, no. 12 (2014): 2321–27.

Ghandnoosh, Nazgol. *Delaying a Second Change: The Declining Prospects for Parole on Life Sentences*. Washington, DC: Sentencing Project, 2017.

Ghandnoosh, Nazgol. "Minimizing the Maximum: The Case for Shortening All Prison Sentences." In *Smart Decarceration: Achieving Criminal Justice Transformation in the 21st Century*, edited by Matthew W. Epperson and Carrie Pettus-Davis. New York: Oxford University Press, 2017.

Ghandnoosh, Nazgol. *The Next Step: Ending Excessive Punishment for Violent Crimes*. Washington, DC: Sentencing Project, 2019.

Ghandnoosh, Nazgol. *U.S. Prison Decline: Insufficient to Undo Mass Incarceration*. Washington, DC: Sentencing Project, 2020.

Ghandnoosh, Nazgol, and Casey Anderson. *Opioids: Treating an Illness, Ending a War.* Washington, DC: Sentencing Project, 2017.

Gibbs, Benjamin R., Robert Lytle, and William Wakefield. "Outcome Effects on Recidivism among Drug Court Participants." *Criminal Justice and Behavior* 46, no. 1 (2019): 115–35.

Gilderbloom, John, and Richard Applebaum. *Rethinking Rental Housing.* Philadelphia, PA: Temple University Press, 1988.

Gilens, Martin. *Why Americans Hate Welfare: Race, Media and the Politics of Antipoverty Policy.* Chicago: University of Chicago Press, 1999.

Goffman, Erving. "Embarrassment and Social Organization." *American Journal of Sociology* 62, no. 3 (1956): 264–71.

Gohara, Miriam S. "Grace Notes: A Case for Making Mitigation the Heart of Noncapital Sentencing." *American Journal of Criminal Law* 41, no. 1 (2013): 41–88.

Goldensohn, Rosa. "They Shared Drugs. Someone Died. Does That Make Them Killers?" *New York Times*, May 25, 2018.

Goldstein, Dana. "How to Cut the Prison Population by 50 Percent: No, Freeing Potheads and Shoplifters Is Not Enough." *Marshall Project*, March 4, 2015.

Goldstein, Paul J. "The Drugs/Violence Nexus: A Tripartite Conceptual Framework." *Journal of Drug Issues* 39 (1985): 143–74.

Gonnerman, Jennifer. "How Prisons and Jails Can Respond to the Coronavirus." *New Yorker*, March 14, 2020.

Goodnough, Abby. "A New Drug Scourge: Deaths Involving Meth Are Rising Fast." *New York Times*, December 17, 2019.

Gordon, Diana R. *The Return of the Dangerous Classes: Drug Prohibition and Policy Politics.* New York: Norton, 1994.

Gottschalk, Marie. "America Needs a Third Reconstruction: The Problem of Mass Incarceration Is a Problem of High Inequality." *Atlantic*, September 18, 2015.

Gottschalk, Marie. *Caught: The Prison State and the Lockdown of American Politics.* Princeton, NJ: Princeton University Press, 2015.

Gottschalk, Marie. "No Way Out? Life Sentences and the Politics of Penal Reform." In *Life without Parole: America's New Death Penalty?*, edited by Carl Olgtree and Austin Sarat. New York: New York University Press, 2012.

Gottschalk, Marie. *The Prison and the Gallows: The Politics of Mass Incarceration in America.* Cambridge: Cambridge University Press, 2006.

Gould, Elise, and Hilary Wething. "U.S. Poverty Rates Higher, Safety Net Weaker Than in Peer Countries." Issue Brief 339. Washington, DC: Economic Policy Institute, 2012.

Gowan, Teresa, and Sarah Whetstone. "Making the Criminal Addict: Subjectivity and Social Control in a 'Strong-Arms' Rehab." *Punishment & Society* 14, no. 1 (2012): 69–93.

Gramlich, John. *America's Incarceration Rate Is at a Two-Decade Low.* Washington, DC: Pew Research Center, 2018.

Green, David A. "U.S. Penal-Reform Catalysts, Drivers, and Prospects." *Punishment and Society* 17, no. 3 (2015): 271–98.

Greenberg, Clair, Marc Meredith, and Michael Morse. "The Growing and Broad Nature of Legal Financial Obligations: Evidence from Court Records in Alabama." *Connecticut Law Review* 48, no. 4 (2016): 1079–120.

Greenberg, David, and Valerie West. "State Prison Populations and Their Growth, 1971–1991." *Criminology* 39 (2001): 615–54.

Greene, Judith, and Marc Mauer. *Downscaling Prisons: Lessons from Four States.* Washington, DC: Justice Strategies and The Sentencing Project, 2010.

Greenwood, Jean E., and Mark S. Umbreit. *National Survey of Victim Offender Mediation Programs in the United States.* Minneapolis: University of Minnesota, Center for Restorative Justice and Peacemaking, 2000.

Griffiths, Curt T. "Sanctioning and Healing: Restorative Justice in Canadian Aboriginal Communities." *International Journal of Comparative and Applied Criminal Justice* 20 (1996): 195–208.

Grinshteyn, Erin, and David Hemenway. "Violent Death Rates: The US Compared with Other High-Income OECD Countries, 2010." *American Journal of Medicine* 129, no. 3 (2016): 266–73.

Grove, R. D., and A. M. Hetzel. *Vital Statistics Rates in the United States, 1940–1960*. Washington, DC: National Center for Health Statistics, National Vital Statistics System, 1968.

Grusky, David B., Bruce Western, and Christopher Wimer, eds. *The Great Recession*. New York: Russell Sage, 2011.

Gullapalli, Vaidya. "Cory Booker's New Sentencing Reform Bill Is about Redemption." *Appeal*, July 19, 2019.

Hackworth, Jason. *The Neoliberal City: Governance, Ideology, and Development in American Urbanism*. Ithaca, NY: Cornell University Press, 2007.

Hagan, John. *Who Are the Criminals? The Politics of Crime Policy from the Age of Roosevelt to the Age of Reagan*. Princeton, NJ: Princeton University Press, 2010.

Hagan, John, and Ruth D. Petersen. "Criminal Inequality in America: Patterns and Consequences." In *Crime and Inequality*, edited by John Hagan and Ruth D. Petersen. Palo Alto, CA: Stanford University Press, 1995.

Hager, Eli. "When 'Violent Offenders' Commit Non-Violent Crimes." *Marshall Project*, April 3, 2019.

Hagar, Eli. "Your Kid Goes to Jail, You Get the Bill." *Marshall Project*, March 2, 2017.

Hagar, Eli, and Bill Keller, "Everything You Think You Know about Mass Incarceration Is Wrong." *Marshall Project*, February 9, 2017.

Halliday, Simon, Nicola Burns, Neil Hutton, Fergus McNeill, and Cyrus Tata. "Street-Level Bureaucracy, Inter-Professional Relations, and Coping Mechanisms: A Study of Criminal Justice Social Workers in the Sentencing Process." *Law and Policy* 31, no. 4 (2009): 405–28.

Halushka, John M. "The Runaround: Punishment, Welfare, and Poverty Survival after Prison." *Social Problems* 67, no. 2 (2019): 233–50.

Haney, Craig. "Condemning the Other in Death Penalty Trials: Biographical Racism, Structural Mitigation, and the Empathic Divide." *DePaul Law Review* 53 (2004): 1557–89.

Haney, Craig. *Criminality in Context: The Psychological Foundations of Criminal Justice Reform*. Washington, DC: American Psychological Association, 2020.

Haney, Craig. "Psychological Secrecy and the Death Penalty: Observations on 'The Mere Extinguishment of Life.'" *Studies in Law, Politics and Society* 16, no. 1 (1997): 3–69.

Haney, Craig. "The Social Context of Capital Murder: Social Histories and the Logic of Mitigation." *Santa Clara Law Review* 35, no. 2 (1995): 547–609.

Haney-Lopez, Ian. "How the GOP Became the White Man's Party." *Salon*, December 22, 2013.

Hanson, Rochelle F., Genelle K. Sawyer, Angela M. Begle, and Grace S. Hubel. "The Impact of Crime Victimization on Quality of Life." *Journal of Traumatic Stress* 23, no. 2 (2010): 189–97.

Hari, Johann. *Chasing the Scream: The First and Last Days of the War on Drugs*. New York: Bloomsbury, 2015.

Harrell, Erika, Lynn Langston, Marcus Berzofsky, Lance Couzens, and Hope Smiley-McDonald. *Household Poverty and Nonfatal Violent Victimization, 2008–2012*. Washington, DC: U.S. Department of Justice, Bureau of Justice Statistics, 2014.

Harris, Alexes. *A Pound of Flesh: Monetary Sanctions as a Punishment for the Poor*. New York: Russell Sage, 2016.

Harris, Alexes, Heather Evans, and Katherine Beckett. "Drawing Blood from Stones: Monetary Sanctions, Punishment, and Inequality in the Contemporary United States." *American Journal of Sociology* 115 (2010): 1753–99.

Harvey, David. *The Condition of Postmodernity: An Enquiry into the Origins of Cultural Change.* Oxford: Blackwell, 1991.

Health in Justice Action Lab. Drug-Induced Homicide Database. Accessed January 21, 2020. https://www.healthinjustice.org/drug-induced-homicide

Healy, Jack, Jack Nicas, and Mike Baker. "A Line of Fire South of Portland and a Yearslong Recovery Ahead." *New York Times,* September 11, 2020.

Heckman, J., L. Malofeeva, R. Pinto, and P. Savelyev. *Understanding the Mechanisms through Which an Influential Early Childhood Program Boosted Adult Outcomes.* Chicago: University of Chicago Press, 2010.

Helms, Ronald, and David Jacobs. "The Political Context of Sentencing: An Analysis of Community and Individual Determinants." *Social Forces* 81, no. 2 (2002): 577–604.

Hepburn, Lisa, and David Hemenway. "Firearm Availability and Homicide: A Review of the Literature." *Aggression and Violent Behavior: A Review Journal* 9 (2004): 417–40.

Herbert, Steve. *Too Easy to Keep: Life-Sentenced Prisoners and the Future of Mass Incarceration.* Berkeley: University of California Press, 2019.

Herbert, Steve, Katherine Beckett, and Forrest Stuart. "Policing Social Marginality: Contrasting Approaches." *Law & Social Inquiry* 43, no. 4 (2017): 1491–513.

Herman, Susan. *Parallel Justice for Victims of Crime.* New York: National Center for Victims of Crime, 2010.

Hernandez, J. "New Jersey Eliminates Cash Bail for People Accused of Some Crimes." *Marketplace,* January 9, 2017.

Herring, Chris. "Complaint-Oriented Policing: Regulating Homelessness in Public Space." *American Sociological Review* 84, no. 5 (2019): 769–800.

Hertz, Daniel Kay. "The Debate over Crime Rates Is Ignoring the Metric That Matters Most: Murder Inequality." *Trace,* July 25, 2016.

Hindelang, Michael J., Michael R. Gottfredson, Christopher S. Dunn, and Nicolette Parisi. *Sourcebook of Criminal Justice Statistics, 1976.* Albany, NY: Criminal Justice Research Center, 1977.

Hinton, Elizabeth. *From the War on Poverty to the War on Crime: The Making of Mass Incarceration in America.* Cambridge, MA: Harvard University Press, 2016.

Ho, Jessica Y. "The Contemporary American Drug Overdose Epidemic in International Perspective." *Population and Development Review* 45, no. 1 (2019): 7–40.

Hoffer, L., and S. J. Alam. "'Copping' in Heroin Markets: The Hidden Information Costs of Indirect Sales and Why They Matter." In *Social Computing, Behavioral-Cultural Modeling and Prediction,* edited by A. M. Greenberg, W. G. Kennedy, and N. D. Bos. Berlin: Springer, 2013.

Hofstader, Richard. "Introduction." In *American Violence: A Documentary History,* edited by Richard Hofstader and Michael Wallace. New York: Knopf, 1970.

Hora, Peggy, William Schma, and John Rosenthal. "Therapeutic Jurisprudence and the Drug Court Movement: Revolutionizing the Criminal Justice System's Response to Drug Abuse and Crime in America." *Notre Dame Law Review* 74 (1999): 439–555.

Horswell, Cindy. "A New Approach: Texas Cuts Costs amid Prison Reform." *Houston Chronicle,* December 15, 2009.

Horwitz, Sari. "Justice Department Set to Free 6,000 Prisoners, Largest One-Time Release." *Washington Post,* October 6, 2015.

Housing Assistance Council. *Race and Ethnicity in Rural America.* Washington, DC: Housing Assistance Council, 2012.

Howard, Daniel. "Race, Neighborhood, and Drug Court Graduation." *Justice Quarterly* 33, no. 1 (2016): 159–84.

Hughes, Caitlyn Elizabeth, and Alex Stevens. "What Can We Learn from the Portuguese Decriminalization of Illicit Drugs?" *British Journal of Criminology* 50 (2010): 999–1022.

Human Rights Watch. *Every 25 Seconds: The Human Toll of Criminalizing Drug Use in the United States* (2016).

Jacobs, David, and Jason T. Carmichael. "The Politics of Punishment across Time and Space: A Pooled Time Series Analysis of Imprisonment Rates." *Social Forces* 80 (2001): 61–89.

Jacobs, David, and Ronald Helms. "Toward a Political Sociology of Punishment: Politics and Changes in the Incarcerated Population." *Social Science Research* 30 (2001): 171–94.

Jacobs, David, and Aubrey Jackson. "On the Politics of Imprisonment: A Review of Systematic Findings." *Annual Review of Law and Social Science* 6 (2010): 129–49.

Jacobs, David, and Richard Klebans. "Political Institutions, Minorities, and Punishment: A Pooled Cross-National Analysis of Imprisonment Rates." *Social Forces* 82, no. 2 (2003): 725–55.

Jaggi, Lena J., Briana Mezuk, Daphne C. Watkins, and James S. Jackson. "The Relationship between Trauma, Arrest, and Incarceration History among Black Americans: Findings from the National Survey of American Life." *Society & Mental Health* 6, no. 3 (2016): 87–206.

James, Doris J. *Profile of Jail Inmates, 2002.* Washington, DC: Bureau of Justice Statistics, 2004.

James, Nathan. "The First Step Act." *Congressional Research Service*, March 4, 2019.

Joint Center for Housing Studies of Harvard University. *The State of the Nation's Housing 2003.* Cambridge, MA: Harvard University Press, 2004.

Joint Center for Housing Studies of Harvard University. *The State of the Nation's Housing 2013.* Cambridge, MA: Harvard University Press, 2014.

Justice Policy Institute. *For Better or for Profit: How the Bail Bonding Industry Stands in the Way of Fair and Effective Pretrial Justice.* Washington, DC: The Justice Policy Institute, 2012.

Kaeble, Danielle. *Probation and Parole in the United States, 2016.* Washington, DC: Bureau of Justice Statistics, 2018.

Kaeble, Danielle, and Mary Cowhig. *Correctional Populations in the United States, 2016.* Washington, DC: Bureau of Justice Statistics, 2018.

Kaeble, Danielle, Lauren Glaze, Anastasios Tsoutis, and Todd Minton. *Correctional Populations in the United States, 2014.* Washington, DC: Bureau of Justice Statistics, 2015.

Kampman, Kyle M. "The Treatment of Cocaine Use Disorder." *Science Advances* 5, no. 10 (2019).

Kang-Brown, Jacob, Oliver Hinds, Jasmine Heiss, and Olive Lu. *The New Dynamics of Mass Incarceration.* New York: Vera Institute of Justice, 2018.

Kang-Brown, Jacob, Chase Montagnet, and Jasmine Heiss. *People in Jail and Prison in 2020.* New York: Vera Institute of Justice, 2021.

Karp, David R., and Olivia Frank. "Anxiously Awaiting the Future of Restorative Justice in the United States." *Victims and Offenders* 11 (2016): 50–70.

Kassie, Emily. "Detained: How the United States Created the Largest Immigration Detention System in the World." *Marshall Project and Guardian*, September 24, 2019.

Katz, Josh, and Amy Goodnough. "The Opioid Crisis Is Getting Worse, Particularly for Black Americans." *New York Times*, December 22, 2017.

Kaye, Kerwin. *Enforcing Freedom: Drug Courts, Therapeutic Communities, and the Intimacies of the State.* New York: Columbia University Press, 2020.

Kaye, Kerwin. "Rehabilitating the 'Drugs Lifestyle': Criminal Justice, Social Control, and the Cultivation of Agency." *Ethnography* 14, no. 2 (2012): 207–32.

Keck, Michelle, and Guadalupe Correa-Cabera. "U.S. Drug Policy and Supply-Side Strategies: Assessing Effectiveness and Results." *Norteamérica* 10, no. 2 (2015): 47–67.

Keen, Bradley, and David Jacobs. "Racial Threat, Partisan Politics, and Racial Disparities in Prison Admissions: A Panel Analysis." *Criminology* 47, no. 1 (2009): 209–38.

Keller, Josh, and Adam Pearce. "This Small Indiana County Sends More People to Prison Than Durham, North Carolina and San Francisco Combined. Why?" *New York Times*, September 2, 2016.

Kempf-Leonard, Kimberley. "Offense Specialization/Expertise." In *Criminology*. New York: Oxford University Press, 2011.

Kentucky Department of Public Advocacy. *The Advocate Newsletter*, February 2017. https://dpa.ky.gov/Public_Defender_Resources/The%20Advocate/Feb%202017%20revised%203.13.17.pdf.

Keyes, Katherine M., Magdalena Cerda, Joanne E. Brady, Jennifer R. Havens, and Sandro Galea. "Understanding the Rural-Urban Differences in Nonmedical Prescription Opioid Use and Abuse in the United States." *American Journal of Public Health* 104, no. 2 (2014): e52–e59.

Killias, Martin, and Marcelo F. Aebi. "The Impact of Heroin Prescription on Heroin Markets in Switzerland." *Crime Prevention Studies* 11 (2000): 83–99.

Kilmer, Beau, Jirka Taylor, Jonathan P. Caulkins, Pam A. Mueller, Allison J. Ober, Bryce Pardo, Rosanna Smart, Lucy Strang, and Peter Reuter. *Considering Heroin-Assisted Treatment and Supervised Drug Consumption Sites in the United States*. Santa Monica, CA: RAND Corporation, 2018. https://www.rand.org/pubs/research_reports/RR2693.html.

Kilpatrick, Dean G., and Ron Acierno. "Mental Health Needs of Crime Victims: Epidemiology and Outcomes." *Journal of Traumatic Stress* 16, no. 2 (2003): 119–32.

King County. Familiar Faces Data Packet. May 2016. Accessed March 2, 2021. https://www.kingcounty.gov/~/media/elected/executive/constantine/initiatives/hhs-transformation/documents/familiar-faces/Population_analysis_combined_6_26_16.ashx?la=en.

King, Ryan S., and Jill Pasquarella. *Drug Courts: A Review of the Evidence*. Washington, DC: Sentencing Project, 2009.

Kneebone, Elizabeth. *The Changing Geography of U.S. Poverty*. Washington, DC: Brookings Institution Press, 2017.

Kneebone, Elizabeth, and Alan Berube. *Confronting Suburban Poverty in America*. Washington, DC: Brookings Institution Press, 2013.

Kohler-Hausmann, Issa. "Misdemeanor Justice: Control without Conviction." *American Journal of Sociology* 199, no. 2 (2013): 351–93.

Kohler-Hausmann, Issa. *Misdemeanorland*. Princeton, NJ: Princeton University Press, 2018.

Kohler-Hausman, Julilly. *Getting Tough: Welfare and Imprisonment in 1970s America*. Princeton, NJ: Princeton University Press, 2017.

Kois, Dan. "America Is a Sham." *Slate*, March 14, 2020.

Kopp, Phillip M. "Is Burglary a Violent Crime? An Empirical Investigation of the Armed Career Criminal Act's Classification of Burglary as a Violent Felony." *Criminal Justice Policy Review* 30, no. 5 (2019): 663–80.

Kroman, David. "Seattle's Arrest Alternative, LEAD, Moves beyond Police." *Crosscut*, July 17, 2020.

Kron, Josh. "Red State, Blue City: How the Urban-Rural Divide Is Splitting America." *Atlantic*, November 30, 2012.

Kupchik, Aaron. *Homeroom Security: School Discipline in an Age of Fear*. New York: New York University Press, 2010.

Kushner, Rachel. "Are Prisons Necessary? Ruth Wilson Gilmore Might Change Your Mind." *New York Times Magazine*, April 17, 2019.

Kuziemko, Illyana. "How Should Inmates Be Released from Prison? An Assessment of Parole versus Fixed-Sentence Regimes." *Quarterly Journal of Economics* 128, no. 1 (2013): 371–424.

Lacey, Nicola, and David Soskice. "American Exceptionalism in Crime, Punishment, and Disadvantage: Race, Federalization, and Politicization in the Perspective of Local Autonomy." In *American Exceptionalism in Crime and Punishment*, edited by Kevin R. Reitz. Oxford: Oxford University Press, 2018.

Lacy, Karyn. "The New Sociology of Suburbs: A Research Agenda for Analysis of Emerging Trends." *Annual Review of Sociology* 42 (2016): 369–84.

Langton, Lynn, and Jennifer Truman. *Socio-emotional Impact of Violent Crime*. Washington, DC: U.S. Department of Justice, Bureau of Justice Statistics, 2014.

Lara-Millan, Armando. "Public Emergency Over-crowding in the Era of Mass Imprisonment." *American Sociological Review* 79, no. 5 (2014): 866–87.

Larimer, Mary E., Daniel K. Malone, Michelle D. Garner, David C. Atkins, Bonnie Burlington, Heather S. Lonczak, Kenneth Tanzer, Joshua Ginzler, Seema L. Clifasefi, William G. Hobson, and G. Alan Marlatt. "Health Care and Public Service Use and Costs before and after Provision of Housing for Chronically Homeless Persons with Severe Alcohol Problems." *Journal of the American Medical Association* 301, no. 13 (2009): 1349–57.

LaSalle, L. *An Overdose Death Is Not Murder: Why Drug-Induced Homicide Laws Are Counter-Productive and Inhumane*. New York: Drug Policy Alliance, 2017.

Lassiter, Mathew D. "Impossible Criminals: The Suburban Imperatives of America's War on Drugs." *Journal of American History* 102, no. 1 (2015): 126–40.

Latimer, Jeff, Kelly Morton-Bourgon, and Jo-Anne Chrétien. *A Meta-Analytic Examination of Drug Treatment Courts: Do They Reduce Recidivism?* Ottawa: Government of Canada, 2006.

Latimore, Amanda D., and Rachel S. Bergstein. "'Caught with a Body' yet Protected by Law? Calling 911 for Opioid Overdose in the Context of the Good Samaritan Law." *International Journal of Drug Policy* 50 (2017): 82–89.

Law Enforcement Assisted Diversion (LEAD). *Referral and Diversion Protocol*. Seattle, 2018.

Lee, Hedwig, Tyler McCormick, Margaret T. Hicken, and Christopher Wildeman. "Racial Inequalities in Connectedness to Imprisoned Individuals in the United States." *Du Bois Review* 12, no. 2 (2015): 269–82.

Lee, Hedwig, Christopher Wildeman, Emily Wang, Niki Matusko, and James S. Jackson. "A Heavy Burden? The Health Consequences of Having a Family Member Incarcerated." *American Journal of Public Health* 104, no. 3 (2014): 421–27.

LEAD National Support Bureau. Advancing Criminal Justice Reform in 2021. Accessed March 3, 2020. https://www.leadbureau.org/

Lees, Tom Slater, and Elvin Wyly. *Gentrification*. New York: Routledge, 2008.

Leigh, Courtney, Elizabeth Pelletier, Sarah Eppler-Epstein, Ryan King, and Leah Sakala. *A Matter of Time: Causes and Consequences of Rising Time Served in America's Prisons*. Washington, DC: Urban Institute, 2017.

Lennard, Natasha. "Oregon's Decriminalization Vote Might Be Biggest Step Yet to Ending War on Drugs." *Intercept*, November 4, 2020. https://theintercept.com/2020/11/04/oregon-drugs-decriminalization/.

Lerman, Amy E., and Vesla M. Weaver. *Arresting Citizenship: The Democratic Consequences of American Crime Control*. Chicago: University of Chicago Press, 2014.

Lichter, Daniel T., Domenico Parisi, and Michael C. Tacquino. "The Geography of Exclusion: Race, Segregation and Concentrated Poverty." *Social Problems* 59 (2012): 364–88.

Liebertz, Scott, and Jaclyn Bunch. "Examining the Externalities of Welfare Reform: TANF and Crime." *Justice Quarterly* 35, no. 3 (2017): 477–504.

Lilley, David R. "Did Drug Courts Lead to Increased and Punishment of Minor Drug Offenses?" *Justice Quarterly* 34 (2017): 673–98.

Lilley, David R., Kristen DeVall, and Kasey Tucker-Gail. "Drug Courts and Arrest for Substance Possession: Was the African American Community Differentially Impacted?" *Crime & Delinquency* 65, no. 3 (2019): 352–74.

Lilley, David R., Megan C. Stewart, and Kasey Tucker-Gail. "Drug Courts and Net-Widening in U.S. Cities: A Reanalysis Using Propensity Score Matching." *Criminal Justice Policy Review* 31, no. 2 (2020): 287–308.

Lipari, Rachel N., Eunice Park-Lee, and Struther Van Horn. *America's Need for and Receipt of Substance Use Treatment in 2015*. Washington, DC: Substance Abuse and Mental Health Services Administration, September 29, 2016.

Lipsky, Michael. *Street-Level Bureaucracy: Dilemmas of the Individual in Public Services*. New York: Russell Sage, 1980.

Llewellyn, J., and R. Howse. *Restorative Justice: A Conceptual Framework*. Ottawa: Law Commission of Canada, 1998.

Löbmann, R., and U. Verthein. "Explaining the Effectiveness of Heroin-Assisted Treatment on Crime Reductions." *Law and Human Behavior* 33, no. 1 (2009): 83–95.

Lofstrom, Magnus, and Steven Raphael. "Incarceration and Crime: Evidence from California's Public Safety Realignment Reform." *Annals of the American Academy of Political and Social Science* 664 (2016): 196- 220.

Lofstrom, Magnus, and Steven Raphael. "Prison Downsizing and Public Safety: Evidence from California." *Criminology & Public Policy* 15, no. 2 (2016): 349–65.

Lopez, German. "The New War on Drugs: Not Every State Is Responding to the Opioid Epidemic with Just Public Health Policies." *Vox*, September 13, 2017.

Lopez, German. "When a Drug Epidemic's Victims Are White: How Racial Bias and Segregation Molded a Gentler Rhetorical Response to the Opioid Crisis." *Vox*, April 4, 2016.

Lopez, German. "The First Step Act, Explained." *Vox,* February 5, 2019.

Love, Michael M., Tracy J. Cohn, Thomas W. Pierce, and Sarah L. Hastings. "Trends in Injection Use among Prescription Opioid-Misusing Individuals in the Rural United States." *Journal of Rural Mental Health* 40, no. 3 (2016): 180–92.

Lowenkamp, Christopher, Alexander Holsinger, and Edward Latessa. "Are Drug Courts Effective: A Meta-Analytic Review." *Journal of Community Corrections* 10 (2005): 5–10.

Lynch, Mona. "Crack Pipes and Policing: A Case Study of Institutional Racism and Remedial Action in Cleveland." *Law & Policy* 33 (2011): 179–214.

Lynch, Mona. *Hard Bargains: The Coercive Power of Drug Laws in Federal Court*. New York: Russell Sage Foundation, 2016.

Lynch, Mona, and Craig Haney. "Looking across the Empathic Divide: Racialized Decision Making on the Capital Jury." *Michigan State Law Review* 2011, (2011): 573–607.

Lynch, Mona, and Marisa Omori. "Crack as Proxy: Aggressive Federal Drug Prosecutions and the Production of Black-White Racial Inequality." *Law & Society Review* 52 (2018): 773–809.

Lynch, Mona, and Marisa Omori. "Legal Change and Sentencing Norms in the Wake of Booker: The Impact of Time and Place on Drug Trafficking Cases in Federal Court." *Law and Society Review* 48, no. 2 (2014): 411–45.

Mack, K. A., C. M. Jones, and M. F. Ballesteros. "Illicit Drug Use, Illicit Drug Use Disorders, and Drug Overdose Deaths in Metropolitan and Nonmetropolitan Areas: United States." *Morbidity and Mortality Weekly Report, Surveillance Summaries* 66, no. 19 (2017): 1–12.

MacCoun, Robert. "Toward a Psychology of Harm Reduction." *American Psychologist* 53 (1998): 1199–209.

Madley, Benjamin. *An American Genocide: The United States and the California Indian Catastrophe, 1846-1873*. New Haven, CT: Yale University Press, 2016.

Maguire, Kathleen, ed. *Sourcebook of Criminal Justice Statistics Online*. Albany, NY: University of Albany, Hindelang Criminal Justice Research Center, 2013.

Maher, Lisa, and David Dixon. "Policing and Public Health: Law Enforcement and Harm Minimization in a Street-Level Drug Market." *British Journal of Criminology* 39 (1999): 488–513.

Malm, Alli, Dina Perrone, and Erica Magaña. *Law Enforcement Assisted Diversion (LEAD) External Evaluation: Report to the California State Legislature*. Long Beach: California State University Long Beach, School of Criminology, Criminal Justice and Emergency Management, 2020.

Marez, JoAnne. "Youngblood, Bailey Guilty of Murder." *Kitsap Sun*, January 1, 1993.

Marijuana Policy Institute. "Decriminalization." Retrieved on September 30, 2020.

Marlatt, G. Alan. *Harm Reduction: Pragmatic Strategies for Managing High-Risk Behaviors.* New York: Guilford Press, 2002.

Marlowe, Douglas B. "Achieving Racial and Ethnic Fairness in Drug Courts." *Court Review* 49 (2013): 40–47.

Marlowe, Douglas B., David S. DeMatteo, and David S. Festinger. "A Sober Assessment of Drug Courts." *Federal Sentencing Reporter* 16, no. 2 (2003): 153–57.

Martin, Jonathan. "Writer's World: Life behind Bars." *Seattle Times*, April 15, 2012.

Martinson, Robert. "New Findings, New Views: A Note of Caution regarding Sentencing Reform." *Hofstra Law Review* 7, no. 2 (1979): 243–58.

Maruna, Shadd. "Commentary: Time to Get Rid of the Skid Bid? What Good Are Short Term Stays of Incarceration?" *Journal of the American Academies of Political and Social Science* 665, no. 1 (2016): 98–102.

Maruschak, Laura M., Marcus Berzofsky, and Jennifer Unangst. *Medical Problems of State and Federal Prisoners and Jail Inmates, 2011–12.* Washington, DC: Bureau of Justice Statistics, 2015.

Maruschak, Laura M., and Todd D. Minton. *Correctional Populations in the United States, 2017–18.* Washington, DC: Bureau of Justice Statistics, 2020.

Massey, Douglas S., and Chiara Capoferro. "The Geographic Diversification of American Immigration." In *New Faces in New Places: The Changing Geography of American Immigration*, edited by Douglas S. Massey. New York: Russell Sage, 2008.

Matassa, Mark, Kery Murakami, and David Postman. "O.K. Boys Ranch—How a House of Horrors Stayed Open—System Gets Blame, but People Failed to Heed Warnings." *Seattle Times*, December 14, 1995.

Mather, Mark, and Beth Jarosz. *Poverty and Inequality Pervasive in Two-Fifths of U.S. Counties.* Washington, DC: Population Reference Bureau, 2016.

Mauer, Marc. "A Twenty Year Maximum for Prison Sentences." *Democracy: A Journal of Ideas* 39 (Winter 2016). Accessed June 3, 2020. https://democracyjournal.org/magazine/39/a-20-year-maximum-for-prison-sentences/

Mauer, Marc, and Ashley Nellis. *The Meaning of Life: The Case for Abolishing Life Sentences.* New York: New Press, 2019.

Maynard, Mark. "Kentucky Incarceration Rate Surges." *Kentucky Today*, April 29, 2019.

McCold, Paul, and Benjamin Wachtell. *Restorative Policing Experiment: The Bethlehem Pennsylvania Police Family Group Conferencing Project.* Bethlehem, PA: Community Service Foundation, 1998.

McKinley, Jesse. "The Bail Reform Backlash That Has Democrats at War," *New York Times*, February 14, 2020.

Meares, Tracey L., and Vesla M. Weaver. "Abolish the Police?" *Boston Review*, August 21, 2017.

Medina, Daniel A. "The Progressive Prosecutors Blazing a New Path for the Justice System." *Guardian*, July 23, 2019.

Mendleberg, Tali. *The Race Card: Campaign Strategy, Implicit Messages and the Norm of Equality.* Princeton, NJ: Princeton University Press, 2001.

Miller, Lisa. *The Myth of Mob Rule.* Oxford: Oxford University Press, 2016.

Miller, Reuben Jonathan. "Devolving the Carceral State: Race, Prison-Reentry, and the Micro-Politics of Urban Poverty Management." *Punishment & Society* 16, no. 3 (2014): 305–35.

Mitchell, Andreas, and Brie Williams. "Compassionate Release Policy Reform: Physicians as Advocates for Human Dignity." *American Medical Association Journal of Ethics* 19, no. 9 (2017): 854–61.

Mitchell, Ojmarrh, David B. Wilson, Amy Eggers, and Doris L. MacKenzie. "Assessing the Effectiveness of Drug Courts on Recidivism: A Meta-Analytic Review of Traditional and Non-Traditional Drug Courts." *Journal of Criminal Justice* 40, no. 1 (2012): 60–71.

Møllmann, Marianne, and Christine Mehta. *Neither Justice nor Treatment: Drug Courts in the United States*. Washington, DC: Physicians for Human Rights, 2017.

Monnat, Shannon M. "Factors Associated with County-Level Differences in U.S. Drug-Related Mortality Rates." *American Journal of Preventative Medicine* 54, no. 5 (2018): 611–19.

Morris, Martina, and Bruce Western. "Inequality at the Close of the Twentieth Century." *Annual Review of Sociology* 25 (1999): 623–52.

Muhammad, Khalil Gibran. *The Condemnation of Blackness: Race, Crime and the Making of Urban America*. Cambridge, MA: Harvard University Press, 2011.

Murphy, Jennifer. *Illness or Deviance? Drug Courts, Drug Treatment, and the Ambiguity of Addiction*. Philadelphia, PA: Temple University Press, 2015.

Myers, Sage R., Charles C. Branas, Benjamin C. French, Michael L. Nance, Michael J. Kallan, Douglas J. Wiebe, and Brendan G. Carr. "Safety in Numbers: Are Major Cities the Safest Places in the United States?" *Annals of Emergency Medicine* 62, no. 4 (2013): 408–18.

Nadelmann, Ethan. "Thinking Seriously about Alternatives to Drug Prohibition." *Daedalus* 121 (2002): 85–97.

Nagin, Daniel. "Deterrence in the Twenty-First Century: A Review of the Evidence." *Crime & Justice: A Review of the Research* 42 (2013): 199–263.

Napatof, Alexandra. "Misdemeanors." *Annual Review of Law & Social Science* 11 (2015): 255–67.

National Academies of Sciences, Engineering and Medicine. *Decarcerating Correctional Facilities during COVID-19: Advancing Health, Equity, and Safety*. Washington, DC: National Academies Press, 2020.

National Academies of Sciences, Engineering and Medicine. *Medications for Opioid Use Disorder Save Lives*. Washington, DC: National Academies Press, 2019.

National Alliance to End Homelessness. *A Plan, Not a Dream: How to End Homelessness in Ten Years*. Washington, DC, 2000.

National Association of Criminal Defense Lawyers. *The Trial Penalty: The Sixth Amendment Right to Trial on the Verge of Extinction and How to Save It*. Washington, DC, 2018.

National Association of Drug Court Professionals, Drug Court Standards Committee. *Defining Drug Courts: The Key Components*. Washington, DC: Bureau of Justice Assistance, 2004.

National Center on Addiction and Substance Abuse at Columbia University. *Behind Bars II: Substance Abuse and America's Prison Population*. New York: Columbia University Press, 2010.

National Conference of State Legislatures. *Drug Sentencing Trends*. Washington, DC, 2016.

National Institute of Corrections. *Correctional Health Care: Addressing the Needs of Elderly, Chronically Ill and Terminally Ill Inmates*. Washington, DC: National Institute of Corrections, 2004.

National Low Income Housing Coalition. *The Crisis in America's Housing: Confronting Myths and Promoting a Balanced Housing Policy*. Washington, DC: National Low Income Housing Coalition, 2005.

Neal, Derek, and Armin Rick. "The Prison Boom and the Lack of Black Progress after Smith and Welch." Working Paper No. 20283. National Bureau of Economic Research, 2014.

Neller, Daniel J., Robert L. Denney, Christina A. Pietz, and R. Paul Thomlinson. "The Relationship between Trauma and Violence in a Jail Inmate Sample." *Journal of Interpersonal Violence* 21, no. 9 (2006): 1234–41.

Nellis, Ashley. *Life-Sentenced Population Outnumbers Population of All Prisoners at the Dawn of Mass Incarceration*. Washington, DC: Sentencing Project, 2019.

Nellis, Ashley. *No End in Sight: America's Enduring Reliance on Life Imprisonment*. Washington, DC: Sentencing Project, 2021.

Nellis, Ashley. *Still Life: America's Increasing Use of Life and Long-Term Sentences*. Washington, DC: Sentencing Project, 2017.

NENA: The 9-1-1 Association. *9-1-1 Statistics*. Accessed April 21, 2021. https://www.nena.org/page/911Statistics

Netherland, Julie, and Helena B. Hansen. "The Drug War That Wasn't: Wasted Whiteness, Dirty Doctors and Race in Media Coverage of Prescription Opioid Misuse." *Culture, Medicine and Psychiatry* 40, no. 4 (2016): 664–86.

Netherland, Julie, and Helena B. Hansen. "White Opioids: Pharmaceutical Race and the War on Drugs That Wasn't." *BioSocieties* 12, no. 2 (2017): 217–38.

Nichanian, Daniel. "Voters beyond Big Cities Rejected Mass Incarceration in Tuesday's Elections." *Appeal*, November 7, 2019.

Nolan, James L., Jr. *Reinventing Justice: The American Drug Court Movement*. Princeton, NJ: Princeton University Press, 2001.

O'Connor, Maureen. *The Hidden Disaster of State Issue* 1. Supreme Court of Ohio, Chambers of the Chief Justice, August 28, 2018. http://ohiopa.org/oconnor1.pdf.

O'Donnell, Guillermo. "On the State, Democratization and Some Conceptual Problems: A Latin American View with Glances at Some Postcommunist Countries." *World Development* 21 (1993): 1355–69.

O'Hear, Michael, and Darren Wheelock. 2020. "Violent Crime and Punitiveness: An Empirical Study of Public Opinion." *Marquette Law Review* 103, no. 3 (2020): 1035–71.

Oppel, Richard A., Jr. "Sentencing Shift Gives New Leverage to Prosecutors." *New York Times*, September 25, 2011.

Oppel, Richard A., Jr. "A Cesspool of a Dungeon: The Surging Population in Rural Jails." *New York Times*, December 13, 2019.

Opportunity Agenda. *An Overview of Public Opinion and Discourse on Criminal Justice Issues*. Washington, DC: Opportunity Agenda, 2014.

Organisation for Economic Co-operation and Development, Statistics Directorate. "Income Inequality Update: Rising Inequality: Youth and Poor Fall Further Behind. Insights from the OECD Income Distribution Database." June 2014. https://www.oecd.org/social/OECD2014-Income-Inequality-Update.pdf.

Orth, Ulrich. "The Effects of Legal Involvement on Crime Victims' Psychological Adjustment." In *Social Psychology of Punishment of Crime*, edited by Margit Oswald. New York: Wiley & Sons, 2009.

Owens, Emily. "Truthiness in Punishment: The Far Reach of Truth-in-Sentencing Laws in State Courts." *Journal of Empirical Legal Studies* 8 (2011): 239–61.

Page, Joshua. "Prisoners Officer Unions and the Perpetuation of the Penal Status Quo." *Criminology and Public Policy* 10, no. 3 (2011): 735–70.

Page, Joshua. *The Toughest Beat: Politics, Punishment and the Prison Officers Union in California*. Oxford: Oxford University Press, 2011.

Pager, Devah. *Marked: Race, Crime and Finding Work in an Era of Mass Incarceration*. Chicago: University of Chicago Press, 2007.

Pager, Devah, Bruce Western, and Bart Bonikowski. "Discrimination in Low Wage Labor Markets." *American Sociological Review* 74 (2009): 777–79.

Papachristos, Andrew V., and Sara Bastomski. "Connected in Crime: The Enduring Effect of Neighborhood Networks on Spatial Patterning of Violence." *American Journal of Sociology* 124 (2018): 517–68.

Pare, Paul-Philippe, and Richard Felson. "Income Inequality, Poverty and Crime across Nations." *British Journal of Sociology* 65, no. 3 (2014): 432–58.

Parsons, Jim, and Tiffany Bergin. "The Impact of Criminal Justice Involvement on Victims' Mental Health." *Journal of Traumatic Stress* 23, no. 2 (2010): 182–88.

Patterson, E. J., and S. H. Preston. "Estimating Mean Length of Stay in Prison: Method and Applications." *Journal of Quantitative Criminology* 24 (2008): 33–49.

Payne, Allison Ann, and Kelly Welch. "Restorative Justice in Schools: The Influence of Race on Restorative Discipline." *Youth and Society* 2013 (2013): 1–26.

Pérez, Myrna. "7 Years of Gutting Voting Rights." New York: Brennan Center for Justice, 2020.

Petersilia, Joan, and Francis T. Cullen. "Liberal but Not Stupid: Meeting the Promise of Downsizing Prisons." *Stanford Journal of Criminal Law and Policy* 2 (2015): 1–43.

Pettit, Becky. *Invisible Men: Mass Incarceration and the Myth of Racial Progress.* New York: Russell Sage, 2012.

Pettit, Becky, and Bryan Sykes. "State of the Union 2017: Incarceration." Stanford, CA: Stanford Center on Poverty and Inequality, 2017.

Pettit, Becky, and Bruce Western. "Mass Imprisonment and the Life Course: Race and Class Inequality in U.S. Incarceration." *American Sociological Review* 69 (2004): 151–69.

Pew Center on the States. *One in 100: Behind Bars in America.* Philadelphia, PA: Pew Charitable Trusts, 2008.

Pew Center on the States. *Time Served: The High Cost, Low Return of Longer Prison Terms.* Washington, DC: Pew Center on the States, 2012.

Pew Charitable Trusts. *Imprisonment: Crime Fell in 30 States over Five Years.* Washington, DC: Pew Charitable Trusts, Public Safety Performance Project, 2015.

Pew Charitable Trusts. "Issue Brief: Punishment Rate Measures Prison Use Relative to Crime." Washington, DC: Pew Charitable Trusts, 2016.

Pew Charitable Trusts. *Prisons and Crime: A Complex Link.* Washington, DC: Pew Charitable Trusts, Public Safety Performance Project, 2014.

Pfaff, John F. *Locked In: The True Causes of Mass Incarceration—and How to Achieve Real Reform.* New York: Basic Books, 2017.

Pfaff, John F. "Micro and Macro Causes of Prison Growth." *Georgia State University Law Review* 28, no. 4 (2013): 1237–72.

Pfaff, John F. "The Myths and Realities of Correctional Severity: Evidence from the National Corrections Reporting Program on Sentencing Practices." *American Law and Economics Review* 13, no. 20 (2011): 491–531.

Pierson, Paul. "Increasing Returns, Path Dependence, and the Study of Politics." *American Political Science Review* 94, no. 2 (2000): 251–67.

Pilgram, David. "The Brute Caricature." Ferris State University, Jim Crow Museum, 2012. http://www.ferris.edu/jimcrow/brute/.

Pinto, Nick. "Bailing Out: Criminal Justice Reformers Are Rethinking the Crusade against Cash Bail." *New Republic*, April 6, 2020.

Porter, Nicole D. *Repurposing: New Beginnings for Closed Prisons.* Washington, DC: Sentencing Project, 2016.

Pranis, Kay. "Restorative Justice in Minnesota and the USA: Development and Current Practice." *Visiting Experts' Papers, 123rd International Senior Seminar, Resource Material Series* 63 (2004): 111–23.

"Prison Sentences Revised." *Spartanburg Herald-Journal*, June 3, 2010.

Provine, Doris Marie. *Unequal under the Law: Race in the War on Drugs.* Chicago: University of Chicago Press, 2007.

Psick, Zachary, Cyrus Ahalt, Rebecca T. Brown, and Jonathan Simon. "Baby Boomers: Policy Implications of Aging Prison Populations." *International Journal of Prison Health* 13, no. 1 (2017): 57–63.

Purnell, Derecka, and Marbre Stahly-Butts. "The Police Can't Solve the Problem. They Are the Problem," *New York Times*, September 26, 2019.

Quinones, Sam. *Dreamland: The True Tale of America's Opiate Epidemic.* New York: Bloomsbury Press, 2015.

Rakoff, Jed S. "Why Innocent People Plead Guilty." *New York Review of Books*, November 20, 2014.

Ramirez, Mark D. "Americans' Changing Views on Crime and Punishment." *Public Opinion Quarterly* 78, no. 2 (2014): 560–63.

Ranapurwala, Shabbar I., Meghan E. Shanahan, Apostolos A. Alexandridis, Scott K. Proescholdbell, Rebecca B. Naumann, Daniel Edwards Jr., and Stephen W. Marshall. "Opioid Overdose Mortality among Former North Carolina Inmates: 2000–2015." *American Journal of Public Health* 108 (2018): 1207–13.

Rankin, Bill. "Drug Court Grads Have Reason to Smile: Defendants Work, Stay Sober, Get Treatment in Dawson County." *Atlanta Journal-Constitution*, August 20, 2012.

Raphael, Steven, and Michael A. Stoll. *Job Sprawl and the Suburbanization of Poverty.* Washington, DC: Brookings Institution, 2010.

Raphael, Steven, and Michael A. Stoll. *Why Are So Many Americans in Prison?* New York: Russell Sage Foundation, 2013.

Reding, Nick. *Methland: The Death and Life of an American Small Town.* New York: Bloomsbury Press, 2009.

Reeves, Jimmie L., and Richard Campbell. *Cracked Coverage: Television News, the Anti-Cocaine Crusade and the Reagan Legacy.* Durham, NC: Duke University Press, 1994.

"Reform Sentencing." Editorial. *Spartanburg Herald-Journal,* February 18, 2008.

Reimer, Norman L., and Martin Antonio Sabelli. "The Tyranny of the Trial Penalty: The Consensus That Coercive Plea Practices Must End." *Federal Sentencing Reporter* 31, nos. 4–5 (2019): 215–21.

Reinarman, Craig, and Harry G. Levine. "The Crack Attack: Politics and Media in the Drug Scare." In *Crack in America: Demon Drugs and Social Justice*, edited by Craig Reinarman and Harry G. Levine. Berkeley: University of California Press, 1997.

Reinarman, Craig, and Harry G. Levine. "Crack in Context: America's Latest Demon Drug." In *Crack in America: Demon Drugs and Social Justice*, edited by Craig Reinarman and Harry G. Levine. Berkeley: University of California Press, 1997.

Rempel, Michael, Janine M. Zweig, Christine H. Lindquist, John K. Roman, Shelli B. Rossman, and Dana Kralstein. "Multi-Site Evaluation Demonstrates Effectiveness of Adult Drug Courts." *Judicature* 95, no. 4 (2012): 154–57.

Renaud, Jorge. *Eight Keys to Mercy: How to Shorten Excessive Prison Sentences.* Northampton, MA: Prison Policy Initiative, 2018.

Renaud, Jorge. *Grading the Parole Release Systems of All 50 States.* Northampton, MA: Prison Policy Initiative, 2019.

Reosti, Anna. "We Totally Go Subjective: Discretion, Discrimination, and Tenant Screening in a Landlord's Market." *Law and Social Inquiry* 45, no. 3 (2020): 618–57.

Reuter, Peter. "On the Multiple Sources of Violence in Drug Markets." *Criminology & Public Policy* 15, no. 3 (2016): 877–83.

Reuter, Peter. "Systemic Violence in Drug Markets." *Crime, Law and Social Change* 52, no. 3 (2009): 275–84.

Reuter, Peter, and Domenic Schnoz. *Assessing Drug Problems and Policies in Switzerland, 1999–2008.* Accessed January 4, 2020. https://assmca.pr.gov/BibliotecaVirtual/Sustancias/Assessing%20Drug%20Problems%20and%20Policies%20in%20Switzerland.pdf

Rezansoff, Stefanie N., Akm Moniruzzaman, Elenore Clark, and Julian M. Somers. "Beyond Recidivism: Changes in Health and Social Service Involvement Following Exposure to Drug Treatment Court." *Substance Abuse Treatment, Prevention, and Policy* 10 (2015): 1–12.

Rhodes, Tim, and Dagmar Hedrich, eds. *Harm Reduction: Evidence, Impacts and Challenges.* Lisbon: Office for Official Publications of the European Communities, 2010.

Rios, Victor M. 2011. *Punished: Police in the Lives of Black and Latino Boys.* New York: New York University Press.

Roberts, Anna. "LEAD Us Not into Temptation: A Response to Barbara Fedders's Opioid Policing." *Indiana Law Journal Supplement* 94, no. 5 (2018): 91–103.

Rodgers, Simon, and Feilding Cage. "Full US 2012 Election County-Level Results to Download." *Guardian*, November 14, 2012.

Rhine, Edward E., Joan Petersilia, and Kevin R. Reitz. "Improving Parole Release in America." *Federal Sentencing Reporter* 28, no. 2 (2015): 96–104.

Rich, Josiah, Scott Allen, and Mavis Nimoh. "We Must Release Prisoners to Lessen the Spread of Coronavirus." *Washington Post,* March 17, 2020.

Robina Institute of Criminal Law and Criminal Justice. "New Model Penal Code Approved by the American Law Institute." *Robina Institute Blog,* June 5, 2017.

Roeder, Oliver. "A Million People Were in Prison before We Called It Mass Incarceration." *FiveThirtyEight,* September 18, 2015.

Rogeberg, Ole. "Drug Policy, Values and the Public Health Approach: Four Lessons from Drug Policy Reform Movements." *Nordic Studies on Alcohol and Drugs* 32 (2015): 334–62.

Rossman, Shelli B., Michael Rempel, John K. Roman, Janine M. Zweig, Christine H. Lindquist, Mia Green, P. Mitchell Downey, Jennifer Yahner, Avinash S. Bhati, and Donald J. Farole. *The Multi-Site Adult Drug Court Evaluation: The Impact of Drug Courts.* Washington, DC: Urban Institute, 2011.

Rottman, David, and Pamela Casey. "Therapeutic Jurisprudence and the Emergence of Problem-Solving Courts." *National Institute of Justice Journal* (1999): 12–19.

Roussell, Aaron, and Daniel Gascón. "Defining 'Policeability': Cooperation, Control, and Resistance in South Los Angeles Community-Police Meetings." *Social Problems* 61, no. 2 (2014): 237–58.

Sabik, Iyengar. "The Dangerous Shortage of Domestic Violence Services." *Health Affairs* 28, Supplement 1 (2009): w1052–65.

Sabol, William J. *Survey of State Criminal History Information Systems, 2012.* Washington, DC: Bureau of Justice Statistics 2014.

Sabol, William J., Thaddeus L. Johnson, and Alexander Caccavale. *Trends in Correctional Control by Race and Sex.* Washington, DC: Council on Criminal Justice, 2019.

Saez, Emmanuel, and Gabriel Zucman. *The Triumph of Injustice: How the Rich Dodge Taxes and How to Make Them Pay.* New York: Norton, 2019.

Saloner, Brendan, Kalind Parish, Julie A. Ward, Grade DiLaura, and Sharon Dolovich. "COVID-19 Cases and Deaths in Federal and State Prisons." *JAMA* 324, no. 6 (2020): 602–3.

Sampson, Robert J. "Criminal Justice Processing and the Social Matrix of Adversity." *Annals of the Academy of Social and Political Sciences* 651 (2014): 296–301.

Sampson, Robert J. *Great American City: Chicago and the Enduring Neighborhood Effect.* Chicago: University of Chicago Press, 2012.

Sampson, Robert. *Toward a Theory of Race, Crime and Urban Inequality.* In *Crime and Inequality,* edited by John Hagan and Ruth D. Petersen. Stanford, CA: Stanford University Press, 1995.

Sampson, Robert, and John Laub. "Life Course Desisters? Trajectories of Crime among Delinquent Boys Followed to Age 70." *Criminology* 41, no. 3 (2003): 301–40.

Sampson, Robert, and Charles Loeffler. "Punishment's Place: The Local Concentration of Mass Incarceration." *Daedalus* Summer (2010): 20–31.

Sanger-Katz, Margot. "Bleak New Estimates in Drug Epidemic: A Record 72,000 Overdose Deaths in 2017." *New York Times*, August 15, 2018.

Sarat, Austin. *The Killing State: Capital Punishment in Law, Politics, and Culture.* Oxford: Oxford University Press, 1999.

Satterberg, Dan. "My Sister's Drug Addiction—And What It Taught Me." *Crosscut,* May 17, 2018.

Savage, Joanne, and Bryan Vila. "Changes in Child Welfare and Subsequent Crime Rate Trends: A Cross-National Test of the Lagged Nurturance Hypothesis." *Applied Developmental Psychology* 23, no. 1 (2002): 51–82.

Savelsberg, Joachim J. "Knowledge, Domination, and Criminal Punishment." *American Journal of Sociology* 99 (1994): 911–43.

Sawyer, Wendy, and Peter Wagner. *Mass Incarceration: The Whole Pie, 2019*. Northampton, MA: Prison Policy Initiative, 2019.

Schauffler, R., R. LaFountain, S. Strickland, K. Holt, and K. Genthon, eds. "Court Statistics Project DataViewer." Court Statistics, November 20, 2019. www.courtstatistics.org.

Schedler, Andreas. "What Is Democratic Consolidation?" *Journal of Democracy* 9, no. 2 (1998): 91–107.

Schenwar, Maya, and Victoria Law. *Prison by Any Other Name: The Harmful Consequences of Popular Reforms*. New York: New Press, 2020.

Scholl, L., P. Seth, M. Kariisa, N. Wilson, and G. Baldwin. "Drug and Opioid-Involved Overdose Deaths." *Morbidity and Mortality Weekly Report* 67 (2019): 1419–27.

Schram, Sanford F., Joe Soss, and Richard C. Fording. "Deciding to Discipline: Race, Choice and Punishment at the Frontlines of Welfare Reform." *American Sociological Review* 74, no. 3 (2009): 398–422.

Schwartzapfel, Beth, Katie Park, and Andrew Demillo. *One in Five Prisoners in the United States Has Had Covid-19*. Marshall Project, December 2020. Accessed March 4, 2021. https://www.themarshallproject.org/2020/12/18/1-in-5-prisoners-in-the-u-s-has-had-covid-19

Seeds, Christopher. "Bifurcation Nation: American Penal Policy in Late Mass Incarceration." *Punishment & Society* 19, no. 5 (2017): 590–610.

Seitz-Wald, Alex, and Elahe Izadi. "Criminal Justice Reform, Brought to You by CPAC." *National Journal*, March 7, 2014.

Sen, Amartya. "Development as Capability Expansion." *Journal of Development Planning* 19 (1989): 41–58.

"A Sensible Call for Sentencing Reform." Editorial. *Roanoke Times*, October 13, 2008.

Sered, Danielle. *Until We Reckon: Mass Incarceration and the Road to Repair*. New York: New Press, 2019.

Sevigny, Eric, Brian Fuleihan, and Frank Ferdik. "Do Drug Courts Reduce the Use of Incarceration? A Meta-Analysis." *Journal of Criminal Justice* 41 (2013): 416–25.

Sevigny, Eric L., Harold A. Pollack, and Peter Reuter. "Can Drug Courts Help to Reduce Prison and Jail Populations?" *Annals of the American Academy of Political and Social Science* 647, no. 1 (2013): 190–212.

Sewell, Abigail, and Kevin Jefferson. "Collateral Damage: The Health Effects of Invasive Police Encounters in New York City." *Journal of Urban Health* 93, Supplement 1 (2016): 42–67.

Sewell, Abigail, Kevin Jefferson, and Hedwig Lee. "Living under Surveillance: Gender, Psychological Distress, and Stop-Question-and-Frisk Policing in New York City." *Social Science and Medicine* 159 (2016): 1–13.

Shade, Damion. "HB 1269 Makes 780 Retroactive but Leaves Issues Unresolved." Oklahoma Policy Institute, May 28, 2019. https://okpolicy.org/hb-1269-makes-780-retroactive-but-leaves-issues-unresolved/.

Shaffer, Deborah Koetzle. "Looking inside the Black Box of Drug Courts: A Meta-Analytic Review." *Justice Quarterly* 28, no. 3 (2011): 493–521.

Shah, Sanjay, David DeMatteo, Michael Keesler, Jennie Davis, Kirk Heilbrun, and David S. Festinger. "Addiction Severity Index Scores and Urine Drug Screens at Baseline as Predictors of Graduation from Drug Court." *Crime & Delinquency* 61, no. 9 (2015): 1257–77.

Sharkey, Patrick, Gerard Torrats-Espinosa, and Delaram Takyar. "Community and the Crime Decline." *American Sociological Review* 82, no. 6 (2017): 1214–40.

Shaw, Michael. "Photos Reveal Media's Softer Tone on Opioid Crisis." *Columbia Journalism Review*, July 26, 2017.

Shepherd, Katie. "Portlanders Call 911 to Report 'Unwanted' People More Than Any Other Reason: We Listened In." *Willamette Week*, February 6, 2019.

Sherman, Lawrence W., Heather Strang, Evan Mayo-Wilson, Daniel J. Woods, and Barak Ariel. "Are Restorative Justice Conferences Effective in Reducing Repeat Offending?" *Journal of Quantitative Criminology* 31, no. 1 (2015): 1–24.

Shifter, Michael. "Tensions and Trade-Offs in Latin America." *Journal of Democracy* 8, no. 2 (1997): 114–28.

Shuler, Jack. "Overdose and Punishment." *New Republic*, September 10, 2018.

Silbey, Susan, and Austin Sarat. "Critical Traditions in Law and Society Research." *Law & Society Review* 21, no. 1 (1987): 165–74.

Simes, Jessica. "Place and Punishment: The Spatial Context of Mass Incarceration." *Journal of Quantitative Criminology* 34, no. 2 (2018): 513–33.

Simmons, Catherine A. "Getting By after a Loved One's Death: The Relationship between Case Status, Trauma Symptoms, Life Satisfaction, and Coping." *Violence and Victims* 29, no. 3 (2014): 506–22.

Simon, Jonathan. *Governing through Crime: How the War on Crime Transformed American Democracy and Created a Culture of Fear.* New York: Oxford University Press, 2007.

Simon, Jonathan. *Mass Incarceration on Trial: A Remarkable Court Decision and the Future of Prisons in America.* New York: New Press, 2016.

Simon, Jonathan. "The Second Coming of Dignity." In *The New Criminal Justice Thinking,* edited by Sharon Dolovich and Alexandra Natapoff. New York: New York University Press, 2017.

Simon, Jonathan, and Stephen A. Rosenbaum. "Dignifying Madness: Rethinking Commitment in an Age of Mass Incarceration." *University of Miami Law Review* 70 (2015): 1–52.

Sledjeski, Eve M., Brittany Speisman, and Lisa C. Dierker. "Does Number of Lifetime Traumas Explain the Relationship between PTSD and Chronic Medical Conditions? Answers from the National Comorbidity Survey-Replication (NCS-R)." *Journal of Behavioral Medicine* 31, no. 4 (2008): 341–49.

Sliva, Shannon, and Carolyn Lambert. "Restorative Justice Legislation in American States: A Statutory Analysis of Emerging Legal Doctrine." *Journal of Policy Practice* 14 (2015): 77–95.

Small, Deborah. "Cause for Trepidation: Libertarian's Newfound Concern for Prison Reform." *Salon*, March 22, 2014.

Smeeding, Timothy. "Poor People in Rich Nations: The United States in Comparative Perspective." *Journal of Economic Perspectives* 20, no. 1 (2006): 69–92.

Smiley, Calvin John, and David Fakunle. "From 'Brute' to 'Thug:' The Demonization and Criminalization of Unarmed Black Male Victims in America." *Journal of Human Behavior and Social Environments* 26, nos. 3–4 (2016): 350–66.

Smith, Jason P., and David M. Merolla. "Black, Blue, and Blow: The Effect of Race and Criminal History on Perceptions of Police Violence." *Sociological Inquiry* 89, no. 4 (2019): 624–44.

Smith, Kevin B. "The Politics of Punishment: Evaluating Political Explanations of Incarceration Rates." *Journal of Politics* 66, no. 3 (2004): 925–38.

Smith, Neil. *The New Urban Frontier: Gentrification and the Revanchist City.* New York: Routledge, 1996.

Smith, Robert. "England and Wales Expand the Meaning of Domestic Abuse." National Public Radio, December 29, 2015.

Smith, Rich. "New Data Analysis Shows the Astonishing Breadth of Racial Disparity in Drug Possession Convictions." *Stranger*, March 17, 2021.

Snyder, Howard N., Alexia D. Cooper, and Joseph Mulako-Wangota. "Arrests in the United States, 1980 to 2014." Washington, DC: Bureau of Justice Statistics. www.bjs.gov, July 15, 2020.

Soss, Joe, Richard C. Fording, and Sanford F. Schram. *Disciplining the Poor: Neo-liberal Paternalism and the Persistent Power of Race.* Chicago: University of Chicago Press, 2011.

Steinberg, Darrell, David Mills, and Michael Romano. *When Did Prisons Become Acceptable Mental Healthcare Facilities?* Stanford, CA: Stanford Law School, 2015.

Stellin, Susan. "Is the Drug War Over? Arrest Statistics Say No." *New York Times*, November 5, 2019.

Stillman, Sara. "Black Wounds Matter." *New Yorker*, October 15, 2015.

Stone, Elizabeth. "Is There 'Hope for Every Addicted American'? The New U.S. War on Drugs." *Social Science* 7, no. 3 (2018).

Streiker, Carol S., and Jordan M. Streiker. "Judicial Developments in Capital Punishment Law." In *America's Experiment with Capital Punishment: Reflections on the Past, Present and Future of the Ultimate Penal Sanction*, edited by James R. Acker, Robert M. Bohm, and Charles S. Lanier. Durham: Carolina Academic Press, 2014.

Stuart, Barry. *Building Community Justice Partnerships: Community Peacemaking Circles*. Ottawa: Canadian Department of Justice, 1997.

Stuart, Forrest. *Down, out and under Arrest: Policing and Everyday Life in Skid Row*. Chicago: University of Chicago Press, 2016.

Stuart, Forrest, Amada Armenta, and Melissa Osborne. "Legal Control of Marginal Groups." *Annual Review of Law & Social Science* 11 (2015): 235–54.

Stuntz, William J. *The Collapse of American Criminal Justice*. Cambridge, MA: Harvard University Press, 2011.

Subramanian, Ram, Christian Henrichson, and Jacob Kang-Brown. *In Our Own Backyard: Confronting Growth and Disparities in Local Jails*. New York: Vera Institute of Justice, 2015.

Subramanian, Ram and Rebecka Moreno. *Drug War Détente: A Review of State-Level Drug Law Reform, 2009–2013*. New York: Vera Institute of Justice and Center on Sentencing and Corrections, 2014.

Substance Abuse and Mental Health Services Administration. *Key Substance Use and Mental Health Indicators in the United States: Results from the 2017 National Survey on Drug Use and Health*. Washington, DC: Substance Abuse and Mental Health Services Administration, 2018.

Sundt, Jodi, Emily J. Salisbury, and Mark G. Harmon. "Is Downsizing Prisons Dangerous? Effect of California's Realignment Act on Public Safety." *Criminology & Public Policy* 15 (2016): 315–41.

Sutton, John R. "Symbol and Substance: Effects of California's Three Strikes Law on Felony Sentencing." *Law & Society Review* 47, no. 1 (2013): 37–71.

Sykes, Bryan, and Becky Pettit. "Mass Incarceration, Family Complexity, and the Reproduction of Childhood Disadvantage." *Annals of the American Academy of Political and Social Sciences* 654, no. 1 (2014): 127–49.

Thorpe, Rebecca. "Perverse Politics: The Persistence of Mass Imprisonment in the 21st Century." *Perspectives on Politics* 13, no. 3 (2015): 618–37.

Tiger, Rebecca. *Judging Addicts: Drug Courts and Coercion in the Justice System*. New York: New York University Press, 2017.

Tiger, Rebecca. "Race, Class and the Framing of Drug Epidemics." *Contexts* 16, no. 4 (2013): 46–56.

Toda, Dean. "Something's Got to Give with Prison Population." *Gazette*, May 17, 2009.

Tonry, Michael. *Sentencing Fragments: Penal Reform in America, 1975–2025*. Oxford: Oxford University Press, 2018.

Tonry, Michael, and D. P. Farrington. "Punishment and Crime across Time and Space." *Crime and Justice* 33 (2005): 1–39.

Travis, Jeremy. "Summoning the Superheroes: Harnessing Science and Passion to Create a More Effective and Human Response to Crime." In *25th Anniversary Essays*, edited by Marc Mauer, and Kate Epstein. Washington, DC: Sentencing Project, 2012.

Travis, Jeremy, Bruce Western, and Steven Redburn, eds. *The Growth of Incarceration in the United States: Exploring Causes and Consequences*. Committee on Causes and Consequences of High Rates of Incarceration. Washington, DC: National Academies Press, 2014.

Truman, Jennifer L., and Lynn Langton. *Criminal Victimization, 2014*. Washington, DC: U.S. Department of Justice, Bureau of Justice Statistics, 2015.

Uggen, Christopher, Jeff Manza, and Melissa Thompson. "Citizenship, Democracy and the Civic Reintegration of Criminal Offenders." *Annals of the American Academy of Political and Social Science* 605, no. 1 (2006): 281–310.

Ullman, Sarah E., and Judith M. Siegel. "Traumatic Events and Physical Health in a Community Sample." *Journal of Traumatic Stress* 9, no. 4 (1996): 703–20.

Ulmer, Jeffrey T. and Brian D. Johnson. "Organizational Conformity and Punishment: Federal Court Communities and Judge-Initiated Guidelines Departures." *Journal of Criminal Law and Criminology* 107, no. 2 (2017): 253–92.

Umbreit, Mark, and Marilyn Armour. *Restorative Justice Dialogue: An Essential Guide for Research and Practice*. New York: Springer, 2011.

Umbreit, Mark S., Betty Vos, and Robert B. Coates. "Restorative Justice Dialogue: Evidence-Based Practice." *Contemporary Justice Review* 10, no. 1 (2007): 23–41.

Umbreit, Mark S., Betty Vos, Robert B. Coates, and E. Lightfoot. "Restorative Justice in Action: Restorative Justice in the Twenty-First Century." *Marquette Law Review* 89, no. 2 (2005): 251–304.

United Nations Office on Drugs and Crimes. International Homicide Statistics Database. Accessed April 22, 2021. https://data.worldbank.org/indicator/VC.IHR.PSRC.P5?locations=NO.

Unlock the Box. *Solitary Confinement Is Never the Answer*. June 2020. Accessed February 7, 2021. https://static1.squarespace.com/static/5a9446a89d5abbfa67013da7/t/5ee7c4f1860e0d57d0ce8195/1592247570889/June2020Report.pdf

Unnever, J. D., and Francis T. Cullen. "The Social Sources of American's Punitiveness: A Test of Three Competing Models." *Criminology* 48 (2010): 99–129.

U.S. Bureau of Labor Statistics. "Employment Situation Summary." Economic news release. October 2, 2020. https://www.bls.gov/news.release/empsit.nr0.htm.

U.S. Department of Health and Human Services. *The AFCARS Report*. Washington, DC: Administration for Children and Families, 2015.

U.S. Department of Justice. *Crimes against Persons with Disabilities*. Washington, DC: Office for Victims of Crime, 2017.

U.S. Government Accountability Office. *Adult Drug Courts*. Washington, DC: U.S. Government Accountability Office, 2011.

Vallas, Rebecca. *Disabled behind Bars: Mass Incarceration of People with Disabilities in America's Jails and Prisons*. Washington, DC: Center for American Progress, 2016.

Van Dijk, J., and J. van Kesteren. "The Prevalence and Perceived Seriousness of Victimization by Crime: Some Results of the International Crime Victims Survey." *European Journal of Criminal Law and Criminal Justice* 4 (1996): 48–67.

Vansickle, Abbie. "A New Tactic to Fight Coronavirus: Send the Homeless from Jails to Hotels." *Marshall Project*, April 6, 2020.

Venkatesh, Sudhir, and Steven D. Levitt. "An Economic Analysis of a Drug-Selling Gang's Finances." *Quarterly Journal of Economics* 115, no. 3 (2000): 755–89.

Verma, Anjuli. "The Law-Before: Legacies and Gaps in Penal Reform." *Law and Society Review* 49, no. 4 (2016): 847–82.

Vitale, Alex S. *The End of Policing*. London: Verso Books, 2017.

Wacquant, Loïc. *Urban Outcasts: A Comparative Sociology of Advanced Marginality*. Cambridge, UK: Polity Press, 2008.

Wade, James W. "Governor Kasich in Cleveland to Hail New Prison Sentence Reform Law." *Call and Post*, July 13, 2011.

Wagner, Peter, and Bernadette Rabuy. *Mass Incarceration: The Whole Pie 2016*. Northampton, MA: Prison Policy Initiative, 2017.

Wagner, Peter, and Alison Walch. *States of Incarceration: The Global Context*. Washington, DC: Prison Policy Initiative, 2016.

Wakefield, Sara, Hedwig Lee, and Christopher Wildeman. "Tough on Crime, Tough on Families? Criminal Justice and Family Life in America." *Annals of the American Academy of Political and Social Science* 665 (2016): 8–21.

Wakefield, Sara, and Christopher Wildeman. *Children of the Prison Boom: Mass Incarceration and the Future of American Inequality*. Oxford: Oxford University Press, 2013.

Walch, Nastassia. *Addicted to Courts: How a Growing Dependence on Drug Courts Impacts People and Communities*. Washington, DC: Justice Policy Institute, 2011.

Walmsley, Roy. *World Prison Population List*. 12th edition. London: Institute for Criminal Policy Research, 2018.

Wapner, Jessica. "Covid-19: Medical Expenses Leave Many Americans Deep in Debt." *BMJ* 370 (2020).

Warner, Bernard, and Susan Lucas. *Release Options under the Extraordinary Placement Program: 2012 Annual Report to the Legislature*. Olympia, WA: Department of Corrections, 2012.

Washington State Department of Corrections. "Extraordinary Medical Placement (EMP)." Accessed April 22, 2021. http://app.leg.wa.gov/ReportsToTheLegislature/Home/GetPDF?fileName=DOC1PTUM128%40doc.wa.gov_20161010_123135_729221a9-781e-433d-95f4-c14932f71236.pdf.

Weaver, Vesla. "Frontlash: Race and the Development of Punitive Crime Policy." *Studies in American Political Development* 21 (2007): 230–65.

Weidner, Robert R., and Richard S. Frase. "A County-Level Comparison of the Propensity to Sentence Felons to Prison." *International Journal of Comparative Criminology* 1, no. 1 (2001): 1–22.

Weidner, Robert R., and Richard S. Frase. "Legal and Extralegal Determinants of Intercounty Differences in Prison Use." *Criminal Justice Policy Review* 14, no. 3 (2003): 377–400.

Weisberg, Robert, Debbie A. Mukamal, and Jordan D. Segall. *Life in Limbo: An Examination of Parole Release for Prisoners Serving Life Sentences with the Possibility of Parole in California*. Stanford, CA: Stanford Criminal Justice Center, 2011.

Weiser, Benjamin. "Trial by Jury, a Hallowed American Right, Is Vanishing." *New York Times*, August 17, 2016.

Wen, H., B. G. Druss, and J. R. Cummings. "Effect of Medicaid Expansions on Health Insurance Coverage and Access to Care among Low-Income Adults with Behavior Health Conditions." *Health Services Research* 50, no. 6 (2015): 1787–809.

Wenger, Yvonne. "Sanford Backs Prison Reform; Nonviolent Criminals Would Be Given Probation, Parole." *Post and Courier,* April 22, 2010.

West, Heather C. and William J. Sabol. *Prisoners in 2007*. Washington, DC: U.S. Department of Justice, Bureau of Justice Statistics, 2008.

Western, Bruce. *The Challenge of Criminal Justice Reform*. New York: Square One Project, 2019.

Western, Bruce. *Homeward: Life in the Year after Prison*. New York: Russell Sage Foundation, 2019.

Western, Bruce. "The Impact of Incarceration on Wage Mobility and Inequality." *American Sociological Review* 67 (2012): 526–46.

Western, Bruce. "Lifetimes of Violence in a Sample of Released Prisoners." *Russell Sage Journal of the Social Sciences* 1, no. 2 (2015): 14–30.

Western, Bruce. *Punishment and Inequality*. New York: Russell Sage, 2006.

Western Regional Advocacy Project. *Without Housing: Decades of Federal Housing Cutbacks, Massive Homelessness and Policy Failures*. San Francisco: Western Regional Advocacy Project, 2006.

Wexler, David. "Reflections on the Scope of Therapeutic Jurisprudence." *Psychology, Public Policy and the Law* 2 (1996): 220–24.

Whetstone, Sarah, and Teresa Gowan. "Diagnosing the Criminal Addict: Biochemistry in the Service of the State." *Advances in Medical Sociology* 12 (2011): 309–30.

Wiggins, O. "Bail Reform in Maryland Clears Major Hurdle." *Washington Post*, November 18, 2016.

Wildeman, Christopher, and Bruce Western. "Incarceration in Fragile Families." *Future of Children* 20, no. 2 (2010): 157–77.

Williams, Timothy, and Danielle Ivory. "Chicago's Jail Is Top U.S. Hot Spot as Virus Spreads behind Bars." *New York Times*, April 8, 2020.

Wilson, David B., Ojmarrh Mitchell, and Doris L. MacKenzie. "A Systematic Review of Drug Court Effects on Recidivism." *Journal of Experimental Criminology* 2, no. 4 (2006): 459–87.

Wilson, David B., Ajima Olaghere, and Catherine S. Kimbrell. *Effectiveness of Restorative Justice Principles in Juvenile Justice: A Meta-analysis*. Washington, DC: Department of Justice, Office of Juvenile and Delinquency Prevention, 2017.

Wolch, Jennifer, and Michael Dear. *Landscapes of Despair: From Deinstitutionalization to Homelessness*. Princeton, NJ: Princeton University Press, 1987.

Wolch, Jennifer, and Michael Dear. *Malign Neglect: Homelessness in an American City*. San Francisco: Jossey-Bass, 1993.

Wolff, Nancy, Shi Jing, and Jane A. Siegel. "Patterns of Victimization among Male and Female Inmates: Evidence of an Enduring Legacy." *Violence & Victims* 24, no. 4 (2009): 469–84.

Wolfson, Andrew. "Unequal Justice: Kentucky Counties' Prison Rates Vary." *Courier Journal*, October 15, 2016.

Wood, William R. "Why Restorative Justice Will Not Reduce Incarceration." *British Journal of Criminology* 55, no. 5 (2015): 883–900.

Wykstra, Stephanie. "Bail Reform, Which Could Save Millions of Unconvicted People from Jail, Explained." *Vox*, October 17, 2018.

Zehr, Howard. *Changing Lenses: A New Focus for Crime and Justice*. Scottsdale, PA: Herald Press, 1990.

Zehr, Howard. *Little Book of Restorative Justice*. Philadelphia, PA: Good Books, 2002.

Zimring, Franklin E. *The Great American Crime Decline*. New York: Oxford University Press, 2007.

Zimring, Franklin, and Gordon E. Hawkins. *Crime Is Not the Problem: Lethal Violence in America*. New York: Oxford University Press, 1997.

Zimring, Franklin, and Gordon E. Hawkins. *The Scale of Imprisonment*. Chicago: University of Chicago Press, 2001.

Zimring, Franklin, Gordon E. Hawkins, and Sam Kamin. *Punishment and Democracy: Three Strikes and You Are Out in California*. New York: Oxford University Press, 2001.

Index

For the benefit of digital users, indexed terms that span two pages (e.g., 52–53) may, on occasion, appear on only one of those pages.